Ius Comparatum – Global Studies in Comparative Law

Volume 30

More information about this series at http://www.springer.com/series/11943

Académie internationale de droit comparé
International Academy of Comparative Law

Nicolás Etcheverry Estrázulas •
Diego P. Fernández Arroyo
Editors

Enforcement and Effectiveness of the Law - La mise en oeuvre et l'effectivité du droit

General Contributions of the Montevideo Thematic Congress - Contributions générales du Congrès thématique de Montevideo

Éditeur assistant/Assistant Editor: Alexandre Senegacnik

Springer

Editors
Nicolás Etcheverry Estrázulas
School of Law
Universidad de Montevideo
Montevideo, Uruguay

Diego P. Fernández Arroyo
International Academy of Comparative Law
Paris, France

ISSN 2214-6881 ISSN 2214-689X (electronic)
Ius Comparatum – Global Studies in Comparative Law
ISBN 978-3-030-06717-5 ISBN 978-3-319-93758-8 (eBook)
https://doi.org/10.1007/978-3-319-93758-8

This Springer imprint is published by the registered company Springer Nature Switzerland AG
The registered company address is: Gewerbestrasse 11, 6330 Cham, Switzerland

Préface/Preface

Préface

Du 16 au 18 novembre 2016, l'Académie internationale de droit comparé a organisé avec l'Université de Montevideo son 3ème Congrès thématique en Uruguay. L'événement a eu lieu dans le magnifique quartier de Carrasco, en face de la fameuse rambla de Montevideo.

Les congrès thématiques se tiennent tous les quatre ans dans les années intermédiaires où aucun Congrès général n'a lieu. Comme leur nom l'indique, les congrès thématiques abordent un unique sujet général analysé sous plusieurs angles. Le sujet retenu était la mise en œuvre et l'effectivité du droit, sujet particulièrement pertinent dans notre société contemporaine, où les expressions de la loi se multiplient et où le pluralisme juridique semble atteindre son apogée.

Le 3ème Congrès thématique a été précédé d'un congrès introductoire le 16 novembre 2016 afin de présenter un panorama du droit comparé en Amérique latine. Cela a offert une excellente

Preface

On 16 to 18 November 2016, the International Academy of Comparative Law organized its 3rd Thematic Congress in Uruguay with the University of Montevideo. The event took place in the beautiful neighborhood of Carrasco, in front of the famous Montevidean rambla.

Thematic Congresses are held every four years in the intermediate years where no General Congresses take place. As its name indicates, Thematic Congresses address only one general topic analyzed from several perspectives. The selected topic was Enforcement and Effectiveness of the Law, a particularly relevant topic in our contemporary society, in which the expressions of law multiply and legal pluralism seems to reach its peak.

The 3rd Thematic Congress was preceded by an Introductory Congress on 16 November 2016 providing a Panorama of Comparative Law in Latin America. This offered an excellent

occasion de réunir des spécialistes de droit comparé de la région. Après quelques mots d'introduction d'Eduardo Esteva Gallichio (Montevideo) et du Secrétaire général de l'AIDC Diego P. Fernández Arroyo (Paris), une leçon inaugurale a été délivrée par Jorge Esquirol (Miami) sur « le paradigme du droit-et-développement en Amérique latine : l'influence nord-américaine sur le droit de la région ».

La conférence d'ouverture a été suivie d'une première table ronde sur « le droit comparé et l'harmonisation juridique en Amérique latine » – Président : Gonzalo Lorenzo (Montevideo), Intervenants : Jorge Sánchez Cordero (Mexico), Rodrigo Momberg (Santiago), Claudia Lima Marques (Porto Alegre).

Une deuxième table ronde a été consacrée à « l'arbitrage en Amérique latine – entre harmonisation et différenciation (régionale ou mondiale » – Présidente : María Blanca Noodt Taquela (Argentine), Intervenants : Luis Ernesto Rodríguez Carrera (Caracas), Gustavo Tepedino (Rio de Janeiro) Adriana Zapata (Bogotá), Paul Arrighi (Montevideo).

Le Bureau de l'Académie a adopté la structure suivante pour le Congrès thématique : deux conférences, trois tables rondes, six ateliers, deux présentations, générales et deux sujets généraux. L'allocution de bienvenue a été prononcée par Nicolás Etcheverry Estrázulas (Montevideo, Doyen de la Faculté de Droit de l'Université de Montevideo) et la Présidente de l'AIDC, Katharina Boele-Woelki (Hambourg), avant une leçon inaugurale prononcée

opportunity to gather Comparative Law scholars of the region. After some introductory words by Eduardo Esteva Gallichio (Montevideo) and IACL Secretary-General Diego P. Fernández Arroyo (Paris), an Opening Lecture on "Law-and-Development Paradigm in Latin America: US Influence on the Law of the Region" was presented by Jorge Esquirol (Miami).

The Opening Lecture was followed by a first round table on "Comparative Law and Legal Harmonisation in Latin America" – Chair: Gonzalo Lorenzo (Montevideo), Speakers: Jorge Sánchez Cordero (Mexico City), Rodrigo Momberg (Santiago), Claudia Lima Marques (Porto Alegre).

A second round table was dedicated to "Arbitration in Latin America – Between (Regional or Global) Harmonisation and differentiation" – Chair: María Blanca Noodt Taquela (Argentina), Speakers: Luis Ernesto Rodríguez Carrera (Caracas), Gustavo Tepedino (Rio de Janeiro), Adriana Zapata (Bogotá), Paul Arrighi (Montevideo).

The Executive Committee of the Academy adopted the following structure for the Thematic Congress: two keynote lectures, three round tables, six workshops, two general presentations, and two general topics. The Welcome Address was delivered by Nicolás Etcheverry Estrázulas (Dean of the Faculty of Law of the University of Montevideo) and IACL President Katharina Boele-Woelki (Hamburg) before an opening lecture delivered by

par Jürgen Basedow (Hambourg) sur « les multiples facettes de la mise en œuvre du droit. »

Seuls les deux sujets généraux ont été préparés selon le schéma traditionnel de l'Académie, i.e. la préparation d'un rapport général élaboré sur la base de rapports spéciaux. Les thèmes généraux retenus étaient « la mise en œuvre et l'effectivité du droit de la consommation » – Présidente : Bénédicte Fauvarque-Cosson, Rapporteurs généraux Hans-Wolfgang Micklitz (Florence) et Geneviève Saumier (Montréal) – et « la mise en œuvre et l'effectivité du droit de la non-discrimination » – Présidente : Mariana Blengio Valdés (Montevideo), Rapporteurs généraux David Oppenheimer (Berkeley) et Marie Mercat Bruns (Paris).

Les deux tables rondes ont traité de « la mise en œuvre des droits constitutionnels dans les contextes nationaux et supranationaux » – Président : Marek Safjan (Varsovie / Luxembourg), Intervenants : Javier A. Couso (Santiago), David J. Gerber (Chicago) – et « l'effectivité de la résolution internationale des litiges » – Président : Didier Opertti Badán (Montevideo), Intervenants : Makane M. Mbengue (Dakar / Genève), Maria Kaiafa Gbandi (Thessalonique), Mónica Pinto (Buenos Aires), José A. Moreno Rodríguez (Asunción), Catherine Kessedjian (Paris).

Deux exposés généraux sur « le rôle des organisations internationales, des stratégies pour l'application des conventions internationales » ont été offerts par José Angelo Estrella Faria (Rome,

Jürgen Basedow (Hamburg) on "The Multifaceted Enforcement of the Law."

Only the two general topics were developed according to the traditional scheme of the Academy, which consists in a general report elaborated on the basis of special reports. The selected general topics were "Enforcement and Effectiveness of Consumer Law" – Chair: Bénédicte Fauvarque-Cosson, General Reporters Hans-Wolfgang Micklitz (Florence) and Geneviève Saumier (Montreal) – and "Enforcement and Effectiveness of Anti-Discriminatory Law" – Chair: Mariana Blengio Valdés (Montevideo), General Reporters David Oppenheimer (Berkeley) and Marie Mercat Bruns (Paris).

The two roundtables dealt with "Enforcement of Constitutional Rights within National and Supranational Contexts" – Chair: Marek Safjan (Warsaw / Luxemburg), Speakers: Javier A. Couso (Santiago), David J. Gerber (Chicago) – and "Effectiveness of International Dispute Settlement" – Chair: Didier Opertti Badán (Montevideo), Speakers: Makane M. Mbengue (Dakar / Geneva), Maria Kaiafa Gbandi (Thessaloniki), Mónica Pinto (Buenos Aires), José A. Moreno Rodríguez (Asuncion), Catherine Kessedjian (Paris).

Two general presentations on "the Role of International Organizations, Strategies for the Enforcement of International Conventions" were delivered by José Angelo Estrella Faria (Roma,

UNIDROIT) et Hans van Loon (La Haye) – Présidente : Cecilia Fresnedo de Aguirre (Montevideo).

Les six ateliers [workshop] ont offert un nouveau forum académique dynamique et interactif. Les participants ont été invités à choisir deux ateliers parmi deux séries de trois choix et à préparer à l'avance des documents pour les ateliers. Des ateliers ont eu lieu parallèlement dans différentes salles, autorisant les participants à se concentrer sur leurs intérêts académiques personnels :

– A1 : Droit pénal, Président : Pedro Montano Gómez (Montevideo), Coordinateurs : Nora V. Demleitner (Lexington) et Lorena Bachmaier (Madrid);
– A2 : Droit de la concurrence, Président : Joël Monéger (Paris), Coordinateurs : Calixto Salomão Filho (São Paulo);
– A3 : Droit de la famille, Présidente : Graciela Medina (Buenos Aires), Coordinateurs : Isabel Jaramillo Sierra (Bogota) et Salvatore Patti (Rome);
– A4 : Droit du travail, Président : Leonardo Slinger (Montevideo), Coordinateurs : Achim Seifert (Jena) et Dan Wei (Macao);
– A5 : Droit administratif, Président : Pedro Aberastury (Buenos Aires);
– A6 : Droit des contrats, Président : James Douglas (Ville Est, Queensland), Coordinateurs: Giuditta Cordero Moss (Oslo) et Alejandro M. Garro (New York).

George A. Bermann (New York) a prononcé la conférence de clôture sur « les possibilités et limites de la mise en œuvre privée du droit ».

UNIDROIT) and Hans van Loon (The Hague) – Chair: Cecilia Fresnedo de Aguirre (Montevideo).

The six workshops aimed to offer a new dynamic and interactive academic forum. The participants were invited to select two workshops among two series of three choices. Participants were invited to prepare in advance selected materials for the workshops. Workshops were held in parallel rooms and allowed the participants to focus on their personal academic interests:

– WS 1: Criminal Law, Chair: Pedro Montano Gómez (Montevideo), Conveners: Nora V. Demleitner (Lexington) and Lorena Bachmaier (Madrid);
– WS 2: Competition Law, Chair: Joël Monéger (Paris), Conveners: Calixto Salomão Filho (São Paulo);
– WS 3: Family Law, Chair: Graciela Medina (Buenos Aires), Conveners: Isabel Jaramillo Sierra (Bogota) and Salvatore Patti (Rome);
– WS 4: Labor Law, Chair: Leonardo Slinger (Montevideo), Conveners: Achim Seifert (Jena) and Dan Wei (Macao);
– WS 5: Administrative Law, Chair: Pedro Aberastury (Buenos Aires), Convener: Dominique M. Custos (Caen) and Gabriel Bocksang Hola (Santiago);
– WS 6: Contract Law, Chair: James Douglas (City East, Queensland), Conveners: Giuditta Cordero Moss (Oslo) and Alejandro M. Garro (New York).

The Closing Lecture on "Possibilities and Limits of Private Enforcement of the Law" was delivered by George A. Bermann (New York).

Le Secrétaire général de l'AIDC Diego P. Fernández Arroyo (Paris) a conclu avec un bilan du congrès et quelques remarques et informations sur les nouvelles orientations et les activités de l'Académie. Un dîner, aussi charmant que bien servi, a été organisé par l'Université de Montevideo pour célébrer le succès du 3ème Congrès Thématique.

Le prochain Congrès thématique aura lieu en 2020 à Pretoria en Afrique du Sud. Nous sommes confiants que cette nouvelle activité de notre Académie presque centenaire sera aussi riche sur les plans académique et humain comme ce fut le cas à Montevideo.

IACL Secretary-General Diego P. Fernández Arroyo (Paris) concluded with a final review of the Congress and a few remarks and information about the future activities of the Academy. A dinner, as charming as well served, was organized by the University of Montevideo to celebrate the success of the 3rd Thematic Congress.

The next Thematic Congress will be held in 2020 in Pretoria, South Africa. We are confident that this new activity of our nearly 100-year-old Academy will be as enriching on the academic and personal level as it was the case in Montevideo.

Contents

Part I / Partie I Keynote Speeches / Leçons Inaugurale et de Clôture

The Multiple Facets of Law Enforcement 3
Jürgen Basedow

Enforcing Legal Norms Through Private Means 33
George A. Bermann

Part II / Partie II Round-Table Interventions / Interventions à l'Occasion des Tables-Rondes

A Global Adaptive System for Supporting Human Rights? 45
David Joseph Gerber

Jurisdictional Conflicts in Criminal Matters and Their Settlement Within EU's Supranational Settings 57
Maria Kaiafa-Gbandi

Diversité, pertinence et efficacité des mécanismes internationaux de règlement des différends en matière économique 75
Catherine Kessedjian

Effectiveness of International Commercial Arbitration as a Dispute Settlement Mechanism 87
José Antonio Moreno Rodríguez

Part III / Partie III Workshops / Ateliers

Challenges for the Enforcement and Effectiveness of Criminal Law: The Prohibition on Illegal Drugs 109
Lorena Bachmaier Winter and Nora V. Demleitner

Enforcement of Contractual Obligations: Comparative Perspectives . . . 135
Giuditta Cordero-Moss and Alejandro M. Garro

Intra-Family Torts: From Immunity to Special Rules in Criminal and Civil Law 149
Salvatore Patti

Part I / Partie I
Keynote Speeches / Leçons Inaugurale et de Clôture

The Multiple Facets of Law Enforcement

Jürgen Basedow

Abstract Ordering society and economy by means of legal rules is a widespread objective in modern times. The effectiveness of such rules therefore is a common concern in many countries. This paper sheds light upon the relation between substantive laws and enforcement and on the characteristic features of various enforcement tools. One of the trends of modern legal development is the quasi-experimental use of varying enforcement measures of administrative law, private law and criminal law, highlighted by the examples of competition law and consumer law. A second trend outlined in the paper is the one towards alternative dispute resolution (ADR) in its various forms: arbitration, ombudsman complaint procedures, mediation and conciliation. A further part deals with societal, non-legal enforcement mechanisms which are gaining ground especially in cross-border relations increasingly governed by soft law.

1 Introduction

1.1 Substantive Law and Enforcement

For centuries substantive law and the possibility of its enforcement were almost one and the same. Law could even be said to be a kind of appendix to such a possibility. Under the writ system of the common law individual rights were protected only to the extent that a suitable writ could be found from among the traditional forms. In a similar vein the *actiones* of Roman law determined the existence of any kind of entitlement.[1]

[1] See Peter (1957).

J. Basedow (✉)
Max Planck Institute for Comparative and International Private Law, Hamburg, Germany

University of Hamburg, Hamburg, Germany

Institut de droit international, Hamburg, Germany
e-mail: basedow@mpipriv.de

N. Etcheverry Estrázulas, D. P. Fernández Arroyo (eds.), *Enforcement and Effectiveness of the Law - La mise en oeuvre et l'effectivité du droit*, Ius Comparatum – Global Studies in Comparative Law 30, https://doi.org/10.1007/978-3-319-93758-8_1

It was not until the nineteenth century that substantive or material law was stripped of the dominance of formalities and procedure.

Ever since, the principles and rules of substantive law have had a life of their own. They lay down entitlements and rules of conduct for individuals and corporate entities while enforcement deals with their implementation in real life. In modern times the ranking of substance and procedure is sometimes even reversed, procedure being considered as having a "servicing function" vis-à-vis substantive law.[2] Civil procedure, criminal procedure and regulatory procedure have increasingly been discussed in view of their aptness to implement the values enshrined in, and rights granted by, substantive law: in civil law, criminal law and administrative law. Against this backdrop the general theme of the Academy's Congress on the enforcement of law might appear as a return to earlier stages in legal history.

However, the current enforcement debate is more differentiated. A closer look at the growing literature discloses a variety of enforcement mechanisms which can be assigned to three groups:

- First, while the quest for a perfection of procedures in view of a better implementation of substantive law still subsists, it has brought about a greater variety of measures of state law. Thus private enforcement by individuals in civil courts may be supplemented by collective actions or by public enforcement entrusted to administrative agencies; sometimes legislatures even have recourse to criminal enforcement. Conversely, public enforcement may appear as insufficient and be complemented by private enforcement in civil courts, see under Sect. 2.
- Second, we can observe a number of new procedural mechanisms outside the traditional enforcement agencies of states, i.e. outside courts and administrative bodies. While the new mechanisms are structured by rules, they are often organized by private entities. They are generally designated as alternative dispute resolution or ADR, see under Sect. 3.
- A third branch of the enforcement debate focuses on extra-legal, societal mechanisms. This branch has always existed, its recent growth is due to the expansion of non-state substantive law that can be ascertained in many areas. Where private bodies adopt rules and principles the enforcement machinery of states, i.e. courts and administrative agencies, is not necessarily apt or available. The enforcement of various types of private ordering requires a broader look at enforcement mechanisms that may exist beyond the boundaries of law in the social sphere, see under Sect. 4.

The widespread nature of the enforcement debate shows that the concept and purpose of enforcement have broadened over time. Under the traditional dominance of substantive law enforcement was assigned to state bodies which had the task of investigating and giving full effect to a right alleged by an individual party. The judiciary was the arena dedicated to the individual's "struggle for his rights", as it was put by the German jurist *Rudolf von Jhering* in the late nineteenth century.[3] We

[2]Böhmer (1950), p. 95.

[3]von Jhering (1897); the book has its origins in a lecture given in Vienna in 1872; in the German original the word "Recht" covers both the individual entitlement and the law as a body of rules.

shall see that in the modern world of dispute resolution other objectives come to the fore.

1.2 Characteristic Features of Enforcement Mechanisms

Enforcement mechanisms are staked out by procedural rules, often codified and specific to each body: codes or rules of civil procedure for private law, criminal procedure for criminal law and regulatory procedure for administrative agencies and for the judicial review of their decisions. Private entities have their own rules of procedure as well. In every single case the aim is to assert the substantive rights of the parties involved and to implement the substantive law to the fullest extent possible. However, the enforcement mechanisms differ in some fundamental aspects: with regard to the initiator, the selection of the cases, the means of investigation and the effects of a decision.

Individual actions in civil courts are brought by the persons whose rights are at stake. They may apply for an injunction, for a declaratory statement of a right, for the award of damages, the disgorgement of profit, etc. Where they do not go to court, under-enforcement of the law will result, but it is after all their own decision to stay passive. Collective actions, public enforcement and criminal prosecution are however initiated by third persons who are not directly affected by the outcome of a case. Their resources are limited which necessitates a selection of cases and may give rise to discrimination. In respect of collective redress the market for legal services will react to an unsatisfied demand. But this response is not available in public and criminal enforcement. Where they focus on some cases, leaving others unnoticed, the legitimacy of enforcement is in question.

The investigation of a case depends very much on the law of procedure which differs from country to country. But it is fair to say that in civil actions the investigation is very much incumbent on the parties, i.e. with regard to the facts supporting the claim, it is primarily up to the plaintiff to gather them. In public enforcement and criminal prosecution, however, it is up to public bodies, and they can avail themselves of a bundle of powers of fact finding which are not bestowed on private plaintiffs in civil proceedings. Consequently, public enforcement, while being selective, is more apt to disclose infringements of the law in the selected cases.

As to the effects of decisions they differ with regard to the content: injunctions and damages awards are most important in civil enforcement, cease-and-desist orders, fines and blacklisting are available in public enforcement, while criminal verdicts result in fines or imprisonment. The effects of decisions are confined to the relationship between the parties in individual civil actions. Class actions of the opt-out type, however, will often produce effects for a large number of persons included in the plaintiff group. Public enforcement and criminal prosecution focus on specific companies or individuals; but the more serious sanctions are likely to provoke change on a broader scale. Thus, numerous people will indirectly benefit from public and criminal enforcement.

These brief considerations show that much more is involved in the enforcement debate than the effectiveness of substantive law. It is not surprising that the following survey of some major aspects of the debate displays a great variety of approaches and that the straightforward ties between the procedural means and the substantive end have given way to a multi-faceted relationship.

2 Law Enforcement by Varying State Measures

2.1 Survey

Where legal rules confer rights or lay down rules of conduct legislatures will choose enforcement mechanisms from a kind of tool-box containing instruments that pertain to either private law, administrative law or criminal law. Often, the choice of the proper instrument is not even explicitly addressed since it appears obvious that substantive law rules dealing with private relations will be enforced by civil proceedings, that the enforcement of rules relating to the relation between private actors and the state is left to administrative proceedings and that criminal proceedings only deal with serious infringements of rules and values that are essential for social peace.

Not all rights and not all legal rules are enforceable. Wherever an obligor owes a specific conduct over a protracted period of time, performance is sometimes impossible and often impracticable; it would require permanent supervision. Common law and civil law jurisdictions have drawn different conclusions from this fact of life: while the common law basically rejects the obligee's right to specific performance,[4] civil law jurisdictions affirm that right, taking however account of the reduced chance of enforcement by procedural law.[5] Non-enforceable rules of law may be an unattractive notion, but the example, well-known to comparatists, shows that the quest for more effective enforcement sometimes clashes with reality. In such cases modesty may require that unenforceable rules of law should not be adopted. Quite to the contrary, the present debate appears to strive for ever more effective enforcement, regardless of the substantive law involved. Accordingly, the choice of the proper enforcement mechanism has become the object of discussion in several fields of law. Given the servicing function of enforcement vis-à-vis substantive law, the various enforcement mechanisms are progressively rated by their effectiveness. As a result one can observe a certain oscillation of enforcement practices between the different tools which will be highlighted in this part of the paper.

Examples can be provided from various areas of the law: in family law, the enforcement of maintenance obligations, in particular, of child support has always

---

[4] *Co-operative Insurance Society Ltd. v. Argyll Stores*, [1997] UKHL 17, [1997] All ER 297 where Lord Hoffmann said that "any application to enforce the order [for specific enforcement] is likely to be a heavy and expensive piece of litigation."

[5] See Zweigert and Kötz (1998), p. 473 f. for Germany, p. 474 ff. for France.

been a matter of concern. While basically a matter for civil actions this instrument is far too often ineffective where the debtor hides away or urges his or her family not to go to court. From the 1970s onwards more and more countries have therefore charged state authorities with the advance payment of maintenance to the child support creditor. They will in turn be subrogated to the rights to maintenance and it is then up to the public bodies to enforce the subrogated maintenance claims against the debtor.[6] Similar interactions between private law and public law of social security can be found in other contexts as well, in particular, with regard to the financing of higher education.

In commercial law, enforcement tools of private law, public law and criminal law are intertwined in various contexts. Ever since the Great Depression of 1930 capital market regulation and administrative supervision has supported compliance with company law and supplemented its enforcement by the civil courts; as a result the enforcement of the law in this sector has been characterized as "hybrid".[7] Two other areas will be treated in greater detail below: competition law (Sect. 2.2), and consumer law (Sect. 2.3). The comparative analysis points to interesting observations (Sect. 2.4).

2.2 *The Case of Competition Law: Private, Public and Criminal Enforcement*

2.2.1 From Private to Public Enforcement

An area of the law equipped with enforcement mechanisms oscillating between private and public law tools is the law against restrictions of competition. Long before modern antitrust law was introduced in the USA towards the end of the nineteenth century the English common law courts had developed rules protecting competition. They refused to enforce a legal monopoly against competitors,[8] and they invalidated certain agreements in restraint of trade, in particular those involving an unreasonable prohibition of competition in employment contracts or dealership agreements.[9] Moreover, the tort of conspiracy which was often intended to drive

---

[6]For a comparative assessment, see Martiny (2000), pp. 1239–1274, dealing with the laws of Germany, p. 1241, Austria, p. 1248, Switzerland, p. 1254, France, p. 1259, England, p. 1265, and the USA, p. 1267.

[7]Veil and Brüggemeier (2015), p. 302; the authors deal with German law exclusively. In a similar sense for Swiss law, Bohrer (2015), p. 272, calling for a "holistic" concept of capital market enforcement.

[8]*Darcy v. Allein (The Case of Monopolies)*, 77 Eng. Rep. 1260 (K.B. 1603).

[9]See e.g. the early English decision *Mitchel v. Reynolds*, 24 Eng. Rep. 347 (K.B. 1711); Prentice (2015), para. 16-085.

competitors out of the market gave rise to compensation claims of the victims.[10] The enforcement of these rules was left to private initiative and to the civil courts.

In the second half of the nineteenth century periodic depressions drove many US farmers depending on monopolistic railroads into ruin and created an atmosphere of hostility against monopolies in general. The *Sherman* Antitrust Act of 1890[11] was meant to remedy that situation by confirming the substantive principles of the common law, transferring them into federal law, rendering violations punishable and charging the US district attorneys under the direction of the Attorney General with the prosecution of such conduct.[12] Private enforcement was not abolished, but public enforcement gained the upper hand. It was supplemented by the foundation of the Federal Trade Commission in 1914.[13] Law enforcement could now benefit from the investigatory powers available in regulatory and criminal proceedings. After World War II this model was followed, first in the European Union[14] and later on, in particular after the collapse of the socialist systems in Eastern Europe, on a world-wide scale.

2.2.2 From Public to Private Enforcement

Due to limited state resources public enforcement is inevitably selective. It concentrates on flagrant violations and does not concern itself with minor infringements, for example those of a local or regional purview. On the other hand the economic and social benefits of competition arise from a comprehensive protection on *all* markets. In order to fill the enforcement lacunae the US enacted the Clayton Antitrust Act 1914.[15] It encourages private enforcement by the prospect of treble damages, a windfall profit to private plaintiffs who sue infringers of the antitrust laws. In addition the US legal system provides for procedural devices such as the opt-out class action (see under Sect. 2.3.2) and the pretrial discovery of documents which, taken together, facilitate antitrust damages actions.

From a comparative perspective one can ascertain a growing popularity of the additional tool of private enforcement. Some national competition statutes specifically address the compensation of cartel victims, in other jurisdictions the matter is

[10]Halsbury's Laws of England (2015), paras. 712 ff.

[11]An Act to protect trade and commerce against unlawful restraints and monopolies (Sherman Antitrust Act), 26 Stat. 209 (1890), 15 USC §§ 1–7.

[12]The significance of this change is stressed by Areeda et al. (2004), para. 131.

[13]Federal Trade Commission Act, 38 Stat. 717, 15 USC §§ 41–58.

[14]See now, replacing previous legal acts, Council Regulation No. 1/2003 of 16 December 2002 on the implementation of the rules on competition laid down in Articles 81 and 82 of the Treaty, OJ 2003 L 1/1.

[15]An Act to supplement existing laws against unlawful restraints and monopolies, and for other purposes (Clayton Antitrust Act, 2014), Pub.L. 63–212, 38 Stat. 730, 15 USC §§ 12–27.

left to the general law of tort liability.[16] The European Union has recently issued a directive on damages for the infringement of competition law which is intended to ensure the "full effectiveness" of EU competition law and the "practical effect of the prohibitions laid down therein".[17]

However, few other jurisdictions if any incentivize plaintiffs in the same way as the USA by a whole bundle of measures. Some jurisdictions such as Taiwan have allowed for discretionary trebling of damages[18] whereas the EU Directive explicitly excludes "overcompensation, whether by means of punitive, multiple or other types of damages".[19] What is more, legislation outside the USA is generally hostile to reforms of procedural law in support of private damages claims.

As a result and given the tremendous difficulties of fact assessment in private competition litigation plaintiffs in countries other than the USA will usually wait until a competition authority has investigated the case. They will almost exclusively bring follow-on actions in civil courts; stand-alone actions are exceptional. This means that private enforcement is not more than an additional remedy helping to compensate victims who are generally neglected in public enforcement. But it appears doubtful that damages actions can improve the overall enforcement of competition law unless appropriate amendments to procedure strengthen the plaintiff's position in obtaining evidence, provide incentives to go to court and reduce the economic risk of litigation costs.

2.2.3 Criminal Enforcement

Therefore, the call for criminal sanctions of anticompetitive conduct is being heard time and again.[20] As pointed out above, the US antitrust laws specifically provide for criminal enforcement by fines for corporations, and by fines or imprisonment for up to 10 years for individuals. Countries such as France[21] and Japan[22] have likewise established criminal sanctions in their competition legislation, including

[16]For a survey of the law of the Member States of the European Union see Waelbroeck et al. (2004). See also the reports on the laws of the USA (Hannah Buxbaum), Germany (Wulf-Henning Roth), France (Laurence Idot) and Italy (Carlo Castronovo) in Basedow (2007a).

[17]Directive 2014/104/EU of the European Parliament and of the Council of 26 November 2014 on certain rules governing actions for damages under national law for infringement of the competition law provisions of the Member States and of the European Union, OJ 2014 L 349/1; as to its purpose see in particular recital 3.

[18]See Article 32 of the Fair Trade Act of 2011, English translation available on the website of the Taiwanese Fair Trade Commission (www.ftc.gov.tw →laws and regulations →Fair Trade Act).

[19]Article 3(3) of Directive 2014/104/EU.

[20]See for Germany the recent proposals submitted by the Monopolkommission (2015), paras. 196 ff. for hard core cartels.

[21]See Article L.420-6(1) of the Commercial Code; cf. de Giles (2003), pp. 20–28 and 68–73.

[22]See Article 89 of the Japanese Antimonopoly Act, English translation on the website of the Japan Fair Trade Commission (www.jftc.go.jp/en, →Legislation & Guidelines).

imprisonment for individuals. On the other hand, Germany has so far rejected the threat of jail unless the acts in question are covered by general criminal law as is the case for bid-rigging which is punishable as fraud under the Criminal Code.

It is difficult to assess the deterrent effect of the threat of imprisonment which would be the essential contribution to the enforcement of competition law. From the countries listed above few cases of criminal prosecution are reported: in the USA with a market of 320 million people an average of 22 offenders were convicted per year over a period of 11 years from 1999 to 2009[23]; over the whole period only 55 out of the total number of 246 persons were sentenced to prison only, with a median term of 6 months.[24] For France a total number of around 20 criminal convictions is reported for the period from 1988 to 2005; 14 of them dealt with bid-rigging which would be punishable as fraud in many countries anyway.[25] In Japanese practice criminal prosecution of anticompetitive conduct is simply described as "rare".[26]

The small number of criminal convictions is reflected by the absence of the topic of criminal sanctions and related trials in media reports and a lack of public awareness. It is doubtful, however, whether business people who are not sufficiently aware of the punishable character of their acts, but by their very nature are always inclined to engage in business activities promising higher profit, can actually be deterred by the threat of criminal enforcement. The trust in the deterrent effect of criminal enforcement therefore does not appear to be well founded so far as competition law is concerned.

2.3 *The Case of Consumer Protection: Individual, Collective and Administrative Action*

2.3.1 Limits of Traditional Enforcement Through Civil Courts

Consumer law has emerged in many countries since the 1960s and 1970s. To the extent that it deals with consumer health and safety its enforcement is primarily preventive and a matter of public law and administrative procedures. Where it comes to the protection of the consumers' economic interests, however, the matter is of a private law nature and a spin-off of more traditional areas of the law such as contract law, tort law or the law of unfair competition. Consequently, the enforcement of consumer law with regards to economic interests began with civil court actions.

Civil actions require the plaintiff's positive decision to take a dispute to court. However, it became clear early on that this happens far too seldom. Consumers'

---

[23]Howell (2010), p. 5 with figure 1.

[24]Howell (2010), p. 8.

[25]Bout et al. (2015), p. 531, para. 1405 at.

[26]See Ida (2011), para. 75.

self-restraint is explained by several causes: in former times the insufficient information of the average citizen, his or her sense of inferiority or a general fear of engagement in court proceedings involving private attorneys and judges were emphasized. Further motivations underlined in the debate related to a general distrust of the judiciary, a lack of incentives for consumer attorneys and the consumers' fear of the costs of litigation.[27] These observations envisage the consumer as the weaker party or, as it is sometimes put in Brazilian legal writings, as the "vulnerable party",[28] and focus on his or her need to be protected by mechanisms other than traditional court proceedings.

The recent *Zeitgeist* which is more economically-minded rather points to what is called a "rational indifference" as the intelligible ground for the under-enforcement of consumer rights.[29] The reasoning is similar to the one outlined above with regards to specific performance.[30] From this perspective the filing of a lawsuit depends on whether the expected benefits and the chance of winning prevail over the costs of litigation and the risk of losing in the plaintiff's mind. Because of the low amounts which are usually at stake in consumer disputes the expected benefits and the chance of winning are usually considered as comparatively insignificant. On the other hand, the risk of losing entails, in addition to the loss already sustained by the consumer, the obligation to refund the professional for its legal expenses. Since consumers are often risk averse they tend to overweigh the risk of defeat as compared with the chance of winning; consequently many will refrain from going to court.[31]

In addition to a variety of out-of-court mechanisms of dispute settlement which will be discussed further on,[32] two devices of state-driven law enforcement appear to offer a better and more comprehensive implementation of consumer rights: collective actions and the public enforcement of consumer law by administrative authorities. Both depart from the view that, beyond the individual rights involved, there is some kind of public good arising from the enforcement of consumer law.

2.3.2 Collective Actions

Consumer litigation often has two characteristics: low values at stake in the individual dispute and the identity of legal issues arising in a large number of cases. For example, the misleading nature of an advertisement may induce a large number of persons to buy what does not meet their expectations. Since the loss sustained by the individual customers may be minimal they will usually neither apply for an

[27]See e.g. von Hippel (1973) pp. 268–283, revised in von Hippel (1986), § 6.

[28]See the papers published in Lima Marques and Gsell (2016), e.g. Lima Marques (2016), p. 49 f.; several further papers refer to consumers as "vulnerable".

[29]Schäfer (1999), pp. 68, 73 f.

[30]See above at fn. 4 f.

[31]For a general assessment of the theoretical background of litigation from an economic perspective see Shavell (2004), p. 389 f.

[32]See below, Sect. 3.2.

injunction against the company responsible for the advertisement nor sue for damages. Similar situations may occur with regard to goods and services sold at cartelized prices, in respect of securities investments caused by incorrect information or concerning compensation for damage suffered from defective products.

In such cases the individual action appears to be insufficient and traditional justice dysfunctional. Given the public good promoted by law enforcement it would therefore seem to be reasonable that the parallel claims are consolidated and lodged together. Several legal instruments have evolved for this purpose over time.

A traditional legal tool that might be used as a strategic device of law enforcement could be multiple assignments. They would enable the assignee to consolidate the various similar claims and to sue the debtor(s) on his or her own behalf. This mechanism encourages the deliberate setting up of companies which might be used as assignees in a strategic way. A European example is the *Cartel Damage Claims S.A.* which was established to that end in Brussels.[33] It approaches the victims of cartels investigated by a competition authority, purchases their compensation claims, consolidates them and files an action against the cartel members.[34] Obviously this arrangement presupposes that the persons entitled to damages claims, i.e. the assignors are known to the assignee and that both communicate—a condition that is absent in most consumer cases.

In the alternative the several creditors would keep their claims but a single person would be authorized to bring an action reflecting their consolidated claims, on their behalf. The application would have to outline the group of potential creditors; after the court's declaration of admissibility the plaintiff could approach members of the group and invite them to join in the claim. The court's final decision would be binding for those who join in, but not for others. This is the so-called *opt-in class action*. It has generally been recommended by the EU Commission[35] and has been introduced in a number of Member States such as Sweden,[36] Italy[37] and France,[38] however with noteworthy variations.[39]

---

[33]Established in Brussels in 2002; see the website: http://www.carteldamageclaims.com.

[34]For such a case see CJEU 21 May 2015, case C-352/13 (*Cartel Damage Claims (CDC) Hydrogen Peroxide SA v. Akzo Nobel NV and others*), ECLI:EU:C:2015:335; cf. Wurmnest (2016).

[35]Commission Recommendation of 11 June 2013 on common principles for injunctive and compensatory collective redress mechanisms in the Member States concerning violations of rights granted under Union Law (2013/396/EU), OJ 2013 L 201/60.

[36]Lag (2002:599) om grupprättegång, Svensk Författningssamling 2002:599, see in particular § 14 on opting in; on the preparatory work for this law see Dopffel and Scherpe (1999), p. 443 ff.

[37]For the Italian opt-in class action see art. 140*bis* on the *azione di classe* of the *Codice del consumo,* introduced by the Law no. 244 of 24 December 2007 as amended; for a valuable assessment of Italian practice see Afferni (2016).

[38]The French class-action is regulated in Articles L.423-1–L.423-26 of the *Code de la consommation;* for a closer analysis, see Guinchard et al. (2014), paras. 2254-1 ff.

[39]For example, it is available for consumer litigation exclusively in Italy and France, but for all kinds of disputes in Sweden; in France only accredited consumer organizations are entitled to bring such a class action, while in Italy and Sweden every member of the group may initiate the corresponding procedure. In France the compensation of immaterial loss such as pain and suffering is excluded, while Italian law does not provide for such a restriction.

Experience shows that this instrument is of limited value; it only works where the consumer group in question is small and its members are known to plaintiffs. For the plaintiff and for group members the opt-in process is in itself too costly and burdensome where the consumer group consists of many anonymous members which the lead plaintiff will have to find and recruit.[40] Thus, the opt-in model is not a significant step ahead as compared with jurisdictions such as Germany providing for individual damages actions exclusively; the only collective remedy available to accredited consumer organizations that has proven effective under German law so far aims exclusively at injunctive relief.[41]

Where the persons affected cannot be identified because they are too numerous or anonymous the legal instruments presented above will remain futile. It is in this context that the *opt-out class action* is attractive, i.e. a class action brought by a third person on behalf of a group of creditors defined in the petition who have the option to *leave* the group in order not be bound by the court's decision but who are bound if they remain silent. The opt-out class action, which has common law origins, has become an effective tool under the US Federal Rules of Civil Procedure.[42] More recently, it has been introduced in competition law in the United Kingdom.[43] In both cases, the right to bring such actions is not confined to consumers but is also available to professionals.

Class actions, in particular of the opt-out type, shift the initiative for litigation from the persons whose rights are in dispute, to the plaintiffs who may be stakeholder organizations such as consumer associations, but in most cases are law firms. Lawyers are incentivized by their pursuit of profit and by the need to cover the running costs of their firm. Consequently, in class actions there is the risk that the interests of those whose rights are affected and of the plaintiff law firms run apart—a phenomenon addressed by the principal-agent theory developed in institutional economics. Sometimes the legal services provided seem no longer to respond to an actual demand of the clients. The requirement of an approval of the class action by the court is meant to control this risk. Nevertheless, the apprehension that lawyers primarily pursue their own interest is underpinned by US experience; a major issue of the American debate on class actions turns in fact on the lawyers' share of the

---

[40]Afferni (2016), p. 88 explains this "burden of opting-in"; it appears for example manageable where the class of plaintiffs consists of the patients who were treated in a given hospital during a specific period of time, see the case at p. 87, but it is too heavy where all customers of a particular flu shot, invited by public notices in a newspaper, are concerned, see the case at p. 88.

[41]Gesetz über Unterlassungsklagen bei Verbraucherrechts- und anderen Verstößen (Unterlassungsklagengesetz – UklaG) of 26 November 2001, Bundesgesetzblatt I-3422 as amended.

[42]Published on the website of the Legal Information Institute of Cornell University Law School, www.law.cornell.edu/rules/frcp. See Rule 23.

[43]See Article 81 and Schedule 8 of the Consumer Rights Act 2015, 2015 c. 15; Schedule 8 amended the Competition Act 1998 and the Enterprise Act 2002 by introducing appropriate provisions.

litigation proceeds.[44] Therefore, and despite the effectiveness of class actions in terms of law enforcement, most jurisdictions still reject this instrument.

2.3.3 Public Enforcement by State Authorities

Consumers pursue their economic interests in myriad transactions with millions of suppliers of goods and services, i.e. in private relations. Here, the enforcement of the law is usually left to private initiative in civil courts. Where this proves ineffective the idea of public enforcement may come to mind. But since it is not feasible to have a public body surveying the rights of every individual and checking their implementation, public enforcement is by necessity selective. This is confirmed by a comparative analysis which discloses several selection mechanisms.

One of them confines state intervention to disputes arising from *punishable acts* of the professional, thus to acts being particularly flagrant violations of commercial standards. French law has a long tradition in this respect. The Consumer Code threatens criminal sanctions including imprisonment, to sellers of forged or counterfeited foodstuffs and drinks,[45] to business people engaging in misleading commercial practices,[46] and to professionals who exploit the weakness of consumers in doorstep selling operations,[47] or who organize pyramid selling systems[48] etc. France appears to entrust the investigation of such commercial activities to public prosecutors more often than other countries.[49] Given the seriousness of the sanctions prosecutors may, however, refrain from investigations in cases of lower significance.

Public enforcement may also be made dependent on the existence of *supervisory bodies* for specific sectors of the economy. Where specialized authorities have been established e.g. for financial services, telecommunications or other network industries, knowledge about the respective industry is already present in a public body which is charged with economic regulation and has therefore access to the limited number of companies operating in that sector and to the commercial practices prevailing in the market. Such institutions are primed to take over the task of dealing with consumer protection in their respective field.

---

[44] See the data presented by Fitzpatrick (2010), p. 830 ff. At p. 845 the author concludes that in 2006 and 2007 District Court Judges approved 688 class action settlements involving more than $33 billion; of this amount around $5 billion or 15% was awarded to class action lawyers.

[45] Article L.213-1 Code de la consommation; cf. Raymond (2014), paras. 193 ff.

[46] Article 121-3 Code de la consommation; cf. Raymond (2014), paras. 217–222.

[47] Articles 122-8 and 122-9 Code de la consommation; Raymond (2014), paras. 308 f.

[48] Articles 122-6 and 122-7 Code de la consommation; Raymond (2014), para. 409.

[49] See Calais-Auloy and Temple (2010), p. 19 f., para. 18 who refer to former unsuccessful efforts for a "dépénalisation".

In reality, however, such supervisory authorities have very different missions. The Financial Services Ombudsman in the United Kingdom[50] and the corresponding institution in Australia,[51] being linked with the regulatory bodies in the financial markets of the two countries, in fact deal with consumer complaints. On the other hand, the German financial regulator responsible for banking, insurance and capital markets (*Bundesanstalt für Finanzdienstleistungsaufsicht—BAFIN*), while being charged, "within its statutory mission [with the] protection of collective consumer interests"[52] does not have a department that systematically optimizes consumer protection. With regard to telecommunication the German supervisory authority (*Bundesnetzagentur*) has set up, in line with some EU directives, a so-called consumer conciliation board, but its competence is limited concerning both the list of issues which may be submitted to the board and the type of decision it may take.[53]

Public enforcement by an authority of general competence and independent from economic regulation of any particular branch was introduced in Sweden many years ago.[54] A national authority designated as "*Konsumentverket*" and headed by the "*Konsumentombudsmannen*" safeguards consumer interests in various ways. Among others it receives complaints lodged by consumers, investigates the underlying cases and negotiates with the businesses. Where negotiations fail, it may subpoena a practice in minor cases or take the matter to court in others.[55] It does not solve disputes by administrative orders. Whether or not a case will be selected is likely to be determined administratively and will be affected by the limited resources available for public enforcement.

The overall impression emerging from a comparative survey shows that there is no general policy conception. But a certain trend towards the public enforcement of consumer rights is visible in Europe. In 2004, the EU issued a "Regulation on consumer protection cooperation" which is intended to improve the cooperation between national authorities responsible for the enforcement of consumer protection laws.[56] While this instrument only deals with "intra-community infringements"

---

[50]Morris and Little (1999), pp. 43–76; von Hippel (2000), p. 117 ff. With regards to insurance various national ombudsman institutions have been compared by Reichert-Facilides (1999), pp. 169–187.

[51]See Waye and Morabito (2012), pp. 4–7; for a predecessor mechanism see Reich (1992), pp. 809–813; from a comparative perspective Ali and Da Roza (2012), p. 500 ff.

[52]See § 4(1a) Gesetz über die Bundesanstalt für Finanzdienstleistungsaufsicht (Finanzdienstleistungsaufsichtsgesetz—FinDAG) of 22 April 2002, Bundesgesetzblatt I-1310 as amended.

[53]See § 47a Telekommunikationsgesetz (TKG) of 22 June 2004, Bundesgesetzblatt I-1190 as amended.

[54]See Bernitz and Draper (1986), pp. 65–80; Dopffel and Scherpe (1999), p. 431 f. See the website www.konsumentverket.se where information is available in several languages.

[55]Bernitz and Draper (1986), p. 70 ff.; Dopffel and Scherpe (1999), p. 433.

[56]Regulation (EC) No 2006/2004 of the European Parliament and of the Council of 27 October 2004 on cooperation between national authorities responsible for the enforcement of consumer protection laws (the Regulation on consumer protection cooperation), OJ 2004 L 364/1.

resulting from cross-border activities,[57] the Regulation requires Member States to designate competent authorities equipped with certain investigation and enforcement powers.[58] While some Member States appear hesitant in complying with this obligation, it is likely to pave the way for a more intense role for public authorities in the enforcement of consumer laws in general, perhaps also in the domestic cases of Member States which have so far been opposed to public enforcement.[59]

2.4 Conclusion on State Measures

The inquiry into some legal systems and the enforcement mechanisms of their state machinery discloses a surprising spirit of experimentation. Apparently traditional enforcement procedures have been considered insufficient; the search for more effective tools is visible everywhere. While the US legal system, driven by antitrust concerns, embarked on new paths as early as the end of the nineteenth century, European jurisdictions were much more hesitant, starting enforcement reforms only in the decades after World War II, mainly in the field of consumer law. The solutions espoused by them differ widely, despite the efforts for harmonization made by the EU.

The enforcement measures encountered in various jurisdictions form highly mixed “bundles”. They range from individual civil actions of the traditional type, sometimes encouraged and supported by public subsidies[60] or particular incentives, to opt-in class actions and opt-out class actions, to criminal enforcement and the establishment of special administrative agencies entrusted with dispute settlement upon complaint. The mix varies from country to country; as shown at the beginning of this paper, the enforcement mechanisms also differ in some basic aspects.[61] It is difficult to recommend a specific “bundle” as being superior.

The policies pursued are complex: (1) Changes in enforcement mechanisms have always been driven by the wish for more effective implementation of individual rights and substantive laws. (2) On the other hand, the expansion of traditional law enforcement in civil courts to new areas has raised the costs of the judicial system to

[57]See Articles 2(1) and 3(b) of Regulation (EC) No 2006/2004.

[58]See Article 4 of Regulation (EC) No 2006/2004.

[59]This tendency emerges from recent policy papers of the European Commission, see Report from the Commission to the European Parliament and the Council assessing the effectiveness of Regulation (EC) no. 2006/2004 of the European Parliament and of the Council of 27 October on the cooperation between national authorities responsible for the enforcement of consumer protection laws (the Regulation on consumer protection cooperation), COM(2016) 284 final of 25 May 2016; Proposal for a Regulation of the European Parliament and oft he Council on cooperation between national authorities responsible for the enforcement of consumer protection laws, COM (2016) 283 final of 25 May 2016 which is intended to repeal and replace Reg. 2006/2004.

[60]See on legal aid in Germany below, fn. 79.

[61]See above, Sect. 1.2.

a critical threshold which is of concern for legislatures. (3) Moreover, traditional views on the role of the various institutions and professions involved in law enforcement—courts, private attorneys, state authorities, all with vested interests—have at all times exercised a strong conservative influence. Few countries—such as Sweden—have succeeded in transferring the bulk of the enforcement of a whole area of the law—consumer law—from the judiciary to a state body. (4) This was possible because the amicable arrangement between the parties to a dispute became the primary objective to be achieved by negotiations between the consumer board (*konsumentverket*) and the professional. This gradual shift in the objectives of enforcement is even more eye-catching when we look at alternative measures.

3 *Alternative* Dispute Resolution (ADR)

3.1 Survey

Law enforcement by the judiciary has certain drawbacks. It costs time and money. It may disclose confidential facts to third parties or to the public. It may deter people who prefer private dealings to contacts with state power in general or with specific states. It turns the parties into bystanders, assigning the leading role to counsel and the court. Its adversarial nature may exacerbate conflicts while the parties involved are basically interested in maintaining peaceful relations. It may be in the hands of judges who, knowing very little about the circumstances of the court's investigation, may not deliver an outcome that is accepted as just. Each of these drawbacks provides an incentive to certain groups of parties to look for alternative dispute resolution.

The resulting development of the law started at an early stage and brought about rather diverse procedures. The common designation of these procedures as "ADR" signals a negative commonality: they are alternatives to proceedings in state courts, usually organized by private initiative. This does not mean, however, that state power is irrelevant for them; we can often observe a mix of private and state activities. Moreover, state power often plays a role in support or review proceedings. The purpose of ADR is the resolution of disputes with the assistance of third persons, usually outside state courts. ADR is generally said to comprise several types of mechanisms[62]: (assisted) negotiation, conciliation, arbitration (Sect. 3.2), ombudsman complaint procedures (Sect. 3.3) and mediation (Sect. 3.4) are the most important ones; only the latter three types will be further explored in this paper.

---

[62]For a general survey see Nolan-Haley (2013); the author dedicates special chapters of her book to negotiation, mediation, arbitration, dispute resolution in the court system and hybrid dispute resolution procedures, including ombudspersons. Esplugues and Barona (2014), p. 11 f. distinguish negotiation *inter partes* from the mechanisms involving a neutral third person, either devoid of decision-making powers (mediation, conciliation, ombudsman), or equipped with such power (arbitration).

The role of the third person varies in the mechanisms listed above: in arbitration that person is entrusted with the power of decision although not with its execution; in ombudsman complaint procedures he or she is entrusted with the task of investigating the other party's behaviour, at the request of, or upon complaint by one party, and of proposing a solution to the dispute; in mediation he or she is entrusted with the mission of finding, through discussions with the parties, possible strands of compromise. While the concepts differ from country to country and the borderlines between them are blurred by mixed techniques, grouping the various mechanisms into several broad categories may help to clarify the discussion and to further legal development.[63]

3.2 Arbitration

The oldest technique is arbitration. As early as the Middle Ages arbitration institutions emerged in Europe, for example in England the so-called Piepowder courts,[64] and in maritime trade along the European coasts, in particular in the *Consulados del Mar* in the Mediterranean countries, on the island of *Oléron* off the French Atlantic coast and in *Visby* on the island of *Gotland* in the Baltic Sea.[65] Everywhere, the reasons for these foundations were similar: itinerant merchants, before traveling on to their next destination, needed their disputes to be resolved quickly by persons with an insider knowledge of the respective trade and its customs. The flexibility required was not available in the general courts and the tribunals set up by the seigneurs which operated in a much more formal way.

Arbitration tribunals specific to particular industries or segments of industries have always existed: at various trading places, special arbitration tribunals can be found for particular goods and services, e.g. for fresh or tinned produce,[66] coffee,[67] and diamonds.[68] Contrary to a widespread belief in the law and economics literature, arbitration is, however, not confined to the closed circles of businesses of the same origin and operating in the same industry. Commercial arbitration, consumer arbitration, labor arbitration, medical malpractice arbitration and investment arbitration

[63]For a recent comparative survey with 12 national reports from Australia, China, England and Wales, Hong Kong, India, Indonesia, Ireland, Japan, Korea, Philippines, Singapore, Thailand and the United States see Esplugues and Barona (2014).

[64]See Pirenne (1933), here cited from the 4th edition of the German translation, UTB 1976, p. 55 f.

[65]On the formation of maritime law in these places see Wagner (1906), pp. 40–45.

[66]See e.g. the Court of Arbitration of the Waren-Verein der Hamburger Börse e.V. https://www.waren-verein.de/en/court-of-arbitration.

[67]See e.g. for the German coffee import association, Deutscher Kaffeeverband e.V., the arbitration rules at www.kaffeeverband.de/der-verband/leistungen-ziele-aufgaben/schiedsgericht.

[68]In the law and economics literature a number of publications by Lisa Bernstein have been very influential; see, for diamonds, Bernstein (1992), pp. 117–121 on trade custom, pp. 124–130 on the arbitration system.

are nowadays common dispute resolution mechanisms, albeit in a limited number of countries.

Whether preference is given to arbitration or to state courts depends on a variety of factors rooted in the legal systems of the various jurisdictions. Two examples: where regular legal proceedings at first instance last for several years a short-track procedure will be an attractive alternative for consumers' low-value disputes despite the risk of bias. And investment arbitration has emerged from the fact that private investors lack confidence in the impartiality of the judiciary of certain host states. The choice of arbitration is made in every country in the shadow of the law that ensures the operation of the judiciary: the better and cheaper the courts, the lower the incentive to opt for arbitration. It follows that in the law enforcement market comparative enquiry plays a significant role in party choice.

The poor functionality of the judicial system in a large number of countries has prompted the international community ever since World War II to improve the framework conditions for certain types of arbitration. The 1958 New York Convention has been ratified by more than 160 States and provides for an almost worldwide recognition and enforcement of foreign arbitral awards in commercial matters.[69] Arbitration rules adopted by the International Chamber of Commerce[70] and by the United Nations Commission on International Trade Law (UNCITRAL)[71] allow for the conduct of proceedings in accordance with standards approved by neutral international bodies. And the UNCITRAL Model Law on Commercial Arbitration[72] has made available a blueprint for national arbitration laws favoring arbitration. These and other measures have encouraged the use of commercial arbitration considerably. Over a period of 20 years the number of institutional arbitrations conducted in some major international arbitration centers has in fact quadrupled.[73]

3.3 *Ombudsman Complaint Procedures*

3.3.1 Law Enforcement in Consumer Disputes

As pointed out above, the rise of consumer protection from the 1960s onwards has disclosed important deficits of law enforcement in this area which have been explained in a variety of ways.[74] But irrespective of its reasons the insufficient

[69]Convention on the Recognition and Enforcement of Foreign Arbitral Awards, Done at New York on 10 June 1958, 330 UNTS 38.

[70]See the most recent version, the 2012 Arbitration Rules, available at www.iccwbo.org.

[71]UNCITRAL Arbitration Rules, several versions on the website of UNCITRAL: www.uncitral.org.

[72]UNCITRAL Model Law on International Commercial Arbitration 1985 with Amendments as adopted in 2006, www.uncitral.org.

[73]See the table in Basedow (2015), p. 382.

[74]See above, Sect. 2.3.

enforcement of consumer rights is generally perceived as a deficit of the legal system and, because of the economic consequences, as a threat to the operation of consumer markets.

Various forms of relief have been probed in a large number of countries[75]: the foundation of special authorities in Sweden entrusted with the investigation of consumer complaints[76] and the establishment of similar but specialized institutions linked with regulatory bodies, *viz.* the Financial Ombudsman Services in the United Kingdom[77] and in Australia[78] have already been mentioned. In terms of traditional enforcement mechanisms some states such as Germany,[79] subsidize litigation in state courts both in respect of court costs and legal fees. Further institutions deserve attention: special tribunals and fast-track procedures for small claims, especially in some states of the US[80] and in Sweden[81]; mediation procedures which may be voluntary or a compulsory precondition for actions in state courts like in Argentina[82]; the creation, by state legislation, of a legal framework for consumer complaint institutions which are then set up by cooperating business and consumer associations in Denmark.[83]

The list is not exhaustive; the variety of forms is great. Some measures listed above try to preserve the central role of the judiciary for dispute resolution and to make it operational for small claims, others strike a new path outside the courts. Of particular interest in this section is the establishment of bodies—public or private—which are usually devoid of decision-making power, but are charged with the task of receiving complaints from consumers, investigating the facts of the dispute, communicating their findings to the parties, and eventually urging a party to acknowledge a breach of its obligations or helping the parties to settle the dispute. First probed in the Nordic countries, the Scandinavian expression *ombudsman* has become common for this type of mechanism.

3.3.2 ADR in the US and the EU

In line with the aforementioned characteristics, federal legislation in the US defines the procedures of alternative dispute resolution as "any process or procedure [...] in

[75]See von Hippel (1986), p. 159 ff.

[76]See above, the text at fn. 52–55.

[77]See above, fn. 50.

[78]See above, fn. 51.

[79]Gesetz über die Prozesskostenhilfe of 13.6.1980, Bundesgesetzblatt (Federal Law Gazette; hereinafter BGBl.) I 677; Gesetz über die Rechtsberatung und Vertretung für Bürger mit geringem Einkommen of 18.6.1980, BGBl. I 689.

[80]*Cf.* von Hippel (1973), p. 271 ff.

[81]Dopffel and Scherpe (1999), p. 433 on the Market Court—*marknadsdomstolen*.

[82]Sievers (2001). For mediation see below Sect. 3.4.

[83]Scherpe (2002), pp. 110 ff., 171 ff.

which a neutral third party participates to assist in the resolution of issues in controversy, through processes such as early neutral evaluation, mediation, minitrial, and arbitration [. . .]".[84] The EU Directive on alternative dispute resolution refers to out-of-court resolution procedures conducted by an "entity which proposes or imposes a solution or brings the parties together with the aim of facilitating an amicable solution".[85] While the US definition is of a general purview, the ADR Directive concerns itself only with disputes between professionals and consumers.

Both definitions attest to the difficulty in precisely defining ADR. While the borderline between ADR and court proceedings is undisputed the entities organizing ADR may be private or public,[86] and the procedures at issue range from those aiming at amicable solutions, on the one hand, to those conducted with a view to the decision of the dispute, on the other.[87] Both mediation and arbitration are included in US law, whereas the ADR Directive does not cover consumer arbitration agreed upon before the dispute arises as a binding mechanism and as a substitute to court proceedings.[88]

The general terms employed by the definitions take account of the diversity of forms of ADR created within the various sister states of the US and in the Member States of the EU by public and private initiatives; almost all of them are intended to be covered. As a consequence, the regulatory precision of both instruments is low. Both instruments, and in particular the ADR Directive, enunciate primarily principles of general importance: expertise as well as neutrality and impartiality of the ADR entity; transparency of proceedings which is to be assured by the supply of huge amounts of information to the consumer; effectiveness in terms of easy and gratuitous access to, and fairness of, the proceedings and their voluntary character which does not exclude action in court.[89]

In the context of law enforcement the principle of legality laid down in art. 11 ADR Directive is of particular significance. The provision makes clear that solutions "imposed" by ADR shall not deprive consumers of the protection afforded by mandatory rules of their country of habitual residence. Thus the mandatory provisions of that country either have to be applied themselves or have to be assessed as a yardstick for the solution of the dispute. The minimum protection is, however, only prescribed for ADR procedures that end up in an "imposed" solution. That

[84]28 U.S. Code § 651 as amended by Pub.L. 105–315 of 30 October 1998, 112 Stat. 2998.

[85]Directive 2013/11/EU of the European Parliament and of the Council of 21 May 2013 on alternative dispute resolution for consumer disputes and amending Regulation (EC) No. 2006/2004 and Directive 2009/22/EC (Directive on consumer ADR), OJ 2013 L 165/63 (henceforth: ADR Directive).

[86]The German statute implementing the ADR Directive explicitly deals with dispute resolution entities established by public authorities, see § 28 of the Gesetz über alternative Streitbeilegung in Verbrauchersachen of 19 February 2016, Bundesgesetzblatt (BGBl.) I-254.

[87]Both are explicitly listed in 28 U.S. Code § 651(a).

[88]See Article 10 ADR Directive and recital 43.

[89]See Articles 6–10 ADR Directive.

attribute requires that the parties are informed in advance of the binding nature of the solution and that the consumer specifically agrees to it.[90]

An example of both "imposed" and other solutions can be found in the activities of the German Insurance Ombudsman.[91] On a consumer's complaint the Ombudsman will investigate the case exclusively on the basis of documentary evidence; as a result it will reject the complaint, recommend a solution or decide the case. A decision is binding for, or "imposed" on, the insurer where the value of the dispute does not exceed 10,000 €; the insurer's adherence to the scheme would be considered, by any court, as a *pactum de non petendo* rendering a subsequent claim for less than 10,000 € inadmissible. Conversely, the Ombudsman's decision is never binding for consumers whose right to a court action is highlighted in the rules of procedure. Consequently, Article 11 ADR Directive does not apply to policyholders lodging a complaint with the Insurance Ombudsman; while the Ombudsman, in proposing an amicable solution, is not bound by mandatory provisions of law, these provisions will be applied under the pertinent rules of procedure, where a decision is taken.

These observations again give evidence of divergent objectives which are hidden under the camouflage of the common designation "ADR". While some of these procedures aim at the enforcement of individual rights by the application of law, others pursue the objective of conflict termination, irrespective of the application of rules of law.

3.4 Mediation and Conciliation

Contrary to the complaint procedures conciliation and mediation exclusively aim at an amicable resolution of a dispute, irrespective of which party is right or wrong. A rule such as Article 11 ADR Directive requiring the application of law for "imposed" solutions therefore does not apply to conciliation or mediation procedures. They are characterized by the absence of any decision-making powers on the part of the neutral entity or person involved. On the basis of a broad comparative investigation *Hopt* and *Steffek* have suggested the following definition for mediation[92]: "Mediation is a procedure based on the voluntary participation of the parties, in which an intermediary (or multiple intermediaries) with no adjudicatory powers systematically facilitate(s) communication between the parties with the aim of enabling the parties to themselves take responsibility for resolving their dispute."

The same could be said for conciliation. The two concepts "are frequently used interchangeably both in practice and academic study", although conciliators will

[90]See Article 10(2) ADR Directive.

[91]See the rules of procedure (Verfahrensordnung) on the website www.versicherungsombudsmann.de; for a general survey and appraisal see Basedow (2007b), pp. 49–63.

[92]Hopt and Steffek (2013), p. 11; for a more recent comparative assessment of the law relating to mediation and additional national reports see Esplugues and Marquis (2015).

often "exert more [. . .] influence on the result of agreement, in particular by means of a (non-binding) conciliation decision."[93] The EU Directive on cross-border mediation which defines its scope with similar words therefore explicitly adds that it applies to such a process, "however named or referred to".[94]

While mediation procedures are generally aimed at an amicable solution of the dispute, i.e. a voluntary commitment of the parties, these procedures are not always voluntary themselves. In jurisdictions such as Argentina[95] and also in some of the German *Länder*[96] parties are required to proceed to mediation before they can litigate their case in court. The admissibility of the action will depend on the presentation of a certificate giving evidence of an unsuccessful mediation. On a private basis legal cost insurers may establish similar requirements in the insurance contracts.[97] But mediation is also voluntary in many instances. Parties may prefer mediation to court proceedings and arbitration because they may wish a less legalistic conduct of the proceedings or because they fear a loss of confidentiality engendered by the publication of awards and judgements.

For the purpose of this study it follows from the goal of mediation, i.e. the amicable solution of a dispute, that mediation cannot be classified as a means of law enforcement strictly speaking. It pursues other objectives, namely the cooling-down of a conflict; the achievement of a situation where both parties involved prefer the end of the argument to its continuation even if they cannot fully obtain what they had initially sought. In general, the alleged rights are not clearly proved in mediation. Nevertheless, the overall enforcement of the law may be considered to improve in a statistical sense since more people will have their claims satisfied at least in part than under the traditional system of enforcement through litigation. Mediation is attractive to the extent that people are deterred by litigation and therefore abstain from seeking enforcement of their claims. From this perspective, enforcement measured in statistical terms supersedes individual enforcement.

---

[93]Hopt and Steffek (2013), p. 16.

[94]Directive 2008/52/EC of the European Parliament and of the Council of 21 May 2008 on certain aspects of mediation in civil and commercial matters, OJ 2008 L 136/3; see for a closer analysis, Esplugues (2014), pp. 485–771; this long report is based on 22 reports on the laws of EU Member States contained in the same volume.

[95]See above at fn. 82.

[96]According to § 15a of the Introductory Law of the Code of civil procedure it is up to the single *Länder*, i.e. the German states to decide whether mediation is compulsory or not. For example, the biggest German *Land* North Rhine-Westphalia initially required a certificate on unsuccessful mediation as a precondition for any lawsuit involving a value of less than 1200 DM (about 600 €), see Article 1 § 10 Gesetz zur Ausführung von § 15a EGZPO of 9 May 2000, Gesetz- und Verordnungsblatt Nordrhein-Westfalen (GV NRW) 2000, 476, but repealed this requirement some years later by the law of 20 November 2007, GV NRW 2007, 583. The mediation requirement has been maintained for disputes in matters of discrimination and between neighbours.

[97]Such contract terms have explicitly been upheld by the German Federal Court (Bundesgerichtshof, BGH), see BGH 14 January 2016, Verbraucher und Recht 2016, 227 with an annotation by *Burkhard Lensing*.

4 Extra-Legal, Societal Enforcement Mechanisms

The enforcement of the law has never been an exclusive domain of legal mechanisms. Morality and ethics have always played an important role. Children know that if they do not respect each other's rights they will lose friends who do not want to play with them any more. These mechanisms operate prior to, and regardless of, any information about law. What matters in the context of this inquiry is that these extra-legal or societal enforcement mechanisms appear to become more structured and gain significance in the public domain. This can best be observed in connection with the rise of what usually is referred to as soft law, in particular in international relations.

4.1 The Advancement of Soft Law

In recent times, more and more sets of non-binding rules have been adopted, especially for cross-border activities.[98] In view of the difficult approval of binding legal provisions in an international setting, non-binding rules appear to provide at least a common orientation. Such sets of non-binding rules are sometimes authored by intergovernmental organizations such as UNIDROIT, the Hague Conference on Private International Law, the Organization for Economic Cooperation and Development (OECD), particular units of the United Nations system, or sometimes by private bodies, e.g. the International Chamber of Commerce (ICC) or the Baltic and International Maritime Conference (BIMCO). The addressees are often private actors but may also be states and their institutions. The instruments bear various designations: codes of conduct, principles, guidelines, best practices, etc. They are intended to guide the conduct of people and companies or distribute the risks flowing from specific activities. In this respect, international conventions that have not taken effect are of a similar nature. All this is often covered by the term *soft law*.

Some examples should demonstrate the great variety of such texts: as early as 1980 the United Nations Conference on Trade and Development (UNCTAD) tried to harmonize competition law by a set of multilaterally agreed equitable principles and rules for the control of restrictive business practices.[99] Since that time UNIDROIT has drafted the Principles of international commercial contracts which have been published in several versions.[100] In the same field the ICC continues to revise the

[98]For surveys of the many aspects of this phenomenon, see Jansen and Michaels (2008); Calliess (2014); Cafaggi (2012).

[99]The UN-RBP Code is contained in UN Doc. TD/RBP/Conf./10 of 2 May 1980; also published in Wirtschaft und Wettbewerb (WuW) 1982, p. 32.

[100]The most recent version is UNIDROIT Principles of International Commercial Contracts, UNIDROIT 2010.

so-called Incoterms,[101] and the Hague Conference has recently adopted the Hague Principles on Choice of Law for International Commercial Contracts.[102] In capital market law, the International Accounting Standards Board, a private body, is committed to the development of global accounting standards as a common benchmark for the valuation of companies; its work product are the International Financial Reporting Standards (IFRS).[103] The International Labour Organization (ILO) has drafted, alongside a large number of binding conventions, the non-binding 1998 Declaration on Fundamental Principles and Rights at Work which emphasizes, *inter alia*, the right to collective bargaining and the prohibition of child labour.[104] A final example is provided by the Guiding Principles on Business and Human Rights endorsed by the Human Rights Council of the United Nations which lay down obligations of states and of corporations aiming at a better protection of human rights in business life, in particular in countries which do not provide for sufficient protection of human rights under their own national law.[105]

These instruments and many similar texts are meant to serve as persuasive authority and to urge individuals and companies to act accordingly. They are, however, not binding in a legal sense unless states give some legal recognition to them. This happens time and again; it improves the prospect for compliance but is not indispensable to it. Non-legal enforcement mechanisms may have a similar effect.

4.2 Enforcement and Compliance

4.2.1 Support by State Law

The term "enforcement" might appear inappropriate where non-binding rules are at issue. But the term compliance would be correct as the addressees' behavior may either deviate from or comply with those rules. And since the authors of such rules aspire for their rules to have a certain social and economic impact, the term enforcement might be acceptable as well. State law can promote compliance with or enforcement of non-binding law by legislation or by case law.

Legislation building on soft law is not uncommon in the corporate law of the EU. For example, the EU has explicitly permitted stock corporations to base their annual accounts on the IFRS irrespective of the national accounting provisions of the

[101]See the ICC website, www.iccwbo.org →products and services →Incoterms 2010.

[102]The Hague Principles and the official Commentary are reproduced in print in both English and French in Uniform Law Review 20 (2015), pp. 365–489.

[103]See the website of the IFRS Foundation, www.ifrs.org.

[104]Available on the website of the ILO, www.ilo.org →Labour standards →Informationa Resources and Publications →Free Trade Agreements and Labour Rights →ILO Declaration on Fundamental Principles and Rights at Work.

[105]United Nations 2011; cf. Ruggie (2007), pp. 819–840.

Member State of incorporation.[106] According to the Annual Accounts Directive, the annual reports of stock companies whose securities are traded on a regulated market have to refer to a corporate governance code which the company either has to apply or voluntarily applies.[107] In some Member States such codes are non-binding regulations established by private bodies. They are, however, upgraded by a comply-or-explain obligation under the Directive: any departure from the rules of the chosen corporate governance code must be disclosed and explained in the report.[108] The mechanism prescribed by legislation leads to what has been called a self-commitment of a company to the compliance with non-state law.[109]

On a similar note the Guiding Principles on Business and Human Rights are treated as a benchmark for the duty of EU corporations to disclose certain non-financial information in their management reports. Companies with a workforce exceeding 500 employees shall include in such a report a statement concerning, *inter alia,* the respect for human rights[110]; according to the recitals of the pertinent directive companies can rely on "international frameworks such as [. . .] the Guiding Principles on Business and Human Rights."[111]

Similar references can be found in other areas of the law as well. In the definition of misleading commercial practices contained in the Directive on Unfair Commercial Practices reference is made to "non-compliance by the trader with commitments contained in codes of conduct" which the trader has indicated to consider as binding.[112] And the conformity of a product to the general safety requirement is

[106]In accordance with Regulation No. 1606/2002 of the European Parliament and of the Council of 19 July 2002 on the application of international accounting standards, OJ 2002 L 243/1 the European Commission, assisted by a special Committee, decides on the application of single accounting standards by Commission Regulation, see for example Commission Regulation (EU) No 183/2013 of 4 March 2013 amending Regulation (EC) No 1126/2008 adopting certain international accounting standards in accordance with Regulation (EC) No 1606/2002 of the European Parliament and of the Council as regards International Financial Reporting Standard 1, OJ 2013 L 61/6.

[107]See Article 46a(1)(a) of Directive 78/660/EEC as amended by Directive 2006/46/EC of the European Parliament and of Council of 14 June 2006 amending Council Directives 78/660/EEC on the annual accounts of certain types of companies, 83/349/EEC on consolidated accounts, 86/635/EEC on the annual accounts and consolidated accounts of banks and other financial institutions and 91/674/EEC on the annual accounts and consolidated accounts of insurance undertakings, OJ 2006 L 224/1.

[108]See Article 46a(1)(b) of Directive 78/660/EEC as amended in 2006; cf. Leyens (2016), p. (401) who presents a survey of similar comply-or-explain rules in some national laws as well, see pp. 380–401.

[109]See Leyens (2015), pp. 611–654.

[110]See Article 19a of Directive 2013/34/EU as amended by Directive 2014/95/EU of the European Parliament and of the Council of 22 October 2014 amending Directive 2013/34/EU as regards disclosure of non-financial and diversity information by certain large undertakings and groups, OJ 2014 L 330/1.

[111]Recital 9 of Directive 2014/95/EU.

[112]See Article 6(2)(b) of Directive 2005/29/EC of the European Parliament and of the Council of 11 May 2005 concerning unfair business-to-consumer commercial practices in the internal market

measured, under the Product Safety Directive, by "product safety codes of good practice in force in the sector concerned".[113]

These are examples of soft law being promoted by legislation; but soft law may of course also be used where courts have to substantiate the meaning of general provisions employed in the applicable law, such as good faith, reasonableness or negligence. Moreover, it may be incorporated by private parties into their contracts which would open the way to the application of general tools of private enforcement.

4.2.2 Societal Enforcement Mechanisms

While legislation may use non-binding rules as a blueprint or as a basis for its own regulatory purposes, this is not always the case. In many instances the rule-makers do not count on any legislative or judicial reinforcement for their own product, but reckon on compliance for other reasons: because the addressees may appreciate the quality of the rules in question, because they trust in their placating nature in times of conflict or their reassuring effect; because they believe that, despite the costs that the rules may generate, they provide a solid basis for running a profitable business, because they fear that rejection of these rules might have detrimental consequences for them.

Not a single of these motivations follows from the operation of legal enforcement mechanisms. All of them are located outside the sphere of law: in psychology, in economics and in sociology. They may be very effective nevertheless, sometimes even more effective than legal enforcement. It is the fear of the detrimental consequences of non-compliance, (the last of the motives referred to above) which comes closest to legal enforcement, since it attributes the effect of non-binding rules to the threat of certain "sanctions", not legal sanctions, but sanctions that may be expected from the social environment of the persons who do not comply.

The operation of such enforcement mechanisms can be studied in connection with declarations such as memoranda of understanding in public international law,[114] letters of intent in commercial law[115] or international framework agreements concluded between multinational enterprises and umbrella organizations of trade unions, usually designated as global union federations in labour law.[116] The binding nature of all these instruments may vary from case to case and is in doubt; in many of

---

and amending Council Directive 84/450/EEC, Directives 97/7/EC, 98/27/EC and 2002/65/EC of the European Parliament and of the Council and Regulation (EC) No. 2006/2004 of the European Parliament and of the Council ('Unfair Commercial Practices Directive'), OJ 2005 L 149/22.

[113] See Article 3(3)(d) of Directive 2001/95/EC of the European Parliament and of the Council of 3 December 2001 on general product safety, OJ 2001 L 11/4.

[114] See e.g. Aust (2000), pp. 18 and 20–21.

[115] See e.g. Lake (1984–85), pp. 331–354; Lutter (1982).

[116] See e.g. Fornasier (2015), p. 288 ff.

them, recourse to legal action or arbitration is even explicitly excluded and replaced by consultation procedures.[117]

But to take only the example of the international framework agreements it nevertheless emerges from these instruments that they aim at affording worldwide a minimum standard to all employees of a multinational enterprise, i.e. the whole group, and in some cases, even to the workers of its suppliers. To this end, they refer to or incorporate soft law instruments such as the above-mentioned ILO Declaration on Fundamental Principles and Rights at Work.[118]

It is not the purpose of this analysis to inquire whether the exclusion of any binding legal effect is valid which may be doubtful in some jurisdictions. But it should be pointed out that non-legal enforcement mechanisms "might be in many cases more effective than legal enforcement."[119] First, international framework agreements provide for the monitoring of compliance in the various countries covered; where non-compliance is disclosed it will be discussed in national or international bodies.[120] Second, there are several sanctions which the enterprise may anticipate[121]: the end of cooperation with the global union federation; industrial action including solidarity strikes; the loss of corporate identity as perceived by the workforce of the various subsidiaries; a loss of reputation in the eyes of banks, investors and consumers, following a media campaign unleashed by the global union federation ("naming and shaming"); and the resulting loss of business.[122]

The operation of those extra-legal mechanisms has the indirect effect of turning the soft law principles incorporated in the international framework agreements into quasi-binding minimum standards. While this is not an enforcement of the workers' individual rights strictly speaking, the effect may be similar: the worldwide workforce of a multinational enterprise can count on the company's compliance with those standards.

5 Conclusion

1. Looking at the law from the perspective of its enforcement reverses the traditional order of investigation in legal scholarship: instead of focusing on rules of conduct and risk distribution intended to solve social problems and to assign losses in society, we start from the performance, characteristic features, efficiency, and

[117] Cf. for international framework agreements the examples provided by Thüsing (2010), p. 92; Fornasier (2015), p. 294.

[118] See fn. 104.

[119] Krause (2012), p. 758.

[120] Fornasier (2015), p. 294 f.; Krause (2012), p. 757.

[121] For a broader survey and analysis not confined to labour law see Scott (2012), pp. 151–156.

[122] On the significance of reputation for the emergence of private ordering see Richman (2004), pp. 2328–2367.

advantages and disadvantages of the various enforcement mechanisms. This may help to realize what kind of rules are susceptible of being enforced and may thus have a beneficial impact on rule-making itself.
2. This report displays a progressive development of the law towards a wide diversity of enforcement mechanisms. A hundred years ago, the bodies of law seemed to be rather clearly assigned to single enforcement devices: private law to civil procedure, criminal law to criminal procedure, administrative law to regulatory procedure. Ever since, legislatures and private actors appear to look for more effective forms of enforcement; as a result, a great variety of enforcement mechanisms has emerged that reminds us of post-modernist culture.
3. The development is driven by a policy-mix that only gradually comes to mind. The traditional search for the effective enforcement of law coincides with the aim of cost reduction, the vested interests of the legal services industry and the growing awareness that the peaceful resolution of conflicts in society may be just as important as the enforcement of individual rights. The different weight given to these goals in the various countries reflects the different mix of enforcement mechanisms employed in a given area of the law.
4. Another result of the policy-mix is an increasing privatization of dispute resolution. Under the heading of alternative dispute resolution (ADR) a large number of different mechanisms, many of them originating in private initiatives, are being tested: some of them are exclusively targeted at amicable solutions, others include the conferral of decision-making powers on third persons. Where these developments might lead remains to be seen.
5. The growing weight given to social concord and the peaceful resolution of disputes directs scholarly attention to extra-legal mechanisms which foster compliance with rules and principles of societal cohabitation. Further research is needed in the area of enforcement as a whole and will have to include the expertise of psychologists, economists and social scientists in order to explore the dynamics of conflicts and the extra-legal conditions for dispute resolution.

References

Afferni G (2016) "Opt-in" class actions in Italy: why are they failing? J Eur Tort Law 7:82–100
Ali S, Da Roza A (2012) Alternative dispute resolution in financial markets – some more equal than others: Hong Kong's proposed financial dispute resolution centre in the context of experience in the UK, US, Australia and Singapore. Pac Rim Law Policy J 21:485–531
Areeda P, Kaplow L, Edlin A (2004) Antitrust analysis, 6th edn. Aspen Publishers
Aust A (2000) Modern treaty law and practice. Cambridge University Press
Basedow J (ed) (2007a) Private enforcement of competition law. Kluwer Law International
Basedow J (2007b) Small claims in a high cost country: The German Insurance Ombudsman. Scand Stud Law 50:49–63
Basedow J (2015) EU law in international arbitration: referrals to the European court of justice. J Int Arbitr 32:367–386
Bernitz U, Draper J (1986) Consumer protection in Sweden: legislation, institutions and practice, 2nd edn. LiberFörläg

Bernstein L (1992) Opting out of the legal system: extralegal contractual relations in the diamond industry. J Leg Stud 21:115–158
Böhmer G (1950) Grundlagen der Bürgerlichen Rechtsordnung, vol 1. Mohr Siebeck, Tübingen
Bohrer A (2015) Kapitalmarktrecht zwischen öffentlich-rechtlicher und privatrechtlicher Normdurchsetzung. In: Fleischer H, Kalss S, Vogt HU (eds) Enforcement im Gesellschafts- und Kapitalmarktrecht 2015. Mohr Siebeck, pp 243–275
Bout R, Bruschi M, Luby-Gaucher, M, Poillot-Péruzzetto S (eds) (2015) Le Lamy Droit Économique. Wolters Kluwer France
Cafaggi F (ed) (2012) Enforcement of transnational regulation. Edward Elgar
Calais-Auloy J, Temple H (2010) Droit de la consommation – Précis Dalloz, 8th edn. Dalloz
Calliess GP (ed) (2014) Transnationales Recht. Mohr Siebeck
de Giles D (2003) Le droit pénal de la concurrence en Europe: 1-Premier bilan et perspectives en France – 2-L'expérience européenne, La semaine juridique – Entreprise et Affaires (JCP-E), 20–28 and 68–73
Dopffel P, Scherpe JM (1999) "Grupptalan" – Die Bündelung gleichgerichteter Interessen im schwedischen Recht. In: Basedow J, Hopt KJ, Kötz H, Baetge D (eds) Die Bündelung gleichgerichteter Interessen im Prozess. Mohr Siebeck, pp 429–451
Esplugues C (2014) Civil and Commercial Mediation in the EU after the Transposition of Directive 2008/52/EC. In: Esplugues C (ed) Civil and commercial mediation in Europe – cross-border mediation. Intersentia, pp 485–771
Esplugues C, Barona S (2014) ADR mechanisms and their incorporation into global justice in the twenty-first century: some concepts and trends. In: Esplugues C, Barona S (eds) Global perspectives on ADR. Intersentia, pp 1–52
Esplugues C, Marquis L (eds) (2015) New developments in civil and commercial mediation. Springer
Fitzpatrick B (2010) An empirical study of class action settlements and their fee awards. J Empir Leg Stud 7:811–846
Fornasier M (2015) Transnational collective bargaining – the case of international framework agreements – a legal analysis. Eurorpäische Zeitschrift für Arbeitsrecht, pp 281–296
Guinchard S, Chainais C, Ferrand F (2014) Procédure civile – droit interne et droit de l'Union européenne, 32nd edn. Précis Dalloz
Halsbury's Laws of England (2015) Vol 97, 5th edn. LexisNexis
Hopt K, Steffek F (2013) Mediation: comparison of laws, regulatory models, fundamental issues. In: Hopt K, Steffek F (eds) Mediation – principles and regulation in comparative perspective. OUP, pp 1–130
Howell B (2010) Sentencing of antitrust offenders: what does the data show? http://www.ussc.gov/sites/default/files/pdf/about/commissioners/selected-articles/Howell_Review_of_Antitrust_Sentencing_Data.pdf
Ida M (2011) Wirtschaftsstrafrecht. In: Baum H, Bälz M (eds) Handbuch Japanisches Handels- und Wirtschaftsrecht. Heymanns, pp 1461–1487
Jansen N, Michaels R (eds) (2008) Beyond the state – rethinking private law. Mohr Siebeck
Krause R (2012) International framework agreements as instrument for the legal enforcement of freedom of association and collective bargaining? The German Case. Comp Labor Law Policy J 33:749–773
Lake R (1984–85) Letters of intent: a comparative examination under English, U.S., French and West German Law. George Wash J Int Law Econ 18:331–354
Leyens P (2015) Selbstbindung an untergesetzliche Verhaltensregeln. Archiv für die civilistische Praxis:611–654
Leyens P (2016) Comply or explain im Europäischen Privatrecht. Zeitschrift für Europäisches Privatrecht (ZEuP), 388–426
Lima Marques C (2016) A vulnerabilidade dos analfabetos e dos idosos na sociedade de consumo brasileira: primeiros estudos sobre a figura do assédio de consumo. In: Lima Marques C, Gsell B

(eds) Novas tendências do direito do consumidor. Thomson Reuters Revista dos Tribunais, pp 46–87
Lima Marques C, Gsell B (eds) (2016) Novas tendências do direito do consumidor. Thomson Reuters Revista dos Tribunais
Lutter M (1982) Der Letter of Intent. Heymann
Martiny D (2000) Unterhaltsrang und -rückgriff, vol 2. Mohr Siebeck
Monopolkommission (2015) Strafrechtliche Sanktionen bei Kartellverstößen, Sondergutachten 72, Nomos
Morris P, Little G (1999) The Ombudsmen and consumer protection. In: Cartwright P (ed) Consumer protection in financial services. Kluwer, pp 43–76
Nolan-Haley J (2013) Alternative dispute resolution in a nutshell, 4th edn. West Publishing
Peter H (1957) Actio und Writ - Eine vergleichende Darstellung römischer und englischer Rechtsbehelfe. Mohr Siebeck, Tübingen
Pirenne H (1933) La civilisation occidentale au Moyen Age du milieu du 15e siècle — Le mouvement économique et social. In: Glotz G, Histoire du Moyen Age, vol. VIII, 2nd section of l'Histoire générale, Paris
Prentice DD (2015) Illegality and public policy. In: Chitty on contracts, vol I – general principles, 32 edn. Sweet & Maxwell
Raymond G (2014) Droit de la consommation, 3rd edn. LexisNexis
Reich N (1992) Die Einrichtung eines Bankenombudsmanns in Australien - ein Modell für selbstverwalteten Verbraucherschutz? Wertpapier-Mitteilungen, pp 809–813
Reichert-Facilides F (1999) Der Versicherungsombudsmann im Ausland - Ein vergleichender Überblick. In: Basedow J, Donath R, Meyer U, Rückle D, Schwintowski HP (eds) Anleger- und objektgerechte Beratung. Private Krankenversicherung. Ein Ombudsmann für Versicherungen, Versicherungswissenschaftliche Studien (VersWissStud 11), Nomos, pp 169–187
Richman B (2004) Firms, courts and reputation mechanisms: towards a positive theory of private ordering. Columbia Law Rev 104:2328–2367
Ruggie JG (2007) Business and human rights: the evolving international agenda. Am J Int Law 101:819–840
Schäfer HB (1999) Anreizwirkungen bei der Class Action und der Verbandsklage. In: Basedow J, Hopt KJ, Kötz H, Baetge D (eds) Die Bündelung gleichgerichteter Interessen im Prozess. Mohr Siebeck, pp 67–100
Scherpe JM (2002) Außergerichtliche Streitbeilegung in Verbrauchersachen - Ein deutsch-dänischer Rechtsvergleich. Mohr Siebeck
Scott C (2012) Non-judicial enforcement of transnational private regulation. In: Cafaggi F (ed) Enforcement of transnational regulation. Edward Elgar, pp 147–164
Shavell S (2004) Foundations of economic analysis of law. Belknap Harvard
Sievers N (2001) Mediation als alternative Konfliktlösungsmöglichkeit auch in Deutschland? - Eine rechtsvergleichende Untersuchung am Beispiel der argentinischen mediación previa, Lang
Thüsing G (2010) International framework agreements: Rechtliche Grenzen und praktischer Nutzen. Recht der Arbeit, pp 78–93
Veil R, Brüggemeier A (2015) Kapitalmarktrecht zwischen öffentlich-rechtlicher und privatrechtlicher Normdurchsetzung. In: Fleischer H, Kalss S, Vogt HU (eds) Enforcement im Gesellschafts- und Kapitalmarktrecht 2015. Mohr Siebeck, pp 279–309
von Hippel E (1973) Besserer Rechtsschutz des Verbrauchers? RabelsZ 37:268–283
von Hippel E (1986) Verbraucherschutz, 3rd edn. Mohr Siebeck, Tübingen
von Hippel T (2000) Der Ombudsmann im Bank- und Versicherungswesen. Mohr Siebeck
von Jhering R (1897) Der Kampf ums Recht, 13th edn. Wien, Manz
Waelbroeck D, Slater D, Even-Shoshan G (2004) Study on the conditions of claims for damages in case of infringement of EC competition rules. http://ec.europa.eu/competition/antitrust/actionsdamages/comparative_report_clean_en.pdf

Wagner R (1906) Handbuch des Seerechts. Einleitung – Personen des Seerechts, 2nd edn. Duncker & Humblot
Waye V, Morabito V (2012) Collective forms of consumer redress: financial Ombudsman case study. J Corp Law Stud 12:1–32
Wurmnest W (2016) International jurisdiction in competition damages cases under the Brussels I regulation: CDC hydrogen peroxide. Com Mkt Law Rev 53:225–248
Zweigert K, Kötz H (1998) An introduction to comparative law, 3rd edn. Oxford University Press

Jürgen Basedow is Director emeritus of the Max Planck Institute for Comparative and International Private Law in Hamburg since 1997 and Professor at the University of Hamburg. Professor Basedow has served on numerous governmental advisory committees, ranging from a Think Tank on Private Enforcement of DG Competition of the European Commission (2004–2006) to an Advisory Board on Insurance of the German Supervisory Authority for Financial Services (BAFIN). From 1988–1991 he served as Vice Chairman of the German Deregulation Committee (Federal Ministry of Economic Affairs), and since 2000 has been a member of the German Monopoly Commission, acting as its Chairman since 2004. He is a titular member and former Secretary-General of the International Academy of Comparative Law.

Enforcing Legal Norms Through Private Means

George A. Bermann

Abstract We ordinarily think of legal norms as not only established through public means, but also enforced through public means—typically by legislatures and courts, or by bodies authorized by law to produce and enforce such norms. That view of legal norms is, however, an incomplete one. Private actors of various stripes also produce norms that, directly or indirectly, exert binding effect. Modes of private law enforcement span a wide range, running from the most private, personal, and informal at one extreme, to the quite formal, on the other. Development of private modes of law enforcement relieves public authorities of carrying the full law enforcement burden. Yet, private law enforcers often work in tandem with public authorities, especially as we move along this spectrum I have identified. Either way, private law enforcement promotes the public good. However, private law enforcement is not an unmitigated good. Each mode of private law enforcement brings along with it a certain number of risks that must be acknowledged and addressed. Ironically, perhaps, these risks sometimes can only be properly addressed with a minimum of intervention of public authorities. In other words, public and private law enforcement are deeply mutually interdependent.

1 Introduction

During the congress, a great many presentations were made on the subject of enforcement of norms, mostly norms legal in nature and enforced mostly through means legal in nature. The congress opened and largely proceeded with an emphasis on the means by which law is enforced publicly, i.e. through public institutions, rather than through private means. But the conference organizers recognized that law enforcement may in various ways also enlist private individuals and entities.

G. A. Bermann (✉)
Columbia Law School, New York, NY, USA
e-mail: gbermann@law.columbia.edu

N. Etcheverry Estrázulas, D. P. Fernández Arroyo (eds.), *Enforcement and Effectiveness of the Law - La mise en oeuvre et l'effectivité du droit*, Ius Comparatum – Global Studies in Comparative Law 30, https://doi.org/10.1007/978-3-319-93758-8_2

To fully appreciate the scope of private law enforcement, it is necessary, at least initially, to conceive of "law" broadly, so as to include consideration of norms, establishing rights and obligations, of non-legal origin. One reason to accept this widening of the lens, is that we can even better appreciate law enforcement through public institutions if we view it against the background of what we might have at our disposal if we had no public law enforcement at our disposal.

Broad consideration of the private law enforcement reveals that such enforcement, like many things, comes in a much larger number of shapes, and a much more diverse set of shapes, than is easily imagined. This presentation seeks to bring a modicum of order to what may seem at first a largely uncharted landscape—the landscape upon which private mechanisms, operating alone or in connection with public mechanisms, contribute to the effective enforcement of legal norms. It does so by presenting "clusters" of ways in which private law enforcement is achieved.

We can identify a certain number of discrete modalities of private law enforcement that may be arrayed on a sliding scale moving from least formal (perhaps, but quite frankly, not necessarily the weakest) to the most formal (possibly, but again not necessarily the strongest) mechanisms. In moving along this spectrum, I shall give examples. I will spend more time on each modality as we progress, for the simple reason that, as we progress, the potential for private law enforcement to work in tandem with public law institutions progressively increases.

The modalities I propose are these:

1. Purely personal enforcement of non-binding norms
2. Law enforcement through institutional or organizational structures
3. Collective private law creation and enforcement
4. Privately developed practices as actual private law norms
5. Private actors as law enforcement actors

2 Purely Personal Enforcement of Non-Binding Norms

A starting premise of this presentation is that rights and obligations may not only be created, but also enforced, outside formal legal systems. We can begin, at the extreme, with norms that are non-binding, that may be purely social in origin and that are enforced, if at all, on a purely personal basis, without support from any institution, public or otherwise. The norm in play in this modality is typically a social norm, by which is meant "a rule of personal conduct that does not depend on government for either promulgation or enforcement."[1] It might include norms governing such banal and basic actions as proper etiquette at the dining table. Judge Richard Posner and Professor Eric Rasmussen call such norms "automatic" because they flow naturally and directly from a party's simple failure to comply with

[1]Posner and Rasmussen (1999).

a given social norm.[2] Exceedingly bad table etiquette can thus lead to social ostracism. Social norms have ready application in the workplace, where they can be sanctioned "informationally." Informational sanctions are those that stem from providing "information about [oneself] that [one] would rather others not know."[3] For instance, using profanity in a job interview may signal to the interviewer that the candidate is unprofessional, resulting in the candidate's rejection.

A more serious example—and one that implicates law as such—is that of the driver driving on the wrong side of the road. That driver may well come into collision with a norm-complying driver driving on the right side of the road. The norm-violator will likely suffer sanctions in the form of bodily harm and property damage, though so too, unfortunately, will likely the norm-complier.[4] The driver is himself his own law enforcement agent, triggering sanctions as a result of his own misconduct. So too is an adulterous spouse who, by his or her own conduct, triggers the alienation of his or her spouse, and may even invite legal consequences such as divorce. This too is not costless to the spouse. (I leave completely aside purely psychological sanctions, notably guilt,[5] the internalized feeling of shame generated by failing to abide by a norm to the detriment of others—a sanction imposing no direct expense to the outside world.)

But we should not dwell here on scenarios such as these. They are mentioned only to illustrate how purely private, even highly personal, conduct can directly unleash the punishment and deterrence we ordinarily associate with public law enforcement.

3 Law Enforcement Through Institutional or Organizational Structures

It is a relatively small step, but nevertheless a step, when we move to enforcement mechanisms that operate not in the purely personal or social sphere, but within institutions. Here too the norms in play may or may not be legally binding on parties, but their violation may result in imposition of institutional sanctions. Companies regularly impose behavioral norms on their employees by creating and enforcing policies and codes to regulate conduct of employees in the workplace through employment manuals and human resource departments. For instance, most companies today have rules to prevent sexual harassment at work and social media policies to regulate conduct of employees on social media platforms. Violation of such policies and codes by employees can generally result in disciplinary sanctions, designed to punish and deter, being imposed on the employees who violate them: from simple reprimand, to pay reduction, to termination. Whether the motivation is

[2]Posner and Rasmussen (1999).

[3]Posner and Rasmussen (1999), p. 371.

[4]Posner and Rasmussen (1999), p. 372.

[5]Posner and Rasmussen (1999), p. 371.

morality, or simply heightened productivity, does not matter.[6] These sanctions are imposed by private entities without the intervention of any public bodies. The norms thereby vindicated may be purely social, but they may also have legal consequences, as in the case of sexual harassment in the workplace.

This is not to say that public law enforcement will not follow. The norms in question may well form a part of the terms of employment (hence contractual), and become a matter for enforcement by employment tribunals and even courts at the request of the workplace victim—for the simple reason that the workplace prohibition has a counterpart legal prohibition. But whether they do or do not, the imposition of privately enforced disciplinary measures is in every sense an exercise in private law enforcement.

4 Collective Private Law Creation and Enforcement

What happens when private actors come together collectively to produce non-binding non-legal norms? Businesses within a single industry agree, explicitly or implicitly, to certain trade and industry norms to ensure better functioning of the industry itself, and possibly accrue to the benefit of consumers.

A good example would be Industry-wide compacts instituting a program for the labelling of good that meet certain safety and health standards. Thus, the organization known as "Fairtrade International" establishes fair trade standards, relating, for example, to the environment or consumer protection, or to protection of youth from forced or abusively badly paid labor.[7] Incentives, rather than sanctions, may first come into play, if, for example, compliance with norms allows an industry-wide organization to place certificates or seals of approval on products, with assumed business advantages. But there will also be monitoring, so that if a producer is found to not conform to a specific standard requirement, it may have its permission to use the Fairtrade label revoked. Membership in a bar association operates in much the same way. Revocation of membership is an act by the bar, not the State, but it surely amounts to law enforcement.[8] What we see here can also fairly be described as the creation and enforcement of what is variously referred to as "codes of conduct" or "best practices, and given effect through "soft law enforcement."

---

[6]Feldman (1984), p. 49.

[7]Standards available at http://www.fairtrade.net/standards/our-standards.html.

[8]The Forest Stewardship Council (FSC) is another private standard-setting organization that creates and enforces standards within the logging and forest industries. The FSC is a non-profit organization that encourages the logging industry, forest owners, and indigenous populations to adopt sustainable forest management practices and deter illegal logging through certification and labeling programs. The organization certifies and labels forests, forest products, and firms that sell those products. Forest owners and managers and retailers that sell certified forest products may receive a premium on products they sell. For more information on the Forest Stewardship Council, see https://us.fsc.org/en-us/what-we-do/mission-and-vision.

But soft law standards may easily morph into hard law. Paramount example include standard-setting organizations (SSOs), which represent "private groups that collaboratively select and adopt uniform technical standards for goods and services."[9] SSOs are "voluntary collectives" and the standards they create are non-binding. Among other things, they may enhance inter-operability of products within a market, particularly in a technology sector.[10]

One of the oldest SSOs is the International Telecommunication Union (ITU), established in Switzerland in 1865 to issue international standards for telephone networks, in relation to "numbering and addressing, traffic management, monitoring and accounting, and quality of service."[11] International accounting standards are the product of much the same process.

To specify a given technology as an industry standards, SSOs may put together so-called FRAND Agreements, the term denoting "fair, reasonable, and non-discriminatory" standards.[12] Through a FRAND Agreement, the holder of a technology patent that is to become the industry standard agrees to license the patents to the other SSO members "on fair, reasonable, and non-discriminatory" (i.e., FRAND) terms." That technology then becomes a standards-body-approved technical standard.

But notice how the stage is then set for recourse to law enforcement through public institutions. Quite obviously, FRANDs, being contracts, are legally enforceable both by the holder of the licensor and other SSO members through pursuit of patent license violations. But there is more. What is there to prevent state and local governments from adopting the resulting standards for purposes of inspections and certifications in the public interest that they themselves perform? One need only think of the inspection and certification of elevators, whether operating in the public or private sector.

It is, moreover, unlikely that these standards will undergo any change upon adoption by state and local governments, as they typically lack the technical expertise or other governmental resources needed to amend them. These standards will have become legal "safe harbors" and private actors will have established them. Though initially driven by purely business considerations, and thus non-binding, such standards have morphed into law, *proprement dit.*

---

[9]Curran (2003), p. 983; Greenbaum (2015), p. 82 ("Our technological era is founded on standards").

[10]Curran (2003), p. 983.

[11]Rysman and Simcoe (2008), p. 1922. The Institute of Electrical and Electronics Engineers (IEEE) is another SSO which has existed in some form since the 1800s. The IEEE has set a wide range of standards within electrical engineering, including rules governing electrical safety, cryptography, and, more recently, specifications for wireless networking (i.e., Wi-Fi).

[12]Kesan and Hayes (2014), p. 237.

5 Privately Developed Practices as Actual Private Law Norms

We can now move to what can only be described as the penetration of privately developed norms into the very fabric of the law. This is particularly apparent in common law countries where wide swaths of private law—both contractual and non-contractual—have been infiltrated by privately established behavioral norms. This process has been mediated by such notions as "the reasonable man" in tort. "Negligence is the omission to do something which a reasonable man, guided upon those considerations which ordinarily regulate the conduct of human affairs, would do, or doing something which a [. . .] reasonable man would not do."[13] To discern what a reasonable person would do or not do, courts rely on all categories of norms thus far discussed in determining reasonableness.[14] A farmer stacks hay in a barn near a fire, and the hay ignites eventually destroying his neighbor's house. The farmer may be held liable for the damages, even though no rule expressly proscribed the farmer from laying hay near the fire. The standard allows the judge to take the factual situation, apply the social norm that people should act reasonably to avoid danger to personal property, and punishes the farmer, if only through an award of damages, for failing to abide by the norm.

When privately developed norms enter the law they typically do so in the form of standards rather than rules, and that makes a difference. Rules are generally costlier for legislatures to create, but standards are costlier for courts to apply.[15] Rules may be more effective than standards in shaping behavior *ex ante* because they are more readily "learned" and "followed" and their application may enjoy benefit from predictability.[16] Yet rules often suffer from over-inclusion, banning conduct that should not be prohibited, or under-inclusion, allowing conduct that should be proscribed.[17] And they run a much greater risk of obsolescence.[18]

I have dwelled too long on the law of tort. What of the law of contract? Norms of private origin make their way into contract law as well, most notably through the notion of "custom and usage." Time and again, courts supplement the literal terms of a contract with consideration of what contracting parties, by virtue of custom and usage, have a right to expect from their contracting partners. This practice emanates from the notion that "[w]hat is usually done may be evidence of what ought to be done."[19] It seems almost impossible to apply principles of good faith in the performance of contracts without reference to what custom and usage leads parties

[13]*Blyth v. Birmingham Waterworks*, 156 Eng. Rep. 1047 (Ex. 1856).

[14]See generally, Gardner (2015): legal standards "allow the law to pass the buck, to help itself *pro tempore* to standards of justification that are not themselves set by the law".

[15]Kaplow (1992), p. 567.

[16]Kaplow (1992), p. 571.

[17]Kaplow (1992), p. 564.

[18]Morse (2010), pp. 562–563.

[19]*Tex. & Pacific Ry. Co. v. Behymer*, 189 U.S. 468, 470 (1903).

reasonably to expect. Here too, privately produced social and business norms enter law as we know it without ever having been formally codified.

6 Private Parties as Law Enforcement Actors

This discussion would not be complete if we did not take the next and final step and examine what law enforcement "in private hands" looks like. Three very different scenarios come quickly to mind.

A first scenario consists of enabling private parties to supplement law enforcement through public institutions by bringing litigation.[20] In the United States, when the law confers on private parties a cause of action for the violation of a norm enacted in the public interest—such as antitrust law, securities law, environmental law, anti-corruption law and even civil rights law—we refer to those private parties as "private attorneys general," precisely because they are "enlisted" to participate alongside public agencies in the enforcement of regulatory norms. The promise of treble or punitive damages, fee allocation or associational or class actions may act as a further inducement. This idea has gained traction around the world, most notably in the European Union, with its encouragement of private damage claims in national courts for violation of EU competition law norms. It has been estimated that of all job discrimination lawsuits brought in the U.S., 98% have been brought by private parties through claims for damages, and only 2% by government.

A striking illustration of the same is the right that private parties enjoy in many civil law systems, by virtue of having been the victim of a crime, to launch the criminal law enforcement process.

A second scenario consists of turning private actors into law enforcement agents, not by incentivizing them through the prospect of big damage awards, but by threat of the government itself. Immigration law affords an excellent example. Employers may become civilly or criminally liable for hiring illegal aliens. Even service providers may become liable for providing services to illegal aliens. These employers and service providers will, against their will, have become law enforcement agents.[21]

A third scenario in which private actors participate directly in law enforcement, i.e., in becoming law enforcers, is of course international commercial arbitration.[22] It is of course the law, after all, that guarantees the enforcement of private agreements to arbitrate, that generally provides the substantive norms according to which commercial disputes will be resolved in arbitration, that organizes the arbitral proceedings that take place on national territory, that determine whether and how courts of the arbitral seat may intervene in the arbitral process, and that guarantee the availability of post-award remedies, in the form of annulment actions and actions for

---

[20] Glover (2012), p. 1137.

[21] Pham (2008), p. 777.

[22] Hay and Shleifer (1998), p. 398.

the enforcement of awards. The use that arbitration makes of our public institutions to ensure its efficacy is fundamental, but the justice that emerges is fundamentally private.

Through these three scenarios, we have finally arrived at a genuine merger of public and private law enforcement, acting in tandem. In each, the applicable law is public, the law enforcement mechanism is public, the guarantee of efficacy is public, but private parties have become the protagonists.

7 Conclusion

As comparative law scholars, it is tempting to hone in on the similarities and differences among national legal systems, viewed as a collection of public institutions. But we rarely take a step back to notice that the law, as enforced through public institutions, is merely one way of providing and order and structure in society. If efficacious, social and other private mechanisms for the enforcement of social and other norms relieve public institutions of some of the burden of governance. But private law enforcement also takes place in tandem with public law enforcement, in all the varying ways I've indicated and doubtless others. This is not a standard way of deploying comparative law, but it is one that resonates especially well with legal efficacy as the overarching theme of this congress.

By way of conclusion, we have first seen that private norms and private actors contribute handsomely to enforcement of the law. The proof is that if we removed all such private enforcement, law enforcement would itself be substantially less effective. We have further seen that private law enforcement is not some single undifferentiated phenomenon. The modalities by which law is enforced privately differ importantly among themselves, not least through the different degree of interface with law enforcement through public means. We have moved from purely personal activity in the absence of any form of public law enforcement, to privately established practices becoming sources of law in civil litigation, to private actors serving as veritable vehicles for the enforcement of law.

It should not be supposed, however, that placing law enforcement in private hands is without risk. Each of the modalities of private law enforcement carries its dangers, not that public law enforcement does not carry its own. Purely personal enforcement of non-binding norms can bring us organized crime, whether in Mafia form or otherwise. Law enforcement through institutional or organizational structures can bring us what is sometimes called "agency capture." When entities produce and enforce norms collectively, they present real threats to market competition and other values promoted by antitrust or competition law. The penetration of private norms in the law of contract and tort has undoubtedly contributed to the indeterminacy of private law. Finally, turning private parties into "private attorneys general" may lead to high levels of frivolous and "nuisance" litigation.

Ironically, if the risks associated with private law enforcement are viewed as serious enough, there is no realistic remedy other than public law enforcement itself.

This only further confirms the interdependency of law enforcement in its public and private forms.

References

Curran PD (2003) Standard-setting organizations: patents, price fixing, and per se legality. Univ Chicago Law Rev 70:983–1009
Feldman DC (1984) The development and enforcement of group norms. Acad Manag Rev 9:47–53
Gardner J (2015) The many faces of the reasonable person. Law Q Rev 131:563–584
Glover JM (2012) The structural role of private enforcement mechanisms in public law. William Mary Law Rev 53:1137–1217
Greenbaum E (2015) Forgetting FRAND: the WIPO model submission agreements. Les Nouvelles 50:81
Hay J, Shleifer A (1998) Private enforcement of public laws: a theory of legal reform. In: AEA Papers and Proceedings
Kaplow L (1992) Rules versus standards: an economic analysis. Duke Law J 42:557–629
Kesan JP, Hayes CM (2014) FRAND's forever: standards, patent transfers and licensing commitments. Ind Law J 89:231–314
Morse AH (2010) Rules, standards and fractured courts. Okla City Univ Law Rev 35:559–605
Pham H (2008) The private enforcement of immigration laws. Georgetown Law Rev 96:777–826
Posner RA, Rasmussen EB (1999) Creating and enforcing norms, with special reference to sanctions. Int Rev Law Econ 19:369–382
Rysman M, Simcoe T (2008) Patents and the performance of voluntary standard setting organizations. Manag Sci 54:1920–1934

George A. Bermann is the Jean Monnet Professor of EU Law, Walter Gellhorn Professor of Law, and the director for the Center for International Commercial and Investment Arbitration (CICIA) at Columbia Law School. He is an affiliated faculty member of the School of Law of Sciences Po in Paris and the MIDS Masters Program in International Dispute Settlement in Geneva. Bermann is an active international arbitrator in commercial and investment disputes; chief reporter of the ALI's Restatement of the U.S. Law of International Commercial Arbitration; co-author of the UNCITRAL Guide to the New York Convention on the Recognition and Enforcement of Foreign Arbitral Awards; chair of the Global Advisory Board of the New York International Arbitration Center (NYIAC); co-editor-in-chief of the American Review of International Arbitration; and founding member of the governing body of the ICC Court of Arbitration and a member of its standing committee. He is a titular member and former President of the International Academy of Comparative Law.

Part II / Partie II
Round-Table Interventions / Interventions à l'Occasion des Tables-Rondes

A Global Adaptive System for Supporting Human Rights?

David Joseph Gerber

Abstract We often fail to see important dimensions of international human rights (HR) protection because we use lenses that do not reveal them. This short article suggests a way of looking at HR protection that I believe has value in many contexts and for many—those who make decisions about human rights and those who suffer from deprivation of those rights. It reveals important factors and forces that influence HR protection, but that conventional lenses often fail to reveal. In doing so it opens up potential avenues for increasing the effectiveness of efforts to improve such protections.

1 Introduction

We often fail to see important dimensions of international human rights (HR) protection because we use lenses that do not reveal them. This short article suggests a way of looking at HR protection that I believe has value in many contexts and for many—those who make decisions about human rights and those who suffer from deprivation of those rights. It reveals important factors and forces that influence HR protection, but that conventional lenses often fail to reveal. In doing so it opens up potential avenues for increasing the effectiveness of efforts to improve such protections.

International human rights protection is generally envisioned and discussed by reference to individual governments and institutions: enforcement by states, sometimes supported by formal arrangements among them and by transnational institutions and nongovernmental organizations (NGOs). In this view, the pieces of the

---

This article is based on a presentation made to the Thematic Congress of the International Academy of Comparative Law, Montevideo, Uruguay, November, 2016. I am grateful to the many participants there who commented on the paper and its potential value.

D. J. Gerber (✉)
Chicago-Kent College of Law, Chicago, IL, USA
e-mail: dgerber@kentlaw.iit.edu

N. Etcheverry Estrázulas, D. P. Fernández Arroyo (eds.), *Enforcement and Effectiveness of the Law - La mise en oeuvre et l'effectivité du droit*, Ius Comparatum – Global Studies in Comparative Law 30, https://doi.org/10.1007/978-3-319-93758-8_3

image are separate. If relationships among them are recognized at all, they tend to be formal—e.g., treaties and policy statements. This view is not incorrect, but it is limited and confining. It misses much of importance that influences human rights protection and may, therefore, impede efforts to improve such protections. Some scholars have recognized the narrowness of this conventional view,[1] but, at least to my knowledge, we have not yet developed an effective means of responding to it.

The response I suggest here expands and deepens our image of international human rights protection. It views institutions for the protection of human rights as components of a global adaptive system. This perspective reveals and highlights the interactions among institutions and decision makers that shape how human rights are understood and how and to what extent they are supported and protected. As a result, this fuller picture makes visible or at least imaginable new avenues for advancing human rights.

My objective in this brief article is to introduce this perspective and identify some potential consequences of using it. We look briefly at the concept of a "global adaptive system". The concept itself combines elements from earlier work of mine in conjunction with new ways of analyzing and thinking that are being developed in the natural and social sciences. The Article then applies this concept to the domain of human rights protection and note some of the potential consequences using it in this area.

2 What Is an "Adaptive System"?

In its simplest form, an adaptive system is a space or field of activity in which diverse, interdependent agents (or participants) interact with each other.[2] They both influence each other and respond to each other's actions. Such a system has its own internal dynamics. It channels information flows among the agents, and it creates incentives and pressures that influence how agents respond to each other. The external environment also shapes these interactions, as individual agents respond to information, incentives and pressures from the environment and, as a consequence, also alter the interactions within the system. In the context of law, these interactions primarily occur through decisions and influences on decisions.[3]

The system is, therefore, continually adapting to both internal and external influences and pressures. The interactions within the system, in turn, produce consequences (e.g., whether a pond's water is clear or green with algae). In the literature of adaptive systems, these are referred to as "emergent properties". The better the system is understood, the greater the potential for foreseeing these consquences.

[1]See, e.g., Koh (1997, 1999).

[2]Miller and Page (2009) and Yang (2008).

[3]For discussion, see Gerber (1998, 2001, 2004).

Such systems are being studied in many branches of the natural and social sciences.[4] A basic example of such a system in the natural sciences is a pond.[5] A pond usually contains aquatic creatures such as fish and amphibian as well as a variety of plants. Each is an agent that interacts with other agents in the system, and their interactions constitute the system. Each agent depends on the water and nutrients in the pond, drawing resources from it for its own use and producing effects on other agents as well as on the water in the pond. How agents interact depends on their own needs and capacities as well as on the environment surrounding the pond (e.g., the temperature of air and water and the introduction of contaminants into the water). If we view the animals, plants and water in the pond individually without seeing them as parts of an adaptive system we have no way of understanding much of what happens in the pond.

3 The Global Adaptive System of Human Rights

We can use this basic concept to create a fuller and more valuable view of the legal protections that governments provide for individuals, focusing specifically on what are conventionally called "human rights." This requires that we identify the field in which the system operates (in our example, the pond), the agents (plants and animals), the interactions (use of resources, impact on resources) and the consequences of the interactions (the characteristics of the water in the pond).

3.1 The Field

The global adaptive system for human rights includes individuals, groups and institutions that make decisions regarding human rights protection as well as those that actively seek such protection. This is the sphere of interactions that constitutes the system. The relevant decisions may be formal (eg, decisions of courts or other government organizations) but they may also be less formal decisions about how an NGO should try to influence decisions or how an individual should seek protection). These are influences by the many forces, pressures and incentives that influence governments and others in relation to human rights issues. Often they relate to a

[4]See Santa Fe Institute, www.santafe.edu/research; Gell-Man (1992) and Narendra and Annaswamy (2012).

[5]Aanother classic example is cells, which make up organisms, which in turn make up an ecosystem. Dodder and Dare (2000) and Waldrop (1992), p. 9 ("Why do ancient species and ecosystems often remain stable in the fossil record for millions of years—and then either die out or transform themselves into something new in a geological instant? Perhaps the dinosaurs got wiped out by an asteroid impact. But there weren't *that* many asteroids. What else was going on?").

particular human rights issue (e.g., the use of torture) or institution (e.g., a national government or a specific office of a national government).

This system is global, because the agents may be located anywhere on the planet, and the interactions take place across territorial borders, often in cyberspace. Political boundaries are often of central importance in these systems, because states and other political institutions define the range of action that governments can take and shape the incentives of decision makers. They may, for example, enable a state to limit communication (for example, by reducing access to cyberspace) although in most cases agents have some access to information from others in the system and some capacity to respond to the actions of other agents.[6]

3.2 Agents and Interactions

The agents that comprise the system include, among others, states, transnational organizations, NGOs, and scholars. All those institutions and individuals who make, influence or try to influence decisions are part of the system. They interact with each other, respond to each other and influence or seek to influence each other. In many ways, they also depend on each other—for information and support. They interact with each other and respond to each other in many ways—including direct contact, support for activities, publication of information, participation in transnational organizations etc.

3.2.1 States

States are central agents in this system. They have power within their territory, and they have extensive authority to use it. The uses of state power and the legitimacy of those uses combine to shape how human rights are understood and treated. For example, they allow a state to violate the rights of individuals and groups on a massive scale and with limited—if any—control from the outside. This makes states the focus of many other agents in the system who must seek to influence state decision makers.

One set of interactions is between states. The interactions occur on many levels. For example, state A may support human rights policies or decisions in State B. It may also facilitate State B's enforcement of laws by taking formal action such as extraditing criminals or using less formal means such as providing information to State B concerning enforcement opportunities.[7] Even more informal measures include providing training for enforcement officials and publicizing the state's own HR decisions, which may encourage encourage (or discourage) other states

[6]Zheng (2013) and Denyer (2016).

[7]See, e.g. von Stein (2015) and Cole (2015).

from taking similar actions. Finally, they interact with each other in the context of transnational organizations. For example, they send representatives to transnational courts such as the Interamerican Court of Human Rights or the European Court of Human Rights.[8] These representatives exercise varying degrees of influence on the decisions of the court, and the court decisions have varying degrees of influence on national decision makers.

3.2.2 Transnational Organizations

Transnational organizations interact with states as well as with other components of the system. These organizations range broadly in power, authority and goals, but they typically play two basic roles. One is to bring relevant decision makers together. They often provide a forum for interactions among other agents in the system. These interactions facilitate network formation as well as promoting the sharing of experiences and ideas.

The other is to influence thinking and decisions among other participants. These organizations range widely in their objectives regarding human rights. Some seek to develop a broader understanding of common problems. Other seek adherents to their own agendas or the agendas of sponsoring states. Often they combine these two basic sets of goals.

Among the most prominent organizations in the field are the UN Commission on Human Rights and regional human rights organizations such as those that operate under the umbrella of the Organization of American States.[9] These organizations seek to influence state decisions. They request information from states, host conferences for other agents attended by other agents in the system and publish material regarding the actions of states.[10] They are often also influenced by states, which may provide much of their funding.[11] Courts such as the European Court of Human Rights and the Interamerican Court of Human Rights have a special status, because they typically hear cases that constitute a public record and issue judgments that are in some sense binding on member states.[12]

---

[8]See Inter-American Court of Human Rights, http://www.corteidh.or.cr/index.php/en; European Court of Human Rights, http://www.echr.coe.int/Pages/home.aspx?p=home; Shelton (1996).

[9]United Nations Commission on Human Rights, http://www.ohchr.org/EN/HRBodies/CHR/Pages/CommissionOnHumanRights.aspx; Organization of American States, http://www.oas.org/en/iachr/.

[10]See United Nations, http://www.un.org/en/sections/priorities/human-rights/.

[11]Amnesty International, for example, receives funding from the United States, the European Commission, the Netherlands, and Norway. NGO Monitor, Amnesty International: Funding, http://www.ngo-monitor.org/ngos/amnesty_international/.

[12]European Court of Human Rights, https://www.echr.coe.int/Pages/home.aspx?p=home; Interamerican Court of Human Rights, http://www.corteidh.or.cr/index.php/en.

3.2.3 Nongovernment Organizations (NGOs)

NGOs are an influential component of the global human rights system. They seek not only to influence government decisions, but to influence thought, public opinion and decisions in many parts of the system. They interact with and often depend on each other in pursuing their respective missions.[13] Organizations such as Amnesty International,[14] Human Rights Watch[15] and many others acquire and reveal information about abuses and put pressure on governments and officials in many parts of the world.[16]

3.2.4 Scholars and Journalists

Finally, scholars and journalists respond to decisions related to HR and present their views and analysis to others in the system.[17] Sometimes they seek to influence specific decisions of specific decision makers. In other cases, they direct their influence more broadly, but in virtually all cases they seek to influence thinking and decisions within the system.

In an adaptive system, each agent can respond to other agents. Responses need not necessarily be immediate or official. Often an agent, for example, an NGO, develops ideas or transfers knowledge or experience to others in the system who recognize it as relevant to their own agendas, because it influences their own decisions about can and should be done. In that sense, they are interdependent. As one scholar has put it, no agent controls the system, but almost every agent influences it.[18]

---

[13]For example, Human Rights Watch considers "strong partnership with other NGOs an essential tool for achieving impact," and works closely with at least over 50 other NGOs, including Amnesty International. https://www.hrw.org/partner-resources. See also Council of Europe, Human Rights Activism and the Role of NGOs, http://www.coe.int/en/web/compass/human-rights-activism-and-the-role-of-ngos.

[14]Amnesty International, https://www.amnesty.org/en/what-we-do/united-nations/.

[15]Human Rights Watch, https://www.hrw.org/about.

[16]For example, Human Rights Watch's most recent investigation in the northwest Central African Republic revealed several human rights abuses that are publicized on through various media campaigns. Human Rights Watch, Central African Republic: Mayhem by New Group, (December 20, 2016), https://www.hrw.org/news/2016/12/20/central-african-republic-mayhem-new-group.

[17]Welch (2000) and Jonassohn and Björnson (1998).

[18]"No agent lives in a vacuum, but typically must interact with other agents to achieve its goals." Littman (1994), pp. 157–163.

4 Some Consequences for Human Rights

Recognizing these interactions as components of a global adaptive system has important consequences.

4.1 Increased Awareness

The interrelationships and interdependencies among the components of the system make both decision makers and victims more aware of potential problems and risks as well as of solutions and opportunities. They identify for each agent what is happening in other parts of the system. For example, a court decision in country A to prevent a form of human rights interference can contribute to the development of a norm shared by others countries in the system or at least encourage others to take similar action.[19] They can also point to successful tactics in litigation or community organizing in one context that might not otherwise be known by other agents or recognized by them as relevant.[20] Finally, they identify obstacles to human rights advancement (e.g. state interference with social media) and to experience—both successes and failures—with strategies for dealing with such obstacles.

4.2 Improved Access, Dialogue, and the Potential for Cooperation

An adaptive systems perspective also identifies opportunities for dialogue and mutual support. For example, where an agent (individual, group, or institution) in one country becomes more aware of what is happening in others parts of the system and of the potential relevance of events and decisions there for its own agenda, it is likely to both seek and receive greater access to information from other agents in the system. This also increases the potential for dialogue among members of the system. Where, for example, an NGO in Latin America sees itself as part of an adaptive system that includes similar institutions in other parts of the world, it is more likely to

[19]For example, a recent landmark decision out of the European Court of Human Rights found for the first time that states have an affirmative obligation to protect against and investigate human trafficking. Rantsev v. Cyprus and Russian Federation, App no 25965/04, IHRL 3632 (ECHR 2010), 7 January 2010.

[20]For example, in response to Russia's illegal use of force against Georgia in 2008, Georgia sued under a human rights treaty for racial discrimination because Russia could otherwise refuse to submit to a legal procedure before the International Court of Justice. By suing under a human rights treaty ratified by Russia, Russia was forced to submit to the ICJ's jurisdiction. Georgia v. Russian Federation, [2008] ICJ Rep 353, ICGJ 348 (ICJ 2008), 15 October 2008, International Court of Justice [ICJ].

recognize the links between them as well as the commonalities they share. This system awareness, in turn, creates a basis for dialogue and interaction that may not exist without it. Finally, increased access and improved dialogue may create opportunities for mutual cooperation among institutions and individuals. Where agents recognize that they are part of the same system and that the relationships within the system shape outcomes, they are more likely to be aware of their shared interests and interdependencies, and this provides a basis for cooperation. Recognizing the basis for cooperation is a step to achieving it.

4.3 Changed Incentives

Such recognition can also alter the incentives of agents. In particular, it can raise the cost to a state of violating human rights protections and thereby create disincentives for the state to take such actions. For example, it may lead to economic sanctions, exclusion from formal or informal networks, reduced status for state representatives in transnational organizations etc. It may also reduce the willingness of those outside the violating state to visit it and/or to invest in it.[21] Such reactions impose costs on the state, and increased costs can be expected to deter harmful state conduct in many (though certainly not all) contexts.

4.4 Content and Framing of Human Rights Norms

Finally, an adoptive systems perspective can influence the content and framing of human rights norms. In some parts of the world human rights protection is often seen as the imposition of "Western" ideas on other countries.[22] Where this happens, decision makers often pay little attention to it, only pretend to pay attention to it, or directly attack what they consider to be the imposition. They may react differently, however, if the issue is reframed. A government may consider itself obligated to improve elements of the welfare of individuals and groups, regardless of whether these obligations are based on "human rights." This means that they may seek the same objectives as a government motivated by concern for what it understands as human rights. In these contexts the actual operational objectives of the governments may be more similar than is often recognized. Both may seek the same objectives and both may recognize an obligation to do so, but they may frame their decisions

[21]For example, China responded to international criticism of their human rights violations in the 1990s after noticing its impact on foreign investment, tourism, and trade. Shi (1993), p. 210. Some organizations, like Tourism Concern, provide information to consumers and investors on how their investments directly impact human rights violations in developing countries. See Tourism Concern: Action for Ethical Tourism, https://www.tourismconcern.org.uk/human-rights/.

[22]See, e.g. Mayer (1993), pp. 309–313.

using different concepts. Viewing the agents as part of a global adaptive system can open content and reframe discussions. It can focus attention on the objectives to be served and the means of achieving them rather than on the concepts used in achieving the results. At least a systems-based perspective provides a basis for dialogue.

China furnishes an example that highlights the issue. The Chinese leadership typically rejects Western demands for human rights protection, and for this reason Chinese individuals often shun the topic entirely in discussions with non-Chinese.[23] Yet Chinese leaders and Chinese government policy have often emphasized the government's responsibility for the welfare of Chinese people (including, e.g. the government's obligation to provide adequate housing, protect against crime etc). These statements and policies are not always vigorously pursued, but the point here is that the protections are framed in terms of the government's obligations rather than the rights of the individual. These may, however, be "two sides of the same coin"—i.e., both may to some extent have the same objectives, and thus finding ways of talking about the issues that respect both ways of framing it can be of significant value. A global adaptive systems perspective facilitates that kind of dialogue.

5 Potential Roles for Comparative Law Tools

Comparative law tools can be of great value in thinking about the global human rights system, its operations and its potential consequences. Some examples:

5.1 Patterning and Mapping

Comparative law has long featured what I call "Patterning and Mapping" tools. These are used to identify patterns and groups in legal systems and their components. They can be particularly valuable in mapping human rights protections, because, as we have seen, these protections often cut across the boundaries of legal traditions and the legal systems of individual states. Careful attention to these systemic relationships and the patterns of decision making among decision makers and institutions in different systems is critical for understanding how the components of a system relate to each other.

[23]See, e.g., Roney (2014); Human Rights Watch, China: Events of 2015, https://www.hrw.org/world-report/2016/country-chapters/china-and-tibet, explaining that China rejects the imposition of Western human rights as "foreign infiltration."

5.2 Function and Context

This method is a standard comparative law tool. It provides a means of more carefully identifying the points of similarity and difference between legal regimes.[24] It focuses on identifying the functions performed within those regimes and then asking how each performs the functions and what factors influence the way it performs them. It is a more finely grained tool of analysis that can identify more specifically where differences are and distinguish apparent differences from operational differences.

5.3 Voices/Formants

Rodolfo Sacco's method of identifying the voices within a system and their relationships to each other adds a further dimension to the tool kit.[25] It emphasizes the multiplicity of voices (what he calls "formants") within any legal system. These include, for example, statutes, regulations, court decisions and so on. Each may play a role in answering the question "What is the law on the subject?" This tool requires that the analyst identify who is saying what in a legal system (courts, legislatures, etc) and how they relate to each other. There is much loose talk about human rights protection, and there can be much value in carefully analyzing these issues in order to clarify which voices have which kinds of influences.

5.4 Decisional Analysis

Finally, what I call "decisional analysis" takes this search further by focusing on decisions and on the factors that influence them.[26] Human rights goals are often easier to talk about than to achieve, and this method provides a means of more carefully identifying the factors that shape decisions—i.e., that lead from goal to decision. The objective is to recognize that legal decisions are embedded in systems and that the systems influence the decisions made within them. On a national level, a system include several basic elements. (1) Authoritative texts—e.g., statutes, regulations and cases—are reference points and sources of justification that influence decisions throughout the system or in identifiable parts of the system. (2) Institutions consist of relationships, procedures, resources and methods that influence incentives resources and methods that shape decisions within them. (3) Communities are networks of personal and social relationships that surround and suffuse the

[24]Michaels (2011).

[25]Sacco (1991).

[26]See Gerber (1998, 2001, 2004).

institutions, distributing status, information and influence. (4) Finally, patterns of thought—values, ideologies and concepts—are attached to or associated with the institutions and communities and help direct goals and decisions. This type of analysis can also be valuable in analyzing a global adaptive system.

These tools have been developed for conventional comparative law purposes such as to better understand similarities and differences among legal systems and to identify and overcome obstacles to communication across the borders of individual legal system. They are, however, also extremely beneficial for analyzing the way a global adaptive system functions. They point to key elements in the operation of such a system. For example, they direct us to questions such as: "What are the differences among the systems?" "How do they influence the flow and dissemination of informatin and influence?" "Who communicates with whom? "Which institutions and individuals have status?" As the tools are used in this new context, they will in some cases have to be modified and further developed, but they can be the basis for effective communication within a network and for honing strategies of cooperation.

6 Conclusions

Viewing the area of international human rights law from a global adaptive systems perspective creates an image of the field, its challenges and its opportunities that differs significantly from most current views. It allows us to what we did not see before: How institutions and agents interact with each other, respond to each other and depend on each other. Human rights protection depends on awareness of harm and support for efforts to deter harm. An adaptive systems perspective can increase both. These insights can be crucial to the continued development of human rights protection.

References

Cole WM (2015) International human rights and domestic income inequality: a difficult case of compliance in world society. Am Soc Rev 80:359–390

Denyer S (2016) China's Scary Lesson to the world: censoring the internet works. Wash Post (23 May 2016). https://www.washingtonpost.com/world/asia_pacific/chinas-scary-lesson-to-the-world-censoring-the-internet-works/2016/05/23/413afe78-fff3-11e5-8bb1-f124a43f84dc_story.html?utm_term=.11f118f1b7e5

Dodder R, Dare R (2000) Complex adaptive systems and complexity theory: inter-related knowledge domains. Research Seminar in Engineering Systems MIT. http://web.mit.edu/esd.83/www/notebook/ComplexityKD.PDF

Gell-Man M (1992) Complexity and complex adaptive systems. In: Gell-Mann M, Hawkins JA (eds) The evolution of human languages, Santa Fe Institute studies in the sciences of complexity, Proc, vol X. Addison-Wesley, Reading, pp 3–18

Gerber DJ (1998) System dynamics: toward a language of comparative law. Am J Comp Law 46:719

Gerber DJ (2001) Globalization and legal knowledge: implications for comparative law. Tulane Law Rev 75:949
Gerber DJ (2004) Authority heuristics and legal knowledge. In: Gambero A (ed) Ordinary language and legal language in public and private law. Milan
Jonassohn K, Björnson KS (1998) Genocid and gross human rights violations. Routledge
Koh H (1997) Why do nations obey international law? Yale Law J 106:2599
Koh H (1999) How is international human rights law enforced? Indiana Law J 74:1397
Littman ML (1994) Markov games as a framework for multi-agent reinforcement learning. In: Proceedings of the 11th International Conference of Machine Learning, pp 157–163
Mayer AE (1993) Universal versus islamic human rights: a clash of cultures or a clash with a construct? Mich J Int Law 15:307
Michaels R (2011) Comparative law. In: Basedow J, Hopt KJ, Zimmermann R (eds) Oxford handbook of European private law, Oxford University Press
Miller H, Page SE (2009) Complex adaptive systems. Princeton University Press
Narendra KS, Annaswamy AM (2012) Stable adaptive systems. Prentice-Hall, Inc. Upper Saddle River
Roney T (2014) China Rejects Human Rights Report from US. The Diplomat (1 March 2014). http://thediplomat.com/2014/03/china-rejects-human-rights-report-from-us/
Sacco R (1991) A dynamic approach to comparative law. Am J Comp Law 39:1–34
Shelton D (1996) The jurisprudence of the Inter-American Court of human rights. Am Univ Int Law Rev 10:333–372
Shi Z (1993), China's just world: the morality of China's foreign policy
von Stein J (2015) Making promises, keeping promises: democracy, ratification and compliance in international human rights law. Br J Polit Sci 46:655–679
Waldrop MM (1992) Complexity: the emerging science at the edge of order and chaos. Simon & Schuste
Welch CE (2000) NGOs and human rights: promises and performance. University of Pennsylvania Press
Yang A (2008) Intelligent complex adaptive systems. IGI Publishing
Zheng H (2013) Regulating the internet: China's law and practice. Beijing Law Rev 4:37–41

David J. Gerber is Distinguished Professor of Law at Chicago-Kent College of Law, Illinois Institute of Technology. He is currently President of the American Society of Comparative Law. He writes and teaches primarily in the areas of antitrust/competition law, comparative law, international economic law and globalization studies. He received his B.A. from Trinity College (Conn.), his M.A. from Yale, and his J.D. from the University of Chicago. In 2013 he was awarded the degree of Honorary Doctor of Laws by the University of Zurich, Switzerland. He is a titular member of the International Academy of Comparative Law.

Jurisdictional Conflicts in Criminal Matters and Their Settlement Within EU's Supranational Settings

Maria Kaiafa-Gbandi

Abstract This paper discusses the fundamental issues surrounding the assignment of jurisdiction in criminal matters and the resolution of jurisdictional conflicts within the supranational setting of the EU. After delving into the interests that lie behind jurisdictional conflicts in criminal matters and their resolution in general, it highlights the settlement models for conflicts of jurisdiction in criminal matters at the national and the international level, and subsequently analyses, comparatively, the EU approach. With regard to the latter, it discusses the notion of the fundamental right based on the ne bis in idem principle enshrined in Article 50 of the CFR as well as the current state of affairs on the basis of the Framework Decision 2009/948/JHA, criticising the existing EU model and opting for a future one for preventing and resolving jurisdictional conflicts in the EU based on firm criteria and the territoriality principle with very slim exceptions.

1 A Fundamental Starting Point

The fundamental issues surrounding the assignment of jurisdiction in criminal matters and the resolution of jurisdictional conflicts within a *supranational* setting such as the EU are important for the unhampered enforcement of criminal law in an international milieu and presently the knottiest riddles in the field. To highlight them, it is useful to begin with a reminder: Criminal law is rigidly bound to the core of state sovereignty.[1] In every legal order, the state has the ius-puniendi-monopol. This explains why criminal law has been so resistant to internationalization and the last one affected by

The text has been published in EuCLR 2017/1, 30 et seq.

[1] See Manoledakis (2000), pp. 42, 45 et seq. (in Greek).

M. Kaiafa-Gbandi (✉)
Research Institute for Transparency, Corruption and Financial Crime, Law Faculty, Aristotle University Thessaloniki, Thessaloniki, Greece
e-mail: kaiafagb@law.auth.gr

N. Etcheverry Estrázulas, D. P. Fernández Arroyo (eds.), *Enforcement and Effectiveness of the Law - La mise en oeuvre et l'effectivité du droit*, Ius Comparatum – Global Studies in Comparative Law 30, https://doi.org/10.1007/978-3-319-93758-8_4

EU law.[2] State sovereignty, as expressed in terms of criminal jurisdiction, aims to protect fundamental legal interests of citizens and the state itself, and simultaneously achieve distinctive goals. Through criminal procedure and the enforcement of a penalty of proportionate magnitude to the committed offense and the offender's guilt, the State attempts to restore public peace and also serve special and general prevention for the future.[3] State sovereignty goes so far in this respect that it even claims the authority to adjudicate violations occurring outside its borders. Each State defines its relevant competence independently and rather inclusively, thus rendering conflicts of jurisdiction inevitable. How such conflicts are resolved over time—and especially in the EU context—can unveil not only the main features of the models utilized to defining jurisdiction and settle relevant conflicts, but also the underlying philosophy.

On the other hand, it should be stressed from the outset that the nullum crimen nulla poena sine processu principle is deep-seated within liberal criminal law systems and seeks to guarantee that a criminal conduct may only be punished by a competent court and with due process.[4] Of course, a criminal process is not carried out to protect the individual from the punishing state, but to urge the protection of society from criminal acts and fulfil the objectives of substantive criminal law as described above. However, limiting the state's criminal repression scope is of paramount significance in democratic societies to maintain the dual identity of criminal law as both an instrument of protecting basic legal interests and a yardstick of civil liberties.[5]

This said, the problems addressed in this paper will refer to criminal acts stretching over more jurisdictions, especially in the EU context which is presently the most sophisticated international milieu. According to its constitutional treaties, the EU comprises both sovereign states and the peoples of Europe, in what has been called "the European Sympoliteia".[6] Member States abide by this supranational organization, in a gradual process of an evolving "federalization".[7] In jurisdictional issues, the layout is pyramid-like: EU interests hold the top and their State and citizen counterparts rest at its basis. In tandem, a gradual shift of sovereignty from the states to the supranational organization becomes evident.

2 Interests Behind Jurisdictional Conflicts in Criminal Matters and Their Resolution

Exercising the right to punish an offense is both reasonable and legitimate, as it aims to protect legal interests within a state's territory, or even beyond it under certain conditions (extraterritorial jurisdiction). In the latter case, such interests belong to the

[2]See e.g. Satzger (2012), p. 44 et seq.

[3]See e.g. Kaiafa-Gbandi et al. (2016), p. 43 et seq. (in Greek).

[4]See e.g. Androulakis (2012), p. 6 et seq. (in Greek).

[5]See Manoledakis (2004), p. 29 (in Greek).

[6]See respectively in Tsatsos (2007), p. 55 et seq. and esp.103 et seq. (in Greek).

[7]See in a comparative perspective with the federal criminal law system of the US Kaiafa-Gbandi (2016), p. 55 et seq.

state itself (state protective principle) or to a state's national (passive personality principle), or are infringed by a state's national abroad (active personality principle) or are universally protected according to relevant international conventions (universality principle).[8] Expanding jurisdiction outside state territory is self-evidently a source of such conflicts, as at least the locus delicti legal order articulates a rightful claim to exercise its relevant competence.

This paper will not discuss the degree to which such an expansion is justifiable.[9] However, its demarcation under set thresholds and the settlement of jurisdictional conflicts are both governed by the same mindset. State extraterritorial criminal jurisdiction targets to eliminate—or at least reduce—punishability loopholes for offenders internationally and also voices the interests of a state's sovereignty. By linking itself to an offence under certain parameters, the state claims to intervene punitively even beyond its strict local confines, in an effort to fulfil the scopes of its criminal law in general. Establishing a conflict-free structure for international cooperation seems to be low in the priorities list.[10] However, while criminal law remains the strictest social control mechanism by severely affecting the legal interests of those criminally accountable, fulfilling its mission as both a protection apparatus of basic legal interests and a benchmark of civil liberties requires its restriction within clearly defined margins. Consequently, while the extraterritorial expansion of criminal jurisdiction aspires to enforce criminal law in a rather wide perspective and aims to the enhanced protection of legal interests and to the self-actualization of a state's sovereignty, drawing the abovementioned crucial limitations and promoting the respective international conflict-settlement regime should pay particular attention to suspects'/defendants' rights.[11] In short, and at least according to a perception of a global justice, the accused should never face dual prosecution and punishment for the same offence.[12]

Every institutional framework regulating criminal jurisdiction at an international level essentially expresses the established relationship between these conflicting aims.[13] The more the balance shifts towards the protection of legal interests and state sovereignty, the less citizen rights are taken into consideration.

Nevertheless, one should consider that such conflicts and their resolution do not only arise in an international context. Federal systems—and especially those envisaging distinct jurisdictions for the same act between local and federal levels and granting leeway for autonomous pursuit—also need to find ways to disentangle respective conflicts arising from their two-tiered criminal law template. In allowing prosecution and punishment for the same offense by both federal and local

[8]For principles of extraterritorial jurisdiction see Satzger (2012), p. 20 et seq. and with regard to the EU framework Böse (2014a), p. 45 et seq.; Zimmermann (2014), p. 70 et seq.

[9]See rel. Zimmermann (2014), p. 70 et seq. and 135–136.

[10]Zimmermann (2014), p. 175.

[11]See especially the analysis of Böse (2014a), p. 44 et seq.; cf. Zimmermann (2014), p. 175 et seq.

[12]In this direction Anagnostopoulos (2008), p. 168 et seq. (in Greek).

[13]Zimmermann (2014), pp. 205–206.

competent authorities, and consequently in acknowledging no institutional safeguard for ne bis in idem (practically but non-bindingly imposed by the so-called "Petite-policy" of the US Attorney General),[14] the USA is in fact the most characteristic example of sovereignty interests gaining the upper hand in regulating jurisdiction in criminal matters in the context of a state itself.[15]

3 Settlement Models for Conflicts of Jurisdictions in Criminal Matters at the National Level

Examining the various models employed for the settlement of jurisdictional conflicts at the national level, one discovers that a popular one recognizes priority to a state's jurisdiction based on territorial, state-protective, or universally defined grounds.[16] The immediate impact of this hidden pecking order can be traced in a number of conflict-settlement procedures. While territoriality often entails the reservation of one's own jurisdiction or the final recognition of a foreign judgement, other principles are merely taken into account in off-set procedures.[17] Taking the Greek legal system as an example, this would imply that on such grounds (e.g. territoriality) prosecution and punishment for the same offence by a foreign legal order does not impede a subsequent equivalent by local authorities. In this case, however, the penalty already served will normally be deducted from the new sentence (Article 10 GPC). On the contrary, in cases of a state's jurisdiction for offenses committed abroad based on the principles of active or passive citizenship, if the perpetrator or victim are own nationals, prosecution not only must obey the double criminality principle but is also impossible if a final conviction has been issued for the same offence *and* the penalty has been served in whole, or by virtue of the statute of limitations (Article 9 GPC).

Therefore, in the presence of a strong link between a criminal act and a specific legal order, state jurisdiction in criminal matters is not actually giving way to a foreign counterpart, thus also expressing its sovereignty through, e.g., territoriality or state protective principle. In such cases, citizens' rights are taken into consideration only minimally, e.g., to the extent that a served penalty deduction is acceptable (Article 10 GPC). Citizens' rights are better off when regulating jurisdiction in the absence of a strong link between state sovereignty and committed offence, e.g. when an own national commits an offense abroad. In these cases, jurisdiction may be blocked not only by the double criminality prerequisite, but also by the previously imposed and served penalty by and within another state's jurisdiction, or by statute of limitations applicable to the same offence (Article 9 GPC).

---

[14]See respectively Abrahms et al. (2016), p. 96.

[15]Kaiafa-Gbandi (2016), p. 110 et seq.

[16]See respectively Meyer (2013), p. 443.

[17]Meyer (2013), p. 443.

This analysis depicts that most states defend their own jurisdiction in criminal matters against their foreign counterparts, especially when the criminal act is strongly linked and directly relevant to their own sovereignty. The same applies to the corresponding conflict resolution: the ne bis in idem principle is dominant in such a settlement when the abovementioned link is weaker, proving that states yield and compromise only if the matter at hand does not challenge their punitive authority in areas under their sovereignty. Even in such cases, however, abstention from prosecution requires the irrevocable imposition of a penalty that is served in full, as well as the legal order's determination to acknowledge the ne bis in idem principle in transnational criminal matters.

4 Settlement Models for Conflicts of Jurisdiction in Criminal Matters at the International Level

The above trend is manifest even at the international level.[18] The Convention Implementing the Schengen Agreement (CISA),[19] agreed between countries of the Schengen Area and not necessarily EU Member-States,[20] is one of the most progressive international instruments in the relevant field. According to its Article 54 CISA obliges its parties to abstain from prosecution for the same facts when the case has been finally and irrevocably tried by one of them, and—in case of a conviction—if the penalty imposed has been, is in the process of being, or can no longer be enforced under the laws of the imposing legal order. However, Article 55 CISA grants its parties the right to express reservations for non-recognition of another State's judicial decision if the act to which the foreign judgment relates:

1. took place in whole or in part in its own territory,[21]
2. constitutes an offence against national security or likewise critical interests of the Member State, or

[18]For the relevant international treaties see Böse (2014c), p. 357 et seq.

[19]Relevant provisions can also be found in two conventions of the Council of Europe (the European Convention on the International Validity of the Criminal Judgments, Hague 28.5.1970, and the European Convention on the Transfer of Criminal Proceedings, Strasburg 15.5.1972) which include similar provisions to Articles 54-55 CISA as mentioned below. However, these conventions have not been widely accepted and their ratification pace is rather slow among signing parties, while major states have not yet sanctioned them. On the other hand, the International Convent on Civil and Political Rights, although arguably introducing the ne bis in idem principle transnationally and unrestrictedly (see Anagnostopoulos (2008), p. 160 et seq.), is—according to the prevailing view (see e.g. van den Wyngaert and Stessens (1999), p. 781 et seq.; Trechsel (2005), p. 385 et seq.)—not to be seen as a basis for the principle's international restricted validity.

[20]See e.g. Gless (2011), p. 154 et seq.

[21]In the latter case, however, the exception does not apply if the acts materialized to some extent in the territory of the party that delivered the judgment.

3. was committed in violation of their formal duties by state officials of the reserving State.

Obviously, CISA parties have to exactly define the categories of offenses for which the above exceptions may apply.[22]

It has been argued that this reservation right was annulled upon enforcement of the Amsterdam Treaty.[23] Nonetheless, even if this were to be true, it would only affect EU Member States that are bound by the TEU/TFEU. At his point, however, the interest is focused on the settlement model for conflicts of jurisdictions in criminal matters at the *international level.*

This reference illustrates that although national parties to an international convention may agree to restrict themselves as to the recognition of foreign judicial decisions in criminal matters, any involvement of their cardinal interests still tips the balance towards their sovereignty rights in settling such conflicts. Thus, citizens are not always shielded against a second prosecution for the same facts, even if they have stood trial for them and were acquitted or finally convicted and wholly served their sanctions. All the same, one has to acknowledge that CISA contributed to a relevant noteworthy progress. Albeit in a restricted area, in binding themselves via international convention its parties took a significant step to recognize a person's right against dual prosecution and trial for the same facts.

In other words, as far as each local ius puniendi, and thus criminal law enforcement, is concerned, the aims of safeguarding state sovereignty and acknowledging the ne bis in idem right to the citizen of the world are still conflicting. The prior is manifestly gaining the foothold, even in an international milieu where States express their fundamental reciprocal confidence by signing a restrictively binding international agreement and recognizing a corresponding right to citizens.

One might, of course, argue that an international recognition of the ne bis in idem principle favors some kind of international "forum shopping". Within its context, an offender could attempt to push for a final judgement by the legal order that applies the most lenient penal regime, and consequently be spared of other potential prosecutions with potentially harsher outcomes. However, this argument seems less convincing nowadays, given the wide range of judicial cooperation options available internationally, and especially for parties in even closer collaboration, as those to CISA.[24] Besides, it has aptly been stressed that a more lenient penal treatment should not be considered a "misfortune", and it is anyhow a minor loss in protecting citizens against double jeopardy.[25] Last but not least, it is also reminded that the "forum shopping" risk also applies to the opposite direction, i.e. when

[22]An exception to the exception—and thus an implementation of the rule—applies when a concerned party has requested a co-signee to launch prosecution for the same acts or has extradited the defendant according to Article 55 §4 CISA.

[23]See respectively Anagnostopoulos (2010), p. 1128; Hecker (2012), p. 467; Plöckinger and Leidenmühler (2003), pp. 82–83.

[24]See respectively Anagnostopoulos (2008), pp. 168–169.

[25]Anagnostopoulos (2008), p. 169.

exercised by prosecuting authorities[26] that will often try to have the case indicted by either the strictest available legal order or the one allowing them a rather unrestricted leeway to act.

Thus, opting for an explicit safeguard of the ne bis in idem principle in criminal matters internationally should still be an international community objective, as this would signify a shift to more anthropocentric legal systems, which would prioritize citizen fortification against dual prosecution over state sovereignty rights and enforcement of sanctioning prowess.

However, the international community is still far from realizing this goal, as evident in the ratifications of the Council of Europe's Conventions on transferring criminal proceedings and rendering international validity to decisions in criminal matters.[27]

5 Resolving and Preventing Conflicts of Jurisdiction in Criminal Matters at a Supranational Level: The EU Approach: A Baffling Challenge

The circumstances are quite different in the EU context. The Union—although at least not yet a federal state—can co-determine its Member-States' criminal law to a decisive extent, going forward to construct a common area of freedom, security and justice for the people living within its borders.[28] In order to achieve this, the EU tries to speed up criminal procedures with transnational characteristics and restricts its interventions to amendments in local procedural provisions to the least possible extent.[29] Hence, in the field of criminal procedure it extensively applies the principle of mutual recognition of criminal decisions and judgments (Article 82 TFEU). One could generally argue that this principle which aspires to pervade the whole criminal procedure (i.e. from the pre-trial stage and up to the enforcement of decisions) promotes a somewhat automatic recognition for judgments delivered by courts of another member state when observant of a minimum form and within the context of the limited power against denial of enforcement. This proves extremely beneficial for the implementation of measures ordered by individual decisions, and doubtlessly empowers the efficiency of crime control. However, mutual recognition can lead to an undermining of existing procedural principles that very much claim to be common between Member States, as palpable e.g. through the EAW provisions that extensively violate the presumption of innocence and the proportionality

[26] Anagnostopoulos (2008), p. 169; Nestler (2004), p. 341 et seq., 349 et seq.; Vogel (2004), p. 40 et seq.

[27] Cf. Böse (2014c), p. 361 et seq.

[28] See e.g. Kaiafa-Gbandi (2016), p. 38 et seq.

[29] See e.g. Asp (2016), pp. 13–14 and 20 et seq.

principle.[30] Evidently, mutual recognition is not destined to never to attain *positive* substance in shaping transnational crime control; nevertheless, such a development is only possible when mutual recognition comes to serve another acknowledged procedural principle, as noticeable in the EU perception of ne bis in idem.[31]

After the Lisbon Treaty, the double jeopardy principle was reformatted in Article 50 of the Union's Charter on Fundamental Rights (CFR), which reads as follows: "Nobody can be prosecuted or be punished with a criminal sanction for an offence for which he/she has been already acquitted of charges or convicted in the frame of the EU with a final decision of a criminal court according to the law". According to the thus far ECJ case-law on the content of the ne bis in idem principle it is argued that[32]:

1. although the provision refers to an offence, it is rather clear that it covers the same facts (idem factum), even under a different legal designation;
2. the term "final decision of a criminal court" implies not only criminal court judgements, but all decisions and rulings under judicial or alternate proceedings that bring final case closure, i.e. reviewable only under exceptional circumstances;
3. Article 50 does not explicitly oblige the enforcement of the sentencing decision, as required by Article 54 CISA, and last but not least,
4. Article 50 allows for no Member-State reservations to the transnational enforcement of the principle, contrary to Article 55 CISA.

This contextual definition of ne bis in idem triggering a conclusive and unrestricted ban against any new prosecution for the same facts is not uncontested, although judicially upheld, e.g., in Greece by a decision of the Supreme Court Plenary (Olomeleia Areiou Pagou).[33] Several scholars[34] and also recently the ECJ itself[35] read the same restrictions of Articles 54 and 55 CISA in Article 50 CFR. However -and even in this mindset, although Article 50 CFR did not repeal the Member States' reservations under Article 55 §1 CISA, such exceptions cannot be held indisputable.[36] On the contrary, they always remain subject to legal scrutiny under Article 52 §1 CFR, that sets the requirements for all fundamental rights limitations, such as that of Article 50 CFR. In particular, such limitations must comply with the principle of proportionality. Hence, it is argued that some Member-State declarations articulated under Article 55 §1 lit b (protection of essential state interests) and c (violation of official duties) CISA, covering offences subjected to harmonization and consequently not restricted to own national interests

[30]See respectively Kaiafa-Gbandi (2010), p. 357 et seq.

[31]Asp (2016), p. 112.

[32]Anagnostopoulos (2008), pp. 173–174 (in Greek).

[33]Areios Pagos (in Plenum) 11/2011.

[34]See authors under fn. 24.

[35]ECJ C-129/27.5.2014, Spasic.

[36]Böse (2014b), pp. 146–147.

(e.g. terrorism, piracy) or not safeguarding essential state interests (e.g. drug trafficking), breach the proportionality principle, and therefore a second investigation and prosecution in another Member State for such cases should be negated. The opposite would unsurprisingly be disproportional. Then again, the overwhelming majority of Member States have not expressed reservation under Article 55 CISA, and this has not had a detrimental impact in a law enforcement. This is seen as proof that a functional coordination mechanism for criminal investigations and proceedings will render the exceptions under Article 55 CISA[37] redundant.

Accounting for even these restrictive views, it is apparent that Article 50 CFR was another step towards prioritizing for civil rights than state sanctioning prowess. Making double prosecution and trial for the same facts impossible for all crimes, leaving very slim reservation rights to the states, and necessitating their adherence to the proportionality principle by abstaining when the adjudicating Member State provides adequate protection of the relevant legal interest, is certainly a significant progress. Besides, judicial cooperation in criminal matters is steadily and dynamically enhanced in the common area of freedom, security and justice,[38] thus adequate protection of legal interests is actually not an issue. This also advocates for a rather unrestricted acceptance of the principle.

In spite of this, many unsolved problems still persist. Ne bis in idem itself does not obstruct more States to prosecute and adjudicate against a person's same act, with the development and conclusion of such cases depending on the procedurally faster Member State, which first finalizes the decision ("first come-first served principle").[39] It is from that point on that ne bis in idem is applicable.

This is substandard for both the states and the persons involved. To date, the most of EU's legislative instruments invite Member States to criminalize certain behaviors, and to establish *extraterritorial* competence for such. Thus, the odds for jurisdictional conflicts are raised.[40] On the other hand, common rules on jurisdiction do not exist on the EU level. Indeed, EU legal instruments exist which bind Member States to coordinate actions when deciding which member state is to prosecute where jurisdictional conflicts arise.[41] However, they provide neither tangible criteria for such coordination, nor a concrete relevant procedure. Eurojust—authorized under Article 85 TFEU to aid in jurisdictional conflict resolution—has issued relevant

[37]Böse (2014b), p. 147.

[38]See European Criminal Policy Initiative (2013), pp. 430–431, 433 et seq., proposing requirements that safeguard individuals' rights to offset this development.

[39]Asp (2016), pp. 91–93.

[40]See, e.g., Article 4 of the Convention on the protection of the European Communities' financial interests; Article 9 §1c, d, e FD 2002/475/JHA; Article 10 §§1b, 2 Directive 2011/36/EU; Article 12 §§1b, 2b Directive 201340/EU.

[41]See respectively FD 2009/948/JHA, as well as e.g. Article 4 the 1995 Convention on the Protection of the European Communities' Financial Interests; Article 9 of the FD 2008/919/JHA on combating terrorism.

guidelines.[42] Though not binding on Member States and lacking a set of fixed criteria, the guidelines propose no hierarchy pattern.[43] This makes foreseeability of competent forum in a transnational case impossible, and thus renders the n.c.n.p.s.l. principle (Article 49 §1 CFR) void, given that the latter also covers criminal act forum,[44] and consequently a person's natural judge in the EU common area of justice. This is intolerable, especially for suspects as frankly jeopardizing their rights, but also for the states themselves, which might be deprived from exercising their punitive power, although they have a stronger link to the case than the legal order that was the first to adjudicate. Framework Decision 2009/948/JHA on the prevention and settlement of conflicts of jurisdiction does not expel such effects either. Actually, in lacking firm criteria and a binding effect of the consultation proceedings outcome, it is likewise defective, envisaging no safeguards whatsoever for the rights of involved persons in the forum choice field.[45] Above all, suspects have to carry the burden of uncertainty until a final decision on their case is issued in one of the Member States, as well as an ambiguity on the exact forum that will adjudicate first; bear in mind that the latter might not even be the locus delicti one, or even one chosen by the prosecuting authorities as the most favorable for them. As a result, in lack of firm criteria for selecting adjudicating forum for transnational cases, forum shopping by offenders cannot be forestalled. Consequently, the questions persist: can we prevent conflicts and regulate jurisdiction of transnational cases in a way that shields the individual adequately versus the risk of defending against multiple jurisdictions for the same case and let ne bis in idem develop its transnational potency in time? Is that not the next appropriate step if priority lies with the rights of suspects and defendants, and even by considering state interests under the proportionality principle? Is this not so, especially in an area which gradually but steadily develops into a common area of prosecutorial powers without the required counter-balance towards a common area of freedom and justice for the individual as well?

These questions still wait for adequate answers in the EU. The existing model shows that the Union practically accepts a priority of its Member States' sovereignty when deciding on forum selection and on possible jurisdictional conflicts. The wider the discretion allowed to States to resolve jurisdictional matters in criminal cases in a non-binding manner, the stronger the threat against citizens' rights.

---

[42]See http://www.eurojust.europa.eu/doclibrary/corporate/newsletter/eurojust%20news%20issue%2014%20(january%202016)%20on%20conflicts%20of%20jurisdiction/eurojustnews_issue14_2016-01.pdf and http://www.ecba.org/extdocserv/conferences/vilnius2016/eurojustguidelines.pdf.

[43]See on the existing EU legal framework the criticism of Böse (2014c), p. 337 et seq., 346 et seq.; Zimmermann (2014), p. 305 et seq.

[44]Böse (2014b), p. 124.

[45]Böse (2014c), p. 357.

6 Reflections on a Future Model for Preventing and Resolving Jurisdictional Conflicts in the EU

A suitable future model for the prevention and/or settlement of jurisdictional conflicts within the EU requires a fundamental understanding that the Union is a *supranational* organization in the process of *a gradual "federalization"*,[46] as far as its status against its Member States goes. This means that the methodology of resolving existing jurisdictional issues in criminal matters has to be by all accounts integrated in the broader framework of this supranational structure, and thus attuned to its concrete principal characteristics. This awareness apparently impacts the focal parameters of future decisions.

When deciding on jurisdiction and the settlement of relevant conflicts *in a national perspective*, a state does not account for interests other than its own. To essentially regulate the expansion of extraterritorial jurisdiction, international law promotes certain principles in this field, which are actually not institutionally binding for States. Furthermore, the latter are never bound in the process of preventing and solving such conflicts. Within *international surroundings*, things are a bit different. If an international treaty regulates jurisdiction and the settlement of relevant conflicts, the ratifying state is correspondingly bound. However, treaties ordinarily settle jurisdictional conflicts favorably for States' sovereignty; otherwise their ratification and enforcement are troublesome. This holds true even for the Convention Implementing the Schengen Agreement (CISA), the most progressive of them all. Besides, when a state signs an international treaty it restricts its own jurisdictional sovereignty only to the extent it wishes. Even if the party later fails to abide by the said provisions, only "soft" institutional enforcement via political pressure of the international community is available to compensate for lack of sanctioning mechanisms.

Things differ significantly within the supranational organization of the EU. Therein, Member States are bound by EU decisions as far as the Union has relevant competence and is aligned to its constitutional treaties (TEU and TFEU). The enforcement of such decisions is institutionally guaranteed.[47] On the other hand, one of the core Union traits in the post-Lisbon era when the Charter on Fundamental Rights became binding, is the placing of the individual at the heart of its activities (Preamble of the Charter, lit. c) and the construction of a common area of freedom, security and justice (Article 3 TEU, Article 67 TFEU) for people's benefit. In this approach, the EU acknowledges in a transnational perspective the ne bis in idem principle as a fundamental right in its Charter (Article 50), covering all its Member States, and providing it with a more substantial content compared to CISA. Thus, even if one believes the principle to be restricted by possible Member States'

[46]See, albeit, the significant differences to a federal system in Tsatsos (2007), p. 55 et seq. and esp. 103 et seq.

[47]See Articles 258 and 260 TFEU granting leeway to sanction Member States for not abiding by EU rules.

reservations in this case, it is only limited and proportional constraints that are acceptable in serving state interests. Given that, it is not tolerable for any regulatory system on the prevention and/or settlement of jurisdictional conflicts within the EU to devalue the priority acknowledged to individual rights over state sovereignty, as expressed in the Charter's preamble and the ne bis in idem principle. Therefore, the message is clear within the EU institutional framework: bringing states together in a common supranational organization is not meant for the shake of a law enforcement without loopholes to jeopardize its peoples' fundamental rights. Selecting to elevate the standard of protection by banning dual prosecution or adjudication for the same facts where intensive judicial cooperation allows for much easier criminal prosecution opens up a new perspective that ought to prevail, regardless of the additional characteristics of the forthcoming model for preventing and/or settling jurisdictional conflicts. For that reason, the model needs to clarify and uphold this fundamental selection in all its manifestations the best possible way.

As a matter of fact, different models could be suggested for the said approach.[48] The one presently incorporated in FD 2009/948/JHA introduces a horizontal design entailing direct interaction and mutual consultation between competent Member State authorities to decide on jurisdiction, supplemented by a vertical component in absence of consensus (cooperation with Eurojust, Article 13 FD 2009/948/JHA). This method covers the *settlement* of jurisdictional conflicts, but not their prevention. An alternative model could also be vertically focused, by envisaging a more active role for Eurojust from the very beginning.[49] However, in the absence of definitive and binding jurisdictional rules on forum selection, procedure, and rights of concerned persons, neither model can properly serve the essence of the EU selection to safeguard ne bis in idem as a fundamental right. The core prerequisite, therefore, is for European rules to cover all relevant issues and hence set a minimum level of required protection and a clear procedural framework. It is of minor importance whether these imperatives will be implemented mostly horizontally (through interaction between competent states' authorities) or vertically (by acknowledging a substantial role to Eurojust and the ECJ)[50] However, other such models already proposed by scholars should also be considered, with an aim to *prevent* jurisdictional conflicts in the first place.[51] Such schemata better convey the essence of the selection made by the European constitutional legislator with the present system of

[48]See e.g. Ambos (2011), §4; Biehler et al. (2003), Bitzilekis et al. (2006), p. 250 et seq., 493 et seq.; Böse et al. (2014), p. 381 et seq.; Eickert (2004), ELI (2017), Fuchs (2006), p. 112 et seq.; Gropp (2012), p. 41 et seq.; Hein (2002), Klip (2005), p. 79 et seq.; Lagodny (2001), Lelieur-Fischer (2006), Schünemann (2006), Sinn (2012), p. 575 et seq.; Thomas (2002), Vander Beken et al. (2002), Zimmermann (2014), p. 369 et seq. For a systematical presentation of the different models proposed to date for the prevention and/or settlement of jurisdictional conflicts in criminal matters and their critical evaluation, see esp. Zimmermann (2014), p. 320 et seq.

[49]This is not the case under Article 13 FD 2009/948/JHA.

[50]To the latter, for example, through a judicial review of settlement decisions that may be filed by suspects or by the Member States themselves.

[51]See e.g. Schünemann (2006), p. 257 et seq.; Bitzilekis et al. (2006), p. 493.

safeguarding ne bis in idem in Article 50 CFR. However, even in the framework of such models one can distinguish between more and less flexible ones.[52] For example, the territoriality-principle could become the rule for jurisdiction assignment and conflict resolution with no exception; when more Member States fulfill the locus delicti territoriality criterion, one of them should be selected to exercise jurisdiction by applying *additional* criteria. The latter could be prioritized according to their degree of relevance to the offence (: locus delicti in terms of majority/center of criminal activities or of criminal outcome, defendant's domicile or habitual residence, location of most important pieces of evidence).[53] Such benchmarks constitute a much more transparent—albeit less flexible—formula when more States fulfill the territoriality criterion.[54] By preventing jurisdictional conflicts before they even arise, such models defend the ne bis in idem principle much more effectively. However, conflicts might still occur when more Member States fulfil the set criteria or when they have foreseen exceptions (e.g. by circumventing the territoriality principle) considered essential to protect legitimate defendant interests[55] or to focus on the alleged acts, considering in particular the subsequent local prerequisites for obtaining evidence.[56]

Preserving the Charter's spirit to prevent and/or settle jurisdictional conflicts in the EU affects a vast array of crucial issues on criminal liability. For example, deciding which State is to be given jurisdictional priority or exclusivity within the EU is not irrelevant in safeguarding foreseeability for the suspect/defendant according to the *n.c.n.p.s.l. principle* (Article 49 §1 CFR). The fora least associated to the commission of the criminal act itself can hardly justify the required foreseeability of a criminal act as articulated by the n.c.n.p.s.l principle.[57] On the other hand, by turning the collection of evidence into a criterion (even linking it with objective elements such as the act itself),[58] the focus is bigotedly transferred to the prosecuting authority, i.e. to states' sovereignty. Through the Union's constitutional treaties—and especially the Charter on fundamental rights, the EU legislator has made a

[52]For rather flexible (and therefore not preferable) proposed models, see Böse et al. (2014), p. 381 et seq.; and Zimmermann (2014), p. 369 et seq. and 449–451, where the consultation process and the exceptions it entails cannot safeguard the foreseeability by the suspect/defendant of the criminal act and its punishment. *Zimmermann* accepts even a new adjudication of a case when special state interests apply (pp. 450–451), while *Böse et al* propose numerous prospects for the transfer of proceedings (p. 443 et seq.).

[53]Bitzilekis et al. (2006), p. 493. Additional criteria to territoriality (e.g. center of criminal activity, etc.) could also be decisive in deciding competent State when multiple associated offences are committed by the same person or when multiple offenders of associated crimes are subject to the jurisdiction of more Member States.

[54]In this direction the model of Schünemann (2006), p. 257 et seq.

[55]See in this direction Bitzilekis et al. (2006), p. 493.

[56]See in this direction Schünemann (2006), pp. 258–259.

[57]See in this respect esp. Zimmermann (2014), p. 228 et seq.; Helenius (2014), p. 163 et seq.; cf. Asp (2016), p. 156 et seq.

[58]In this direction Schünemann (2006), pp. 258–259.

balanced yet clear choice to the citizens' benefit. Foreseeability is also momentous in upholding the *guilt principle* (Article 48 §2); it provides that an error of law is usually not an excuse for a defendant, unless a diligent citizen could not find out what the law is about.[59] A forum with the least possible association to the criminal act does not facilitate citizens to grasp the law, and thus assigning it with jurisdiction to adjudicate and enforce sanctions extensively undermines the functionality of the guilt principle.[60] Nevertheless, stretching the territoriality principle on the other hand beyond its notional confines (locus delicti of violation and outcome) results in granting jurisdiction to States that possibly lack any genuine link to a case. Such an adaptation of the territoriality principle is unfitting to serve both the criminal act foreseeability and the guilt principle.[61]

EU's choice to safeguard ne bis in idem as a fundamental right and integrate it within the framework of rights and principles enshrined in the Charter affects other critical questions. Should prevention of jurisdictional conflicts also cover the investigative phase by excluding parallel investigations? What should be the main characteristics of a procedure that prevents and/or settles jurisdictional conflicts? Should the right to intervene be recognized to the suspect or even to victim? Should settlement decisions be judicially reviewable? One could argue that parallel investigations are neither sensible nor necessary in a common area of freedom, security and justice under gradual yet unremitting enhancement.[62] The dynamics of the current regime of judicial cooperation in criminal matters render this choice understandable. Exclusive jurisdiction models (even including the investigative stage) naturally require a composed and comprehensive regulative framework and a provision for transferring proceedings to another Member State, if at a later point in time investigations push to such a direction.[63] However, such provisions need to safeguard suspects' rights, and should thus foresee that any such transfer does not occur after the conclusion of the investigation stage.[64] On the other hand, allowing suspects to safeguard their rights makes sense, especially where models leave room for a decision upon different or exceptional criteria.[65] The same cannot hold as far as the victim is concerned. Settling or preventing conflicts of jurisdiction is focusing on a criminal procedure whose subject is not the victim but the suspect. The

[59]See Blomsa (2012), p. 464 et seq.

[60]See the interesting proposal of Böse et al. (2014), pp. 381–383, who formulate the following general rule: "Article 1 para 2: Criminal liability under the law of a Member State is subject to the condition that the person is aware (intent) or should be aware (negligence) of the circumstances that make that member State's criminal law applicable".

[61]See the vague notion of "affecting" the territory of a state, used in certain legal orders.

[62]See model in Schünemann (2006), p. 257 et seq.

[63]See, however, the wide possibilities acknowledged for the transference of proceedings in the proposal of Böse et al. (2014), p. 411 et seq. It should be stressed, though, that the wider the transference possibility, the flimsier the safeguarding of the criminal act foreseeability.

[64]So Schünemann (2006), pp. 258–259 et seq. Transference of proceedings should also be exceptionally possible upon request of the defendant for reasons serving his/her interests.

[65]See esp. Articles 12, 13 in the Model Rules in Böse et al. (2014), pp. 444–445.

victim's interests may be affected by the procedure, but the question of parallel or exclusive jurisdiction cannot be determined by them.[66] Otherwise, a lopsided priority is given to prosecuting authorities, given that the victim's interests are normally situated on the same side. To enable them to safeguard their effective participation in the proceedings, victims could be allowed to challenge such decisions when exceptional criteria that serve the interests of the suspect/defendant apply. Arguments related to the essence of the principal mindset to integrate ne bis in idem as a fundamental right in the Charter's framework are also helpful when deciding upon the issue of allowing the suspect to exercise a right to judicial review by the ECJ when the Member State argues for its right to prosecute.[67] Both sides should be heard during a procedure that attempts to weigh their conflicting interests and finalize a State's investigative and adjudicative competence.

7 Conclusion

The preceding analysis should have clarified the following points:

- Multiple prosecutions for the same act, although supporting an unhampered law enforcement, are no longer tolerable within a unified area of sovereign states that are members of a supranational organization. The concept of a common area of freedom, security and justice inescapably leads to a single prosecution and actually to a single investigation for the same act. Thus, preventing and not simply settling jurisdictional conflicts in criminal matters should be a Union objective.
- In defining the proper jurisdiction to prosecute and adjudicate a criminal case within the EU, the Union legislator is bound by the principles and rights safeguarded in EU Treaties and the Charter of Fundamental Rights. These legal instruments endorse the territoriality principle as defined in EU law with very slim exceptions, and especially considering the suspects' interests within an unambiguous procedure, recognizing them the right to be heard (i.e. pleading for an exception that shields their interests), and envisaging a judicial review for relevant decisions. Of course, such a model implies that the supranational organization's interests to facilitate judicial cooperation in criminal matters should not gain the upper hand by substituting states' sovereignty in defining jurisdiction and settling corresponding conflicts. The European Sympoliteia, as already mentioned, is a Union of sovereign states and their peoples, required by its constitutional treaties, even in the field of law enforcement, to express them both alike. Otherwise, the EU can no longer claim to place the individual at the heart of its activities—as it

[66] See thorough argumentation in Zimmermann (2014), pp. 206–208.

[67] See fn. 66.

communicates in the Preamble of its Charter, nor safeguard the core of the fundamental right enshrined in the ne bis in idem principle.

References

Abrahms N, Sun Beale S, Klein RS (2016) Federal criminal law and its enforcement, 6th edn. West Academic Publishing

Ambos K (2011) Internationales Strafrecht, vol 3. Aufl. C.H. Beck

Anagnostopoulos I (2008) Ne bis in idem, European and International Perspectives (in Greek)

Anagnostopoulos I (2010) Ne bis in idem in der Europäischen Union, Offene Fragen. In: Neumann U, Herzog F (eds) Festschrift für W. Hassemer. Verlagsgruppe Hüthig-Jehle-Rehm, pp 1121–1140

Androulakis N (2012) Fundamentals of criminal procedure, 4th edn. (in Greek)

Asp P (2016) The procedural criminal law cooperation in the EU. Förlag

Biehler A, Kniebühler R, Lelieur-Fischer J, Stein S (eds) (2003) Freiburg proposal on concurrent jurisdictions and the prohibition of multiple prosecutions in the European Union, Freiburg im Breisgau: Ed. iuscrim, Max-Planck-Inst. für Ausländisches und Internat. Strafrecht

Bitzilekis N, Kaiafa-Gbandi M, Symeonidou-Kastanidou E (2006) Alternative thoughts on the regulation of transnational criminal proceedings in the EU. In: Schünemann B (ed) A programme for European criminal justice. C.H. Beck

Blomsa J (2012) Mens rea and defences in European criminal law. Intersentia

Böse M (2014a) Fundamental freedoms of the Union. In: Böse M, Meyer F, Schneider A (eds) Conflicts of jurisdiction in criminal matters in the European Union, vol II. Nomos, pp 43–106

Böse M (2014b) Fundamental rights of the EU-charter. In: Böse M, Meyer F, Schneider A (eds) Conflicts of jurisdiction in criminal matters in the European Union, vol II. Nomos, pp 107–168

Böse M (2014c) Models and instruments for solving conflicts of jurisdiction. In: Böse M, Meyer F, Schneider A (eds) Conflicts of jurisdiction in criminal matters in the European Union, vol II. Nomos, pp 335–366

Böse M, Meyer F, Schneider A (2014) Model Rules and Explanation. In: Böse M, Meyer F, Schneider A (eds) Conflicts of jurisdiction in criminal matters in the European Union, vol II. Nomos, pp 381–438

Eickert A (2004) Transstaatliche Strafverfolgung: Ein Beitrag zur Europäisierung, Internationaölisierung und Fortentwicklung des Grundsatzes ne bis in idem. Springer

European Criminal Policy Initiative (2013) A Manifesto on European criminal procedure law. Zeitschrift für Internationale Strafrechtsdogmatik 11:430–446

European Law Institute ELI (2017) Draft legislative proposals for the prevention and the resolution of conflicts of jurisdiction in criminal matters in the Europan union. https://www.europeanlawinstitute.eu/fileadmin/user_upload/p_eli/Publications/Conflict_of_Jurisdiction_in_Criminal_Law_FINAL.pdf

Fuchs H (2006) Zuständigkeitsordnung und materielles Strafrecht. In: Schünemann B (ed) Ein Programm für die europäische Strafrechtspflege. Carl Heymanns Verlag, pp 112–116

Gless S (2011) Internationales Strafrecht, Grundriss für Studium und Praxis. Helbing & Lichtenhahn

Gropp W (2012) Kollision transnationaler Strafegewalten nulla prosecution transnationalis sine lege. In: Sinn A (ed) Jurisdiktionskonflikte bei grenzüberschreitender Kriminalität. V&R Uni Press, pp 41–64

Hecker B (2012) Europäisches Strafrecht, 4th edn. Springer

Hein L (2002) Zuständigkeitskonflikte im internationalen Strafrecht. Ein europäisches Lösungsmodell, Juristische Reihe Tenea/www.jurawelt.com; Vol 11

Helenius D (2014) Straffrättslig jurisdiktion

Kaiafa-Gbandi M (2010) Harmonization of criminal procedure on the basis of common principles: the EU's challenge for a Rule-of-Law transnational crime control. In: Finjaut C, Ouwerkerk J (eds) The future of police and judicial cooperation in the European Union. Brill, pp 357–402
Kaiafa-Gbandi M (2016) The EU and the US criminal law as two-tier models. Sieps - Swedish Institute for European Policy Studies
Kaiafa-Gbandi M, Bitzilekis N, Symeonidou-Kastanidou E (2016) Criminal sanctions, 2nd edn. (in Greek)
Klip A (2005) Substantive criminal law in the European Union. Maklu Uitgevers België
Lagodny O (2001) Empfiehlt es sich eine europäische Gerichtskompetenz für Strafgewaltkonflikte vorzusehen?, Gutachten im Auftrag des Bundesministeriums der Justiz. https://www.uni-salzburg.at/fileadmin/oracle_file_imports/460066.PDF
Lelieur-Fischer J (2006) Comments on the Green Paper on Conflicts of Jurisdiction and the principle of ne bis in idem in criminal proceedings. https://www.mpicc.de/files/pdf2/comments_green_paper_nebisinidem.pdf
Manoledakis I (2000) Reflections on a common European criminal law judicial area. In: Manoledakis I (ed) Reflections on the future of criminal law (in Greek)
Manoledakis I (2004) Criminal law, general theory (in Greek)
Meyer F (2013) Comparative analyses. In: Böse M, Meyer F, Schneider A (eds) Conflicts of jurisdiction in criminal matters in the European Union, vol I. Nomos, pp 411–464
Nestler C (2004) Europäisches Strafprozessrecht. ZStW 116:331–352
Plöckinger O, Leidenmühler F (2003) Zum Verbot doppelter Strafverfolgung nach Art. 54 SDÜ 1990. In: Wistra, pp 81–88
Satzger H (2012) International and European criminal law. C.H. Beck
Schünemann B (ed) (2006) A programme for European criminal justice. C.H. Beck
Sinn A (2012) Jurisdiktionskonflikte bei grenzüberschreitender Kriminalität. Universitätsverlag, Osnabrück
Thomas H (2002) Das Recht auf Einmaligkeit der Strafverfolgung. Vom nationalen zum internationalen ne bis in idem, Nomos
Trechsel S (2005) Human rights in criminal proceedings. OUP
Tsatsos D (2007) The notion of democracy in the European Sympoliteia (in Greek)
Van den Wyngaert C, Stessens G (1999) The international Non bis in idem Principle: Resolving some of the answered questions. ICLQ 48:779–804
Vander Beken T, Vermeulen G, Steverlynck S, Thomaes S (2002) Finding the best place to prosecute. Maklu, Antwerpen
Vogel J (2004) Perspektiven des Internationalen Strafprozessrechts
Zimmermann F (2014) Strafgewaltkonflikte in der Europäischen Union, Ein Regelungsvorschlag zur Wahrung materieller und prozessualer strafrechtlicher Garantien sowie staatlicher Strafinteressen. Nomos

Maria Kaiafa-Gbandi is Professor and Director of the "Research Institute for Transparency, Corruption and Financial Crime" of the Law Faculty of Aristotle University. She is a permanent fellow of the "Alexander von Humboldt" Foundation (Germany). Professor Kaiafa-Gbandi has served as a member of the Special Supreme Court of Greece (2004–2005, 2008–2009 and 2012–2013) and as a President of the Legislative Drafting Committee of the Ministry of Justice for the reform of tax offenses (2015). She is also Council member of the European Law Institute (ELI) based in Vienna, Member of the Commission's Expert Group for European Criminal Policy of the European Union, and a founding member of the academic network European Criminal Policy Initiative (ECPI). She is an associate member of the International Academy of Comparative Law.

Diversité, pertinence et efficacité des mécanismes internationaux de règlement des différends en matière économique

Catherine Kessedjian

Abstract Economic actors have a great variety of dispute resolution methods at their disposal, whether their disputes are against a State or a private party. Efficiency is the key criterion for companies when choosing one mean of dispute resolution over the others. They also have the possibility to strategize their conflict resolution needs and may launch different proceedings one after the other if the previous one did not give them satisfaction. Some may find this unacceptable but, unless clear rules are set to avoid multiple proceedings, the system as it stands now is unavoidable.

1 Introduction

Le contentieux du XXIème siècle offre aux entreprises (le focus de cette contribution) une large diversité de mécanismes de règlement des différends parmi lesquels elles peuvent choisir. La prolifération à laquelle on assiste pour le contentieux entre Etats existe également pour les acteurs économiques. Ces mécanismes sont en concurrence les uns avec les autres, même si certaines complémentarités peuvent exister entre eux. L'objet de cette contribution est non seulement de décrire le phénomène, sans prétendre en donner une image exhaustive, mais également d'en évaluer la pertinence et l'efficacité pour permettre d'en évaluer le développement dans les prochaines années.

C. Kessedjian (✉)
University Panthéon-Assas Paris II, Paris, France
e-mail: catherine.kessedjian@u-paris2.fr

N. Etcheverry Estrázulas, D. P. Fernández Arroyo (eds.), *Enforcement and Effectiveness of the Law - La mise en oeuvre et l'effectivité du droit*, Ius Comparatum – Global Studies in Comparative Law 30, https://doi.org/10.1007/978-3-319-93758-8_5

2 L'état des lieux

Parler de mode international de règlement des différends en matière économique fait immédiatement penser aux panels de l'OMC. Certes, ce contentieux n'est pas ouvert aux entreprises directement puisqu'il s'agit d'un contentieux interétatique. Mais nous savons que, pour peu que le domaine d'activité économique ait une quelconque importance pour l'économie d'un Etat donné, celui-ci ne se fera pas prier longtemps pour porter le contentieux devant un panel de l'OMC alors même que les réels demandeurs sont les entreprises de ce secteur d'activité. Ce contentieux par le truchement des Etats était le lot commun en matière d'investissement avant que les traités bilatéraux d'investissement ne permettent aux entreprises de porter le fer directement contre l'Etat hôte, mettant ainsi fin et des décennies de protection diplomatique en la matière. On peut donc dire que les panels de l'OMC restent aujourd'hui le seul mode international de règlement des différends économiques qui oblige l'Etat à prendre fait et cause pour les entreprises relevant de sa juridiction.

Les juridictions nationales peuvent se transformer en juridiction internationale lorsqu'elles sont appelées à statuer sur un litige international de telle envergure que leurs décisions sont scrutées par une large communauté internationale et analysées pour éventuellement servir de modèle (positif ou négatif) dans d'autres procédures devant des juridictions nationales appartenant à d'autres pays. Trois exemples suffiront à montrer l'importance des juridictions nationales comme juridictions internationales. Le premier tiré d'un litige très politique (en dehors du droit économique) concerne le procès intenté au Royaume Uni contre le général-sénateur, ex-Président, Pinochet pour savoir s'il devait être extradé vers l'Espagne où il pouvait être poursuivi pour les crimes qui lui étaient reprochés devant la justice espagnole. Il ne fait guère de doute que les enseignements de cette affaire et la manière dont elle a été traitée par les juridictions du Royaume-Uni ont été largement analysés dans un très grand nombre de pays au-delà même du cercle des juridictions appartenant au monde du *common law*. Le deuxième exemple est tiré de la jurisprudence des Etats-Unis d'Amérique sur l'interprétation de l'*Alien Tort Statute*[1] et, tout particulièrement, de son application aux actes de violation des droits de l'homme par des entreprises en dehors du territoire des Etats-Unis. L'affaire Kiobel, jugée par la Cour suprême fédérale américaine en 2013,[2] a suscité un très grand nombre de mémoires d'*amicus curiae* dont certains étaient préparés par des Etats étrangers, des ONG étrangères et des fédérations internationales d'entreprises. Elle a

[1]Il s'agit d'une loi adoptée par le premier Congrès des Etats-Unis en 1789, codifiée 28 USC para 1350, prévoyant: « The district courts shall have original jurisdiction of any civil action by an alien for a tort only, committed in violation of the law of nations or a treaty of the United States » (parfois également désigné sous l'acronyme ATCA). Cette loi ouvre les tribunaux américains (*subject matter juridiction*) à des étrangers se plaignants d'actes commis en violation du droit international tel compris aux Etats-Unis. La loi ne précise pas quel lien ces actes doivent avoir avec le territoire des Etats-Unis, ce qu'il est revenu à la jurisprudence de déterminer.

[2]Kiobel v. Royal Dutch Petroleum Co, 569 US (2013). Cette affaire a également donné lieu à plusieurs décisions aux Pays-Bas.

suscité une littérature très abondante partout dans le monde.[3] Enfin, le troisième exemple concerne les actions en dommages et intérêts instituées à la suite d'une condamnation de cartel. En Europe, trois juridictions sont privilégiées par les entreprises qui se disent victimes des sociétés ayant participé au cartel : les Pays-Bas, l'Allemagne et le Royaume-Uni. Comme, la plupart du temps, les cartels sont transeuropéens, voire internationaux, la compétence juridictionnelle (au moins en vertu du Règlement Bruxelles I) ne pose guère de difficulté car il sera facile d'identifier un défendeur dans l'un de ces trois pays et, ensuite, d'utiliser la règle qui permet d'agréger d'autres défendeurs situés ailleurs en Europe. Certains pays possèdent la même règle pour les sociétés situées en dehors de l'Europe, si bien qu'une seule juridiction peut statuer sur les demandes formulées à l'égard d'un grand nombre de défendeurs pour des dommages et intérêts subis dans un grand nombre de pays.

Mais si les juridictions nationales peuvent prendre le rôle de juridictions internationales, il en va également ainsi de tribunaux privés, tels les tribunaux arbitraux ou quasi arbitraux. En matière commerciale internationale, le recours à l'arbitrage est devenu pratiquement une « justice naturelle »,[4] même si aucune étude sociologique d'envergure (et transnationale) ne permet d'avoir une vision exacte de la pratique contractuelle des entreprises, seule apte à démontrer si l'insertion d'une clause compromissoire dans les contrats est devenue une clause habituelle « *a boiler plate clause* » comme certains auteurs le pensent. La Cour de cassation française a même décidé que la sentence arbitrale internationale est une « décision de justice internationale » qui, en tant que telle, n'est rattachée à aucun ordre juridique étatique.[5] Ce faisant elle érige les tribunaux arbitraux internationaux en véritable « juridictions internationales » avec des conséquences qui n'ont pas encore donné tous leurs fruits. Il est certain, en tout cas, que la prolifération des centres d'arbitrage dans le monde dénote au moins la croyance par ceux qui en sont à l'origine que l'arbitrage a de beaux jours devant lui. On peut en tout cas noter pour l'anecdote que certains centres comportent le mot « cour » dans leur intitulé (v. la *London Court of International Arbitration*) ou ont institué en leur sein une « cour » (v. la Cour internationale d'arbitrage au sein de la Chambre de Commerce international), qui ne possède pas grand-chose des attributs habituels d'une telle institution. Mais il est rassurant pour les parties à un litige de savoir que la sentence préparée par un tribunal arbitral statuant sous l'égide de la CCI sera « revue » au moins en ce qui concerne la forme et la cohérence des arguments si ce n'est vraiment sur le fond. Seul, en effet, le tribunal arbitral possède l'autorité pour rendre la sentence qui demeure de sa responsabilité. Le tribunal arbitral n'est donc pas obligé de suivre les observations de la Cour.

---

[3]Pour une analyse récente des tribunaux nationaux comme juridictions internationales, v. « Domestic Courts as International Jurisdictions? », in Moura Vicente (2016), pp. 497–544 (plusieurs auteurs).

[4]Kessedjian (2015), pp. 985–996.

[5]Civ. 1, 29 juin 2007, n°05-18.053, Sté PT Putrabali Adyamulia c. Sté Rena Holding et al.

Le contentieux des investissements, faute d'une juridiction internationale spécialisée, a fait l'objet, de plus en plus fréquemment depuis environ les années 1980,[6] de saisines de tribunaux arbitraux statuant soit sous l'égide du CIRDI,[7] soit sous l'égide d'une autre institution d'arbitrage non spécialisée, soit même de manière *ad hoc*. Le contentieux d'investissement peut s'appuyer soit sur une clause compromissoire insérée dans le contrat passé entre l'investisseur et l'Etat hôte, soit sur l'offre d'arbitrage insérée dans un traité bilatéral d'investissement. C'est pourquoi la concurrence existe également dans ce domaine entre diverses formes d'arbitrage. Plus récemment, en raison d'une insatisfaction croissante vis-à-vis de l'arbitrage d'investissement, plusieurs propositions ont été faites pour créer un tribunal permanent dont l'inspiration a été en partie tirée des panels de l'OMC. Une telle juridiction permanente a été proposée par la Commission européenne dans le cadre du CETA, accord de libre-échange signé entre le Canada et l'Union européenne[8] et acceptée par le Canada, si bien que le texte en cours de ratification à l'heure où nous écrivons comporte des dispositions sur ce tribunal permanent qui fait l'objet d'une critique virulente de la part des milieux de l'arbitrage. Une telle proposition a également été faite aux Etats-Unis d'Amérique qui n'ont pas répondu officiellement sur ce point.[9] Nous ne pouvons analyser en détail ici ces propositions, sauf à donner quelques éléments d'analyse sous l'angle de l'efficacité, thème central du Congrès dans le cadre duquel cette contribution est écrite.[10]

Enfin, depuis quelques années,[11] la médiation vient bouleverser la donne des différends en matière économique en soustrayant ces litiges tant au contentieux classique devant les juridictions nationales ou internationales, qu'au contentieux arbitral, multipliant encore les options qui s'offrent aux entreprises. La médiation

[6]L'arbitrage dans le domaine du contentieux des investissements internationaux a pris un essor sans précédent à partir du premier traité bilatéral de protection des investissements ayant proposé un tel mode de règlement des différends, soit le traité de 1968 entre les Pays-Bas et l'Indonésie. En effet, le premier traité bilatéral d'investissement conclu en 1959 entre l'Allemagne et le Pakistan ne comportait pas une telle offre d'arbitrage.

[7]La Convention de Washington instituant le CIRDI date de 1965. La première affaire à être soumise à un arbitrage sous son égide date de 1972. Mais ce n'est pas avant la fin des années 1990, c'est-à-dire la première crise financière argentine, qu'il a vu ses activités réellement prendre de l'essor.

[8]Pour une analyse de cette proposition, v. A. de Nanteuil, communication à la branche française de l'ILA, sept 2016, à paraître au JDI 2017.

[9]A l'heure où nous écrivons, compte tenu du résultat des élections présidentielles américaines, il est tout à fait incertain que ces négociations seront poursuivies.

[10]Pour une analyse de ces propositions, v. A. de Nanteuil, Communication donnée dans le cadre de la branche française de l'ILA, à paraître au JDI.

[11]La médiation s'est développée tout d'abord dans les pays de *common law* où le coût financier des procès est beaucoup plus important que dans les pays de tradition civiliste. Elle a d'abord été utilisée dans le domaine familial et interpersonnel pour désormais être utilisée dans tous les domaines, y compris les activités commerciales et économiques.

(ou la conciliation[12]) est devenue l'objet de nombreux projets internationaux, même si, pour le moment, il n'existe pas de critères clairs ou uniformes pour les compétences exigées des médiateurs, même au niveau national.[13] En août 2016, le secrétariat de la Charte de l'énergie a publié des lignes directrices pour l'utilisation de la médiation dans le cadre du contentieux d'investissement sur la base du Traité. L'IMI[14] a publié fin 2016 un guide donnant une liste de critères de compétence que les médiateurs en matière d'investissement devraient acquérir pour pouvoir médier ces litiges. L'IBA avait également publié des lignes directrices dans ce domaine en 2015. Tous ces textes n'ont aucune valeur juridique mais font avancer la réflexion et pourraient permettre, à terme, l'élaboration d'un texte international conjoint.[15]

Plus que jamais, dès lors, se révèle parfaitement exact le développement de l'acronyme ADR par le *Chief Justice* de l'Inde, non pas en « *alternative dispute resolution* » (ce qui est généralement l'acception retenue) mais en « *appropriate dispute resolution* ». C'est en effet en termes de pertinence et d'adéquation qu'il convient d'évaluer ces différents modes qui s'offrent aux opérateurs économiques, essentiellement les entreprises. Ce sera notre angle d'attaque, même si nous avons conscience que l'évaluation de l'efficacité peut être faite (doit être faite) également du point de vue de l'Etat, de la société prise collectivement et non pas seulement des parties au différend.

3 La pertinence du choix à travers l'efficacité

Pour les entreprises, il ne fait guère de doute que le choix d'un mode de règlement des différends passe par une évaluation de l'efficacité que chacun d'eux peut déployer. Pour faciliter l'analyse nous nous bornerons à comparer les tribunaux nationaux, l'arbitrage et la médiation.

---

[12]La conciliation permet au tiers impartial qui aide les parties à trouver un accord de donner son avis et de faire des propositions, alors que le médiateur doit normalement s'en garder, suscitant l'accord des parties par des techniques plus subtiles et moins directes. La CNUDCI, dont un des groupes de travail poursuit l'éventuelle adoption d'un texte facilitant l'exécution transfrontière des accords issus de conciliation, traite également, sous le même vocable, des accords issus de médiation.

[13]Un grand nombre de pays, dans tous les continents, sont dotés aujourd'hui de législations visant à encourager le recours à la médiation. Mais l'organisation de la profession est l'un des enjeux qui fait encire l'objet d'âpres discussions.

[14]L'IMI (*International Mediation Institute*), est un organisme privé, situé à La Haye, qui s'est donné pour mission de sélectionner les médiateurs à travers un système d'accréditation.

[15]Le CIRDI a également travaillé sur la médiation/conciliation en matière d'investissement. Mais aussi étrange que cela puisse paraître, le règlement conciliation du Centre est très peu utilisé même si certaines affaires se règlent par des solutions transactionnelles dues à des négociations directes entre les parties.

3.1 La médiation

Si la rapidité et le coût sont les critères d'efficacité pris en considération, la médiation se détache très loin devant n'importe quel autre mode de règlement. Il est possible de régler un conflit en quelques séances de médiation pour un coût qui n'a pas grand-chose à voir avec ceux que les parties doivent exposer si elles ont recours à un mode juridictionnel de règlement des différends. De plus, dans certains pays comme la France, un service public de médiation a été créé au sein du Ministère des Finances. Issu de la crise financière de 2008, il a petit à petit étendu ses activités au-delà des simples questions liées au crédit des entreprises pour aborder la médiation inter-entreprises et la médiation des marchés publics. S'agissant d'un service public, il est gratuit pour les parties qui y font appel ce qui ne favorise pas l'essor d'un marché dans ces domaines, comme c'est le cas au Royaume-Uni ou dans les pays du Nord de l'Europe. Evidemment, l'entreprise doit évaluer le service qui lui est ainsi rendu et le comparer à celui qui lui serait rendu dans le cadre d'une médiation privée.

Ceci étant dit, la médiation n'est pas adaptée à tous les litiges. Pour l'entreprise et ses conseils, la première analyse consiste à se demander non seulement si le différend qui est né (ou que l'on subodore) est de telle nature qu'il peut faire l'objet d'une médiation et si l'autre partie serait susceptible d'accepter une offre de médiation. Par ailleurs, il est fréquent que les contrats comportent une phase obligatoire de médiation avant la saisine d'un tribunal qu'il soit étatique ou arbitral. En droit français, cette phase obligatoire préalable est à prendre très au sérieux car, selon le contenu de la clause et si son caractère comminatoire est clair, son non-respect peut être considéré comme une fin de non-recevoir dans la procédure subséquente[16] et entraîner, par exemple, l'annulation d'une sentence arbitrale qui aurait néanmoins été rendue. Or, cette médiation préalable est souvent inefficace car trop précoce. Les meilleures médiations sont celles qui ont lieu quand le litige est mûr, lorsque les parties ont eu le temps de vérifier les forces et faiblesses de leurs arguments et qu'elles se sont préparées à l'éventualité d'un insuccès au moins partiel. Cet état de conscience est rarement atteint au début du contentieux, mais plutôt quand les parties ont déjà échangé au moins un mémoire de chaque côté. C'est pourquoi, il est souvent préférable de donner au tribunal le pouvoir de suggérer une médiation en cours de procédure, sur tout ou partie du litige, ou, pour le tribunal, de donner aux parties la possibilité de demander à tout moment que la procédure soit suspendue pour leur permettre de négocier avec ou sans l'aide du tribunal arbitral ou d'un tiers. A cet égard, il est utile de noter que se développe une réflexion approfondie autour de processus « mixtes » de règlement des différends, au-delà du traditionnel med-arb ou arb-med, ou med-arb-med, ou arb-med-arb et toute autre combinaison que l'imagination des parties et de leurs avocats peut mettre en place.[17]

---

[16] Sur cette question, Mazeaud (2016), p. 2377.

[17] Un projet de recherche sur ces processus mixtes a été lancé par Thomas Stipanovitch et Véronique Fraser au centre de l'école de droit de Pepperdine University, le Straus Institute for Dispute Resolution. L'auteur de ces lignes est membre de ce groupe de recherche.

Les avocats ont un rôle très important à jouer dans le processus de médiation pour accompagner leur client, notamment, dans ce que l'on appelle en anglais le « *reality check* ». Beaucoup d'avocats reculent encore devant la médiation alors que leur présence est indispensable à une meilleure réussite du processus afin de sécuriser leur client et lui permettre de prendre sa décision en pleine connaissance de cause. Tant que les avocats n'auront pas pris la pleine mesure de leur rôle en médiation, l'efficacité de ce mode de règlement des différends sera moindre.

Un autre point moins favorable à la médiation concerne l'évolution du droit, la sécurité juridique et la prévention. Même si les parties doivent connaître les solutions juridiques que le litige peut recevoir (afin de trouver un accord en pleine conscience de leurs droits), il n'empêche que la médiation se déroule en partie en dehors du droit, en prenant en considération bien d'autres aspects que les aspects juridiques. De plus, la confidentialité qui s'attache aux accords de médiation empêche l'évolution du droit et la prévention des activités en violation de celui-ci. Enfin, chaque accord obtenu à l'issue d'une médiation est très spécifique aux parties en cause et ne peut en aucune manière servir de base pour d'autres accords. En termes d'efficacité systémique, la médiation favorise une société apaisée mais ne sert pas à grand-chose pour éviter, à l'avenir, les comportements déviants.

Il en va différemment lorsque la médiation (ou les bons offices) a lieu dans le cadre d'une procédure transparente et dont les conclusions sont publiées. Il s'agit par exemple des processus de règlement amiable qui sont organisés par les points de contact nationaux (PCN) mis en place dans le cadre des Principes OCDE pour les entreprises multinationales. Généralement saisis par les victimes d'agissements contraires aux Principes OCDE, les points de contact nationaux n'agissent pas tous selon les mêmes processus. Au Royaume-Uni le PCN renvoie les parties devant un médiateur extérieur sans procéder lui-même ni à l'instruction de l'affaire (autrement que de manière préliminaire) ni à une tentative de bons offices. A l'inverse, le PCN français utilise pleinement ses pouvoirs de bons offices pour un processus qui s'apparente à une médiation. Les conclusions publiées sur le site du PCN, que les bons offices réussissent ou non, sont fort utiles, même s'ils sont écrits de manière à préserver les susceptibilités des parties, pour faire évoluer la responsabilité sociétale des entreprises. Dans ces affaires hautement sensibles, une partie du travail du médiateur est d'aider les parties à parvenir à un communiqué commun: pour les victimes, la publicisation des faits et des solutions trouvées fait partie intégrante du processus de réparation alors que, souvent, l'entreprise voudra éviter la publicité. Le travail sur un communiqué commun fait donc partie intégrante de la médiation.

Il n'en demeure pas moins que, malgré tous les points exposés ci-dessus, les parties ont de plus en plus recours à la médiation pour des raisons négatives: elles ne veulent pas des tribunaux nationaux (v. ci-dessous) et sont de plus en plus insatisfaites de l'arbitrage essentiellement pour des raisons de durée, de coûts et d'incertitude dans l'issue du litige.

3.2 L'arbitrage

L'arbitrage, qu'il soit en matière du commerce international ou d'investissement, ne peut guère désormais revendiquer un véritable avantage durée/coût, comme cela avait pu être le cas il y a quelques décennies. Bien évidemment, il est difficile de généraliser car il existe bien des procédures conduites avec célérité et pour un coût raisonnable. Mais l'arbitrage donne parfois l'image d'une procédure qui n'est pas très efficace, suscitant ainsi, de la part des utilisateurs des critiques récurrentes. Les causes en sont connues. Citons quelques-unes d'entre elles : des procédures inadaptées par rapport au litige en cause; une justice de luxe avec trois arbitres dont les agendas sont parfois incompatibles entre eux et avec ceux des cabinets qui assurent la défense des parties; des arbitres qui miment les tribunaux nationaux en multipliant les ordonnances de procédure; l'abus de l'utilisation de témoins pour des litiges qui ne les nécessitent pas; l'abus des « *post hearing briefs* » qui montrent souvent que la procédure n'a pas été suffisamment gérée au fil de l'eau entraînant des questions tardives de la part du tribunal arbitral; des délibérés qui s'éternisent.

C'est pourquoi, les parties devraient mieux reprendre en main leurs litiges et étudier avec le tribunal arbitral les solutions les plus adaptées sans se laisser imposer des modes procédurales inutiles et coûteuses. Dans cette perspective, le *vade mecum* publié par la CCI en 2014 avec l'aide des conseils juridiques en entreprise sur les différentes options qui s'offrent aux parties[18] est d'une grande utilité non seulement pour les parties elles-mêmes, mais aussi leurs conseils et les arbitres. Il appartient, notamment, aux institutions d'arbitrage d'infléchir certaines des tendances constatées. La CCI a déjà pris quelques mesures qui devraient aller en ce sens. Leur succès ce faisant participera du choix que feront les parties des clauses d'arbitrage dans leurs contrats. Ces centres sont en concurrence pour attirer des affaires. Il est difficile pour les nouveaux centres de se faire une place au soleil et ce pour plusieurs raisons. (1) Il y a plusieurs années entre l'insertion des clauses dans les contrats désignant l'un de ces nouveaux centres d'arbitrage et la soumission effective des affaires. Dès lors pour connaître l'ampleur de l'éventuelle désaffection par rapport aux grands centres anciens, seule une étude des pratiques contractuelles serait à même de donner une image fidèle. (2) Même si des clauses sont insérées il est difficile de connaître le pourcentage de contrats qui donnent lieu à un ou plusieurs litiges. Là encore une étude sociologique serait à conduire. (3) Parmi tous les critères qui président au choix de l'arbitrage comme mode de règlement des différends, le choix de la *lex arbitri* est important et n'est pas lié au choix de l'institution. Le choix de la *lex arbitri* peut être direct (rare) ou indirect (par le choix du lieu de l'arbitrage). Il n'en demeure pas moins que l'amélioration de l'efficacité des procédures menées sous leur égide peut constituer un vrai appel concurrentiel pour les nouveaux centres.

Du point de vue du développement du droit, l'arbitrage du commerce international n'est pas idéal puisque le plus grand nombre des sentences demeure encore inconnu. Certaines institutions d'arbitrage procèdent à des publications d'extraits,

[18] International Chamber of Commerce (2014).

mais cela donne une vision tronquée de la pratique arbitrale,[19] car la publication dépend d'un choix opéré par l'institution et les personnes qui en sont chargés. En cela le contentieux devant l'OMC ou le contentieux d'investissement, au moins sous l'égide du CIRDI, présentent une grande supériorité puisque le plus grand nombre des décisions sont connues et peuvent effectivement servir de base à l'évolution du droit et permettre la prévention.

Malgré tous ces inconvénients (qui peuvent être corrigés), l'arbitrage demeure une procédure efficace, notamment du point de vue de l'attente des parties qui peuvent ainsi maîtriser les différents stades de la procédure à condition qu'elles utilisent à bon escient et avec l'aide d'un tribunal actif, l'autonomie de la volonté procédurale dont elles bénéficient[20] qui n'existe pas devant les juridictions nationales.

3.3 Les juridictions étatiques

Les juridictions étatiques sont devenues les juridictions par défaut pour les contentieux économiques internationaux. Cela veut dire qu'elles ne sont saisies que si les parties n'ont pas décidé de leur préférer un autre mode de règlement des différends.

Il n'empêche que, dans certains domaines, on oublie trop souvent que les juridictions étatiques jouent un rôle en tant que juridictions internationales lorsqu'elles sont appelées à statuer sur des litiges mettant en cause le droit international ou des enjeux qui ont une incidence sur les relations économiques internationales ainsi que nous l'avons montré dans la première partie de cette communication. Pour qu'elles puissent jouer ce rôle, encore faut-il que le système judiciaire national auquel est confié une instance inspire confiance aux parties et que la jurisprudence soit aisément accessible et favorable aux intérêts des acteurs économiques.

La confiance est le ressort essentiel de l'efficacité. Or, force est de reconnaître que la plupart des systèmes judiciaires nationaux ne peuvent donner confiance aux parties étrangères tant ils sont soupçonnés de favoriser les parties locales, directement ou indirectement. Cette suspicion, même si elle ne se révèle pas dans des pratiques de corruption directe des juges, constitue d'ailleurs l'une des raisons (certes négatives) du recours à l'arbitrage.

En ce qui concerne la jurisprudence nationale, elle est accessible dans la plupart des grandes démocraties occidentales. Mais elle se développe au gré des forces vives de la vie économique. Ainsi, la France a vu sa jurisprudence en matière d'immunité

---

[19]Nous nous refusons à utiliser le concept de « jurisprudence arbitrale » pour les raisons invoquées in « La pratique arbitrale », in Mélanges en l'honneur du Professeur Jean-Michel Jacquet, Lexis-Nexis, 2013, pp. 121–127.

[20]Kessedjian (2014), p. 1.

d'exécution des Etats enfler assez considérablement dans les dernières années à la faveur d'une série de décisions défavorables à cette immunité, permettant aux créanciers des Etats de saisir un nombre de biens toujours plus large.[21] Cette jurisprudence a été critiquée par certains et a même suscité l'ire de certains pays particulièrement concernés jusqu'à entraîner une tentative de renversement par la loi destinée à rendre plus difficile la saisie de ces biens.[22]

Un autre écueil de la saisine des juridictions nationales concerne la non harmonisation des règles de compétence internationale, sauf quelques textes régionaux, essentiellement en Europe. Chaque Etat étant libre de déterminer ses propres critères de compétence ainsi que l'étendue *ratione loci, ratione personae et ratione materiae* de la compétence de ses tribunaux, des phénomènes de litispendance internationale ou, plus rarement, de déni de justice peuvent voir le jour. La litispendance est possible chaque fois que les parties se voient offrir une compétence non exclusive, ce qui est le cas même dans un ordre juridique harmonisé comme l'est celui de l'Union européenne avec le Règlement Bruxelles I. Mais dans ce cadre, une règle spécifique permet de gérer la litispendance afin d'éviter la multiplication des procédures et l'existence de décisions inconciliables. C'est cela qui manque hors de ce cadre harmonisé si bien que plusieurs tribunaux nationaux peuvent être saisis d'une même affaire ou d'affaires similaires. C'était le cas par exemple dans l'affaire de responsabilité sociétale qui a vu la société Shell attaquée pour ses activités au Nigéria, dans le Delta de la rivière Ogoni, non seulement aux Etats-Unis mais aussi aux Pays-Bas. Dans ce cas, il n'y avait pas de litispendance au sens strict du terme puisque les demandeurs étaient différents dans les deux affaires. Mais les deux affaires étaient issues des mêmes faits et concernaient le même défendeur. Si les juridictions américaines et néerlandaises avaient mis en place une coopération entre elles, une plus grande efficacité procédurale aurait été obtenue. Mais parfois ce sont les parties qui ne souhaitent pas cette coopération car elles préfèrent répartir leurs chances de gagner et s'accommodent très bien de l'existence de multiples fors.[23]

Quant au déni de justice, un grand nombre de pays possèdent une règle qui permet à leurs tribunaux de se déclarer compétent s'il est prouvé qu'aucune autre juridiction au monde ne possède de compétence *de facto* ou *de lege*. Cette hypothèse plus rare ne semble pas avoir donné lieu à un contentieux très abondant.

---

[21]Par ex. en faveur de l'immunité d'exécution: Civ. 1, 28 sept. 2011, n°09-72057, JDI, 2012.668, note G. Cuniberti; Dr. et Patr. mars 2012.86, obs. J.P. Mattout et A. Prüm; Gaz. Pal. 2012, jur. 395, note J. Morel-Maroyer et jur. 474, note Cl. Brenner; Rev. crit. DIP, 2012.125, note H. - Gaudemet-Tallon. En sens inverse, Civ. 1, 13 mai 2015, n°13-17751, Rev. crit. DIP, 2015.652, note H. Muir Watt.

[22]Cavalier législatif de la loi dite Sapin II, adoptée par l'Assemblée nationale le 8 novembre 2016 (art 59 et 60). La loi a été déférée au Conseil constitutionnel les 9 et 15 novembre 2016 (2016-740-DC et 2016-741-DC).

[23]C'est par exemple la stratégie de l'Argentine devant les tribunaux arbitraux du CIRDI.

3.4 *Changer de processus*

Monica Pinto, intervenue avant nous dans la table ronde organisée à Montevideo et d'où est issue la présente contribution, disait en substance si vous n'êtes pas content de la décision alors changez de juge. C'est exactement ce que font les entreprises. Nicolas Binctin l'a bien montré en ce qui concerne la propriété intellectuelle.[24] Les entreprises qui ne sont pas satisfaites du contentieux OMC vont tenter de se placer sous l'égide du CIRDI, opérant ainsi ce que l'auteur appelle une « construction d'une stratégie internationale de propriété intellectuelle » dans laquelle le contentieux prend une part grandissante. Les entreprises titulaires de droits de propriété intellectuelle cherchent à faire qualifier ces droits d'« investissements » afin de bénéficier de la protection des traités bilatéraux d'investissement. Certes, l'auteur se montre prudent sur l'avenir d'un tel contentieux qui dépend en grande partie des tribunaux arbitraux saisis dont on attend les décisions.

Ces stratégies n'ont rien de choquant. Le droit existe, les sujets de la règle peuvent s'en saisir pour construire leur stratégie contentieuse. Des moyens existent pour lutter contre les abus il revient aux tiers indépendants, neutres et impartiaux que sont les médiateurs, les arbitres ou les juges de les utiliser avec discernement mais fermement pour limiter les avantages procéduraux indus dont certaines parties peuvent vouloir bénéficier du fait de l'absence d'harmonisation et de coopération internationale en matière de contentieux.

References

Binctin N (2016) Le renouveau du contentieux international de la propriété intellectuelle. JDI 381

International Chamber of Commerce (2014) Effective Management of Arbitration – A Guide for In-House Counsel and Other Party Representative. https://iccwbo.org/publication/effective-management-of-arbitration-a-guide-for-in-house-counsel-and-other-party-representatives/

Kessedjian C (2014) International arbitration – more efficiency for greater credibility. Fordham Arbitration Series, Brill

Kessedjian C (2015) L'arbitre, 'juge naturel' du commerce international. In: Cecchi-Dimeglio P, Brenneur B (dir) Manuel interdisciplinaire des modes alternatifs de résolution des conflits. Larcier, pp 985–996

Mazeaud V (2016) La (clause de) conciliation à tout prix. Quiproquo sur l'admission des clauses sur le principe de la conciliation, Dalloz

Moura Vicente D (2016) Towards a universal justice? Putting international courts and jurisdictions into perspective. Brill/Nijhoff

[24]Binctin (2016), p. 381.

Effectiveness of International Commercial Arbitration as a Dispute Settlement Mechanism

José Antonio Moreno Rodríguez

Abstract International commercial arbitration has consolidated as a widespread dispute resolution mechanism for solving trans-border business conflicts around the world. This paper concentrates on central features that historically made arbitration very effective. In particular, it highlights the challenges of not losing sight of the cosmopolitan spirit that must guide parties and arbitrators, in light of recent developments.

1 Introduction

Remember Petrocceli? In the seventies, lawyers portrayed heroes in movies and television series. In the nineties, films like The Firm or The Devil's Advocate had, as before, their typical Hollywood happy endings, albeit not anymore glorifying attorneys. In the recent decades, international commercial arbitration has consolidated as a widespread dispute resolution mechanism for solving trans-border business conflicts around the world. The prestige, as will be argued, comes from the good old days of Petrocceli's era in the seventies. Today's question is, however, if current vices can jeopardize its standing... or if a changing scenario will lead to its retreat. This contribution concentrates on central features that historically made arbitration very effective. In particular, it highlights the challenges of not losing sight of the cosmopolitan spirit that must guide parties and arbitrators, in light of recent developments.

This contribution draws upon the oral presentation made by its author at the Thematic Congress on Enforcement and Effectiveness of the Law held in Montevideo, Uruguay, on November 17 and 18 of 2016, organized by the International Academy of Comparative Law.

J. A. Moreno Rodríguez (✉)
Centro de Estudios de Derecho, Economía y Política (CEDEP), Asunción, Paraguay
e-mail: jmoreno@altra.com.py

N. Etcheverry Estrázulas, D. P. Fernández Arroyo (eds.), *Enforcement and Effectiveness of the Law - La mise en oeuvre et l'effectivité du droit*, Ius Comparatum – Global Studies in Comparative Law 30, https://doi.org/10.1007/978-3-319-93758-8_6

2 A Little Bit of History

The new generations *suffer*—emphasis added—the influx of the nineteenth century legacy of the law-centered "statism" then consolidated. For several decades, this idea cornered commercial arbitration, which only strongly rebirthed a few decades ago. However, there is still a widespread conception that the state has the monopoly of creating legal norms via legislation or judicial decisions, and that the mechanical methods of interpreting them can only be reserved to experts in law.

One must not lose sight that the Western legal tradition has been heavily influenced by the ancient Romans, whose law was not originated in the State, as was later conceived, and neither were adjudicators hence "experts" in law. In fact, in Rome, the public authority (the Praetor-Consul) delegated his adjudicating functions in citizens called *arbiter* or *iudex*.[1] The adjudicators were considered regular men with common sense, who did not need to have a thorough knowledge of the law since they acted in close contact with jurists, to whom they requested their opinions.[2]

Similar delegation of functions occurred in the Middle Ages, in which merchants frequently submitted their disputes to the consideration of either their peers—other merchants–, trustworthy third parties, or honourable people—not judges—who acted as arbitrators. The merchants, organized in fairs and corporations, possessed their own statutes. Kings, feudal lords and other authorities allowed them to organize their own justice. And, as a consequence, numerous tribunals were created, frequently considered as arbitral tribunals due to the freedom granted to the parties to choose their adjudicators and because they were expected to apply rules not limited to the local customs.[3]

The later consolidation of State-Nations and the advance of ideas of state sovereignty in the last centuries, among other factors, contributed to the seclusion of arbitration. It is true that in France, for instance, in 1790, the Constituent Assembly had qualified arbitration as "the more reasonable method for terminating disputes among citizens". However, in an emblematic case in 1843 rendered in France, arbitration clauses were ruled invalid, unless exceptional circumstances justified their existence. The French Court went on stating that if arbitration clauses were valid, there was a risk that they would be adopted widely and that individuals would be deprived of basic guarantees recognized by state tribunals. This position remained

[1]Arangio-Ruiz (1994), pp. 87–88.

[2]This was even institutionalized, when in Imperial Rome the Emperor granted a determined group of experts the *ius respondendi ex auctoritate principis*. Among the jurists, historic names such as Papinian, Ulpianus, Modestinus and others can be found. Schulz (1960), p. 13.

[3]Even though, according to David, this must be considered a new form of justice administration from the public authorities rather than, properly, arbitration. Something similar can be said of arbitration in Roman Law. At the time, arbitration could be convened via the *stipulatio*, establishing a sanction (penalty clause) in case the other party failed to comply with what had been decided. Arbitration could also be convened in a "consensual" contract, but in such a case, what had been decided by the arbitrator could be revised by the judge if manifestly unjust or contrary to good faith, see David (1985), p. 13.

unchanged until the 1925 legislative reform of the Code of Commerce, which recognized the possibility to resort to arbitration several disputes that were being solved judicially.[4]

The same fear existed in the *common law*. For a long time, the English judges' pay depended almost exclusively on specific fees that they charged for particular cases in which they intervened. Fixed salaries were non-existent.[5] The situation clearly contributed to the hostility towards arbitration in the country. In the United States, the twist in favor of arbitration began with the Arbitration Act of 1925. It was consolidated in 1932 when the Supreme Court decided that in light of the clear intention of the Congress, there was an obligation to revert the old judicial hostility against arbitration.[6]

In the same sense, states with a high impact in the volume of international commerce have recently reformed their legislations favoring arbitration. Since the last decade of the twentieth century, this turned to be particularly true of Latin American states. Nowadays, arbitration is consolidated in numerous regions of the world. It is massively used in important international commercial transactions involving, for instance, petroleum and natural resources, sales of goods, joint ventures or construction contracts.[7]

Key enactments have boosted the flourishing of arbitration. The New York Convention of 1958 on Recognition and Enforcement of Arbitral Awards is at the forefront. The instrument has been referred to as "the most effective instance of international legislation in the entire history of commercial law".[8] As of today, more than one hundred and fifty countries have ratified the Convention,[9] leading to the availability of a very effective enforcement mechanism for international commercial arbitral awards. Not less important is the massive world-wide adoption in many countries of legislation inspired in the Model Law of the United Nations Commission on International Trade Law (UNCITRAL)[10] as well as in other arbitration-friendly regulations. These legal texts recognize, within the scope of private commercial disputes, the possibility to resort to non-state adjudicators who have the power to judge and put an end to a conflict, with very restricted possibilities of questioning their decision before state courts—only if due process or public policy was clearly affected.

---

[4] Várady et al. (2009), pp. 58–60.

[5] Várady et al. (2009), p. 65.

[6] In light of the clear intention of Congress, the Court understood as its obligation to remove the old hostility towards arbitration (*Marine Transit Corporation v. Dreyfus* (1932)). Mosk (2005), p. 328.

[7] Price Waterhouse Coopers and the Queen Mary University of London conducted a survey in 2013, with the following results: 52% of the businesses surveyed preferred arbitration as a means of resolution of conflicts. This percentage is even higher in sectors such as construction and energy, where 68% and 56% prefer arbitration over other means of dispute resolution. See http://www.arbitration.qmul.ac.uk/research/2013/index.html.

[8] This much cited quote can be found in Mustill (1989), p. 43.

[9] See http://www.uncitral.org/uncitral/es/uncitral_texts/arbitration/NYConvention_status.html.

[10] See http://www.uncitral.org/pdf/english/texts/arbitration/ml-arb/07-86998_Ebook.pdf.

3 National Courts or Commercial Arbitration?

In international transactions, contracting parties commonly have the option of submitting their conflicts to a "national" court or to an "international" arbitration. In the first case there is the risk of having to litigate in another country with adjudicators that will probably handle "national" criteria, ignoring the problems of trans-border commerce. A local judge will generally be influenced by its own legal system. Thus, submitting the resolution of a dispute to a judge of the nationality of the other party represents an important risk to the foreign party. As Humphrey O'Sullivan famously quoted in 1831: "There is little use in going to law with the devil while the court is held in hell".[11]

Moreover, the foreign party will have to recur to lawyers of that jurisdiction, many times unknown or not of its confidence. Further, the process could be conducted in a language that may not be that of the contract, with the consequent complication that the base document of the case must be translated, which again leads to costs and delays, and potential misunderstandings.[12]

In contrast, arbitration provides an effective means to solve international disputes without many of these complications, not few times in places and before neutral arbitrators, competent in technical matters of international commerce and usually with the ability of conducting arbitrations in different languages. The applicable law in arbitrations is frequently "neutral", with a tendency to avoid archaic conflict of laws formulas and, instead, eadoptmploy universal or transnational solutions.[13] Undoubtedly, an adjudicator who is familiarized with comparative law will be either consciously or unconsciously influenced by it. Arbitrators are human beings and as such, they cannot dissociate themselves from their own frames of reference, social influences and networks which surround them.

Undeniably, an international arbitration has features that clearly distinguish it from litigation before national judges. In general, those who choose arbitration often do, in their desire to avoid a "legalist" solution to their commercial conflicts. Merchants frequently feel that the State courts do not understand the realities of commercial exchange, on the one hand. On the other hand, the arbitrators, whose mission derives from the agreement of the parties, are expected to prioritize the rules that the parties themselves had established for their relationships, that is, the terms of their contracts and the usages and practices that normally operate as framework.

The arbitrator is not considered a delegate of the State judge that must abide to local peculiarities in the application of the law. Instead, he is designated directly by the parties. The arbitrator's decisions can be effective, without judicial intervention, even outside the frontiers of the place in which it was rendered. The ambulatory

[11] "Diary of Humphrey O'Sullivan, 6 January 1831", in Park (2006), p. 423.

[12] Blackaby et al. (2009), p. 27.

[13] The tendency to apply transnational law in arbitration is particularly strong in areas in which national laws are developing at different paces, such as frustration, invalidity and interests, see Smit (1998), p. 109.

character of arbitration allows parties to avoid hostile States and, instead, conduct the procedure in places where they can control important aspects of the conflict, both procedural and substantive regarding the applicable law. In matters of substance, the parties can write their own rules and require the application of non-state norms and principles,[14] thus, liberating themselves from inadequate rules for international commerce and aiming instead to a resolution mechanism with transnational criteria.[15]

As stated by Opettit, arbitration registers the phenomena of "juridical acculturation": the arbitrators see themselves obliged to execute their mandate in resemblance of the symbiosis produced in the Middle Ages, where Roman and Canon Law were given prevalence over feudal law and local custom in transactions with foreigners.[16] A novice would say that this leads to a free ride (*carte blanche*), in which the arbitrator could choose whichever rule seems best fit for the dispute without major efforts. This, according to Blessing, is a completely wrong conception. The exact opposite occurs in arbitration. The arbitrator faces the difficult task of comparing the several existing possibilities in the case at hand, and opting for a reasoned solution that will result acceptable in accordance to international standards, exaggerating efforts in argumentation.[17] In words of Lord Goff of Chieveley, "it is better to have a feast of contrasting sources, festering with ideas, than a single hygienic package, wrapped in polythene".[18]

4 The Perils of a "Technocratization" of the Arbitral Process

Arbitration should aim at breaking the so called "technocratization" (neologism that gained popularity not long ago) in which the judges become technocrats in charge of dispute resolution within a State, applying rigid criteria of the orthodoxy of legal reasoning. Particularly in international disputes, parties long to escape from this conception by recurring to arbitration, in which adjudicators are frequently selected based on their knowledge of a business or on their common sense,[19] in the understanding that this method of dispute resolution has only one objective: to serve the merchant.[20]

---

[14]Von Mehren (1992), p. 62.

[15]Juenger (1997), p. 202.

[16]Oppetit (2006), pp. 278–279, footnote. An interesting recent description of the "acculturation" phenomena can be found in Sánchez Cordero (2016), pp. 51 ff.

[17]Blessing (1997), p. 48.

[18]Cited by Smits (2004), p. 239.

[19]Menkel-Meadow et al. (2005), p. 449.

[20]Mustill (1987), p. 149.

David explained that a great number of commercial disputes arise in relation to facts that only an expert can judge, such as, for example, the quality of the goods delivered or the evaluation of the work or services that have been rendered. If a tribunal is requested to decide on those matters, it cannot but base itself on the evidence produced by experts. It is, thus, tempting, to directly recur to the expert and make him the final judge of the dispute, which is exactly what occurs in arbitration. In fact, many commercial controversies are *quality* arbitrations. It could be of the parties' convenience to select someone who, in contrast to a judge, has a better knowledge of commercial usages and principles and who is better suited to understand the psychology of the merchants and therefore, in a better position to interpret a contract and render a decision that could itself become a new commercial usage.[21]

Usages can be expressly incorporated in a contract (as when referring to INCOTERMS Rules of the International Chamber of Commerce, hereafter ICC[22]), but they can also be added implicitly, when it is understood that they would have been desired by the parties. Even in domestic laws, as pointed out by Basedow, usages should be considered incorporated in a contractual relationship as implied consent of the parties, when they are widely known in a given sector of economic activity, and in this sense, they should prevail over suppletive provisions of national laws.[23] This idea goes in hand with solutions found in modern uniform law instruments, such as the Vienna Sales Convention of 1980. Article 9(2) of the CISG acknowledges the notion of implied usages, which means that rules of non-state origin can be imposed to the parties.[24] In such a case, the usage will be applicable even if the parties did not know of its existence, as long as they are amply known and regularly observed in the practice area of commerce concerned, and it can be deduced that the parties should have known it.[25] An analogous solution can be found in Article 1.8 of the UNIDROIT Principles.[26]

A usage is specific to a given activity, but once it gains general acceptance, it becomes a "general principle",[27] as was decided by an arbitral tribunal presided over by Lalive.[28] From the 1930s onwards, the reference to principles was included recurrently in arbitration clauses in petroleum-related contracts. Afterwards, the

---

[21]David (1985), p. 12.

[22]See http://www.iccwbo.org/products-and-services/trade-facilitation/incoterms-2010.

[23]Basedow (2010), pp. 9–10.

[24]Audit (1988), pp. 176–177.

[25]Berman and Dasser (1998), p. 65.

[26]Two categories of usages can be derived from Articles 8 and 9 of the CISG and Article 1(8) of the UNIDROIT Principles, regarding "usages and practices". The first category comprises the usages deriving from commerce itself, and the second category covers practices known by the parties to the contract and observed by them in their business. The UNIDROIT provision is even more direct in the sense that no knowledge of the usage on the part of the actual parties is required. See a discussion in Vogenauer (2015).

[27]Goode (1997), pp. 16–17.

[28]ICC Case 3380/1980, cited by Craig et al. (2000), p. 102.

reference evolved to principles of law "recognized by civilized nations" and other analogue expressions.[29]

In turn, principles, usages and customs of international commercial law have also been referred to as *lex mercatoria* or new *lex mercatoria*, for instance, in the famous English case of 1998 (*Deutsche Schachtbau-und Tiefbohrgesellschaft mbH*).[30] Terminology in the subject is chaotic.[31] Some use the expression transnational law, others refer to *lex mercatoria*, soft law, or several different terms, such as world law, global law, uniform law, and so on. The Hague Conference on Private International Law, in its "Principles" of applicable law to international contracts destined for both the judicial and arbitral setting,[32] recently adopted the expression "rules of law", as equivalent to non-State law and other terms referring to the matter.[33] The terms were chosen to profit from the extraordinary casuistic and doctrinal developments in the world of arbitration with regards to this expression in the past several decades.[34] Originally included in Article 42 of the 1965 Washington Convention relating to investment disputes and the arbitral laws of France and Djibouti, the expression had been adopted by the UNCITRAL Model Law of 1985, thereby echoing the terminology used in the 1976 UNCITRAL Rules of Arbitration (amended in 2010), which inspired arbitration rules all around the world. Herein, *lex mercatoria*, general

---

[29]As general principles of private international law (Aramco Case, 1958); general principles of law (Libia v. Casco y Liamco, 1977; Aminoil v. Kuwait, 1982; Framatome v. Iran, 1982); generally accepted principles (ICC Award, Case 2.152/1972) general principles of law and justice (ICC Award, Case 3.380/1980); general principles of law that must regulate international transactions (ICC Award, Case 2.291/1975); general principles adopted by the international arbitration case law (ICC Award, Case 3.344/1981); widely accepted general principles that regulate international commercial law (ICC Award, Case 3.267/1979); general principles of law applicable to international economic relations (ICSID Award 1983, Asia v. Republic of Indonesia); general principles of law conforming the *lex mercatoria* (ICC Award, Case 3.327/1981); and Rules of Law (ICC Award, Case 1.641/1969).

[30]Goode (1997), p. 29.

[31]It is widely known that extra-State normativity in international commercial transactions became the subject of debate following Berthold Goldman's seminal article published in 1964, see Goldmann (1964), p. 184 et seq. The doctrine of *lex mercatoria* discussed in that paper—and immediately furthered by the subsequent French doctrine on the matter—was once treated as a "phantom" created by Sorbonne Professors. See Teubner (1997), p. 151. After initial strong hesitations (see, for instance Mustill (1987), p. 150), recognition of the doctrine is now undeniable, both in the arbitral world and in large parts of the scholarly sector of commercial law, even though the expression has been severely criticized as a "wicked misnomer" or a "contradiction in terms". Lowenfeld (2002), p. 72. To avoid a contradiction in terms, some, for instance, propose referring to the phenomena as *principia mercatoria*.

[32]Gama and Saumier (2011), pp. 62–63. This results in "levelling the playing field" between arbitration and litigation, at least in countries that have adopted the UNCITRAL Model Law. Pertegás and Marshall (2014), p. 979. It is no longer necessary to include an arbitral clause to assure that the choice of non-State law will be respected.

[33]See Official Comment of UNCITRAL to Article 28. See also the report of the WG of UNCITRAL, 18 meeting, March 1985 (A/CN.9/264), pp. 60–63.

[34]The author of this article has personal knowledge of this due to his participation in the deliberations on the matter.

principles and usages, non-state law and other expressions mentioned in this paragraph, will be used interchangeably.

5 The "Grand-old Men" vs. the "Technocrats"

International commercial arbitration acquired an overwhelming impulse in the modern world from the oil related disputes, particularly in the 1970s,[35] decided by well-known law professors or former judges with a profound knowledge of international private—and even public- law, as Lalive, Judge Lagergren and Lord Mustill, to name a few. These cases had a great impact due to their publicity and to the massive amounts of economic interests they involved. Further, the decisions were highly praised as just solutions that invoked the general principles of law, international usages or *lex mercatoria.*[36]

In the 1980s and 1990s, the situation changed. The informal justice dominated by European academics was transformed into an "offshore" justice system of arbitrations, monopolized by big law firms primarily from the United States and some from England. Ever since, arbitral "technocrats" emerged as opposed to the "grand old men" of arbitration. The technocrats invoke their specialization and technical knowledge, often acquired in important arbitral institutions that hire young lawyers to administer the arbitral cases. They promote the virtues of established precedents and the detailed analysis of the facts. On their behalf, the academics, with an important advantage in theoretical aspects, emphasize transnational law or the *lex mercatoria,* so discussed in numerous publications. When the pendulum is turned towards the great Anglo-american law firms, the role of the *lex mercatoria* is diminished.[37]

The contrast on this matter was clearly visible in two events organized by the ICC in 2014. In one of them, held in Beaune, France, in which conspicuous arbitrators and renowned professors with a solid transnational formation attended, the virtues of the *lex mercatoria* in arbitrations were highlighted.[38] In the other one, held in Miami, attended mostly by practitioners, the technocrat lawyers did not hold back on their critiques of what was discussed in the former event.[39]

Data is contradictory. The defenders of the "technocratic" approach invoke studies that prove ample application of state law. The ICC, for instance, reports that in 85% of disputes referred to ICC arbitration in 2015 the parties included a choice-of-law clause in their contracts, and in 99% of the cases they chose national

[35]Dezalay and Garth (1996), p. 75.

[36]Dezalay and Garth (1996), chapter 2.

[37]Dezalay and Garth (1996), chapter 3.

[38]See in http://www.adejesus.com.

[39]This was brought to my attention by attendants to this event, held annually in the month of November in Miami.

laws. The ICC notes that the choices do not necessarily correspond to the law actually applied to the merits of the dispute.[40] However, some years ago, a study conducted by Berger among 2733 lawyers, found that approximately a third of them indicated that they knew of at least one case in their practice in which parties had referred to transnational law in their contracts, and more than 40% had knowledge of at least one arbitral proceeding in which the term had been used.[41] Later in 2010, using 136 extensive questionnaires and qualitative data based on 67 in-depth interviews, found that the use of transnational law is fairly common in the arbitral setting (approximately 50% of those interviewed used the term at least "sometimes").[42] Even more recently, in 2014, a survey on the use of soft law instruments in international arbitration was open for responses at the Kluwer Arbitration Blog. The users were asked to report on their real-life encounters with the UNIDROIT Principles of International Commercial Contracts, the *lex mercatoria* and similar expressions. The outcome for the UNIDROIT Principles and the *lex mercatoria* was strikingly similar, which may suggest that they are used interchangeably. Around 50% of the responses stated that they had used both occasionally, whereas about 20% specified that they used them always or regularly.[43]

6 The Dangers of "Technocratization"

The technocratization of arbitration leads to what has been referred to as "the increasing judicialization of international arbitration", with the adoption of judicial procedures, judicial style regulation and judicial behavioral norms. As a result—Horvath mentions—the simple and idealistic understanding of international

[40]English law and the law of the United States were more frequently chosen, accounting for a quarter of all contracts. Other choices were the laws of Switzerland, France and Germany. ICC Dispute Resolution Bulletin, 2016, Issue 1, p. 17. Cuniberti conducted an empirical study of more than 4400 international contracts concluded around 12,000 parties based on an analysis of data published with respect to the contractual practices of parties participating in ICC arbitrations (the "ICC Arbitration Data"). His study (from 2007 to 2012) reveals that, when international commercial parties agree to go for a law other than their own, they generally choose the law of one of five jurisdictions: England, Switzerland, United States, France and Germany, see Cuniberti (2014), pp. 3–5. However, as it was pointed out, the selection of non-state law did was not comprised in this research, see Boele-Woeli (2016), p. 97.

[41]See in Drahozal (2003), p. 30.

[42]2010 International Arbitration Survey: Choices in International Arbitration, Queen Mary, University of London, School of International Arbitration (SIA) and White & Case, http://www.arbitration.qmul.ac.uk/docs/123290.pdf, pp. 11 ff.

[43]The survey was conducted within the Fondecyt (National Foundation for Scientific and Technological Development, Chile) Project No. 1110437. Elina Mereminskaya, Bofill Mir & Alvarez Jana Abogados, for ITA, Results of the Survey on the Use of Soft Law Instruments in International Arbitration, 6 June 2014, http://kluwerarbitrationblog.com/blog/2014/06/06/results-of-the-survey-on-the-use-of-soft-law-instruments-in-international-arbitration.

arbitration has become increasingly less accurate. If this drift continues, the risk is that a highly effective and successful dispute resolution mechanism will be lost to the international business community.[44] In fact, in a recent survey conducted by Queen Mary University and White and Case, some interviewees have expressed concerns over the "judicialization" of arbitration, the increased formality of proceedings and their similarity with litigation, pointing out that the trend is potentially damaging to the attractiveness of arbitration.[45]

Not surprisingly, the technocrat approach, which leads to a nationalistic application of the law in arbitrations, is recurrently criticized by renowned law professors, who, at the same time, have been involved in numerous important arbitral cases. In this regard, Blessing, for instance, argues that though companies that act in the international market can select a national law to govern their contracts, if a dispute arises, it is necessary for arbitral tribunals to render a decision based on the fundamental notions and general principles in accordance with the expectations of the parties. The arbitrator cannot act as a slave or mechanic who blindly applies the local tools to find a solution to the conflict.[46]

Further, it should also be borne in mind that judges are generally ill-prepared to apply foreign domestic laws. This was reflected in the famous and frequently cited Rheinstein research regarding a renowned casebook on Private International Law, in which of the forty cases applying national law, only four reached the correct outcome, albeit for the wrong reasons.[47] Kaufmann-Kohler, remembering the cases in which she acted as arbitrator, governed by the laws of Germany, France, England, Poland, Hungary, Portugal, Greece, Turkey, Lebanon, Egypt, Tunisia, Morocco, Sudan, Liberia, Korea, Thailand, Argentina, Colombia, Venezuela, Switzerland, Illinois and New York, asked herself whether she actually knew these legal systems. She answered that, except for the law of New York, which she learnt years ago and does not pretend to know today, and the law of Switzerland, which she actively practices, the answer is clearly no.[48] Therefore, the possibilities of erring in the application of a foreign law and its interstices are clearly high!

Glenn makes the point that matters get worse in many countries where judicial corruption is widespread, being difficult to predict the outcome because of precedents of dubious origin.[49] David, in turn, highlights than many national systems are ill-prepared for international transactions. For instance, the refusal of the buyer to accept goods is much more serious in an international sale, in which it would be

[44]Horvath (2011), pp. 251–271.

[45]In-house counsel value the features of the arbitration process that distinguish it from litigation, Queen Mary 2013, http://www.arbitration.qmul.ac.uk/research/2013/index.html.

[46]Blessing (1997), p. 42.

[47]See, for example, Lando (2003), p. 126.

[48]International Commercial Arbitration Committee's Report and Recommendations in Ascertaining the Contents of the Applicable Law in International Commercial Arbitration, Arbitration International 2010/2, p. 198.

[49]Glenn (2001), pp. 58–59.

desirable that, even though the buyer may have those rights, certain obligations such as conservation or resale of the goods should be burdened upon him.[50] As expressed by Juenger, "nationalizing" an international transaction equates to pretending the quadrature of a circle.[51] State judges frequently recur to "escape clauses" such as the manipulation of Private International Law notions of characterization, *renvoi*, international public policy and others, or even invoke "constitutional"[52] or "human rights"[53] to arrive to a "material justice" over a "substantive justice.[54]

The above paragraphs evidence the dangers of the technocrat approach. Lalive well said that the international arbitrator has to be "neutral" not only in respect to the countries from which the parties come from and their political systems, but also in respect to the legal systems from those states. This means that the arbitrator has to have an international way of thinking. The neutrality and objectivity of the arbitrators must therefore necessarily involve a high level of "international mindedness" and comparative approach, the exact opposite of legal nationalism.[55] It is promising that young generations of students participating in arbitration "moots" all around the world easily grasp the cosmopolitan approach in arbitration and the use of soft law instruments and other comparative law techniques.[56]

7 The Legitimate Expectation of the Parties

According to Derains, the above expression must not be confused with "will" of the parties. The express or implicit selection of a governing law does not exclude the possibility that, in certain cases, it would be legitimate to expect an arbitrator to take into account the operation of a rule that the parties did not specify as applicable to the

[50]It must be taken under consideration that, commonly, transnational transactions involve particular factors, such as the distance between buyers and sellers, or certain requirements as the licenses to import and export that depend of the authorities, or prohibitions for currency transfers and endless eventualities. David (1969), pp. 11–12.

[51]See Juenger (2000), pp. 1139–1140.

[52]See recently Micklitz (2016), p. 168 ff.

[53]The Constitutional Court of Germany rendered a landmark decision in this sense on the year 1971, followed by others, such as one of the Italian Court in 1987. In addition, the Court of Justice of the European Union, in at least one occasion, based its decision on the European Convention on Human Rights, for instance, when it held that the scope of the exception of public policy of the duty of recognizing civil rulings of other member states must be interpreted pursuant to said convention (*Krombach v Bamberski*, Case C-7/98, (2000) ECR I-1935), see Reimann (2006), pp. 1392–1393.

[54]This terminology, coined by Kegel, is well explained by Symeonides. Material justice limits the objective of Private International Law to simply choosing the State that will provide the applicable law without considering to the content and the substantive quality of the arrived solution. Substantive justice looks for the better substantive solution to a multi-State case, see Symeonides (2001), pp. 125–128.

[55]Lalive (1984), p. 28.

[56]See, for instance, Fernández Arroyo (2016), pp. 271–272.

contract or that they did not expressly exclude. This can happen, for instance, in matters related to public policy or imperative norms.[57] In words of Moura Vicente, legitimate expectations suppose the intervention of the adjudicator to safeguard the expectations generated in the other party or third parties or the commutative justice in exchanges.[58]

Here's an example. The Swiss superior tribunal dismissed an annulment claim based in that the arbitrator used both the Vienna Convention and the UNIDROIT Principles to determine what constituted "material breach" according to Swiss law, even though the parties had selected Swiss law as applicable. Confirming the arbitral award, the Tribunal explained that the reference to these instruments did not suppose the application of international law. On the contrary, it sustained that the reference both to the Vienna Convention and the UNIDROIT Principles is perfectly legitimate according to Swiss law, considering that the parties in an international commercial contract could reasonable have the expectation of adopting concepts of both instruments previously mentioned.[59]

When parties choose a third country's law, they do so mainly with the aim of finding a neutral solution but rarely with an in-depth knowledge of its content. The subtleties of its rules as distilled from the case law may be surprising to a foreign party.[60] As an example, Berger asks if when parties choose German law as neutral without any knowledge of its subtleties, the arbitral tribunal should apply and awkward long-standing case law in Germany requiring certain standard term clauses to be "bargained for in detail". While the strict formula makes sense in consumer transactions, German law also applies this formula to business transactions, where the presumption of the professional competence of the parties would not require the same degree of legal protection. The matter was addressed in an interim award of January 2001, rendered by an arbitral tribunal in ICC arbitration No. 10279. The tribunal decided not to apply the local interpretation, considering that they were dealing with experienced international businesspeople and companies and that it "would be inconsistent with commercial reality".[61]

According to Berger, in cases like this the answer depends largely on the parties' expectations. A fair assumption is that in choosing arbitration instead of domestic courts the parties expect the adjudicators "to refrain from a 'mechanical' application of the law". Instead, arbitrators should take into account the economic circumstances of the case and the international context in which the parties operated. Most arbitration laws and rules include the mandate to the arbitrators of considering the trade usages which "underscores the objective of arbitration to provide resolutions of

---

[57]Derains (1995), II.2. As creatures of the parties' consent, arbitrators must show special fidelity to shared expectations expressed in the contract or treaty, Park (2016), p. 893.

[58]Vicente (2016), p. 74.

[59]Schweizerisches Bundesgericht (Switzerland), December 16, http://www.unilex.info.

[60]Bortolotti (2014), p. 8.

[61]Berger (2014), pp. 80–84.

international disputes in a manner that accord with the commercial expectations of the parties and practices in the trade concerned".[62]

Of course, the situation will be different in cases in which the foreign parties, following the advice of their lawyers, have selected a law like the German for the very reason that it provides a strict law on general contract terms.[63]

This whole matter, of course, calls for careful scrutiny. Brunner proposes a case-by-case analysis to consider the legitimate interest of the parties. If a party chose a national law because it desired a rigid solution for a specific case, it can express so, thus, excluding the possibility of considering other laws or transnational law.[64] Otherwise, the judge should have discretion to reach an appropriate solution taking into consideration the circumstances of the contract and the international environment in which the relationship developed.

8 A "Broader Brush"

Goode coined the expression "broader brush" in reference to the interpretation of national laws in transnational contracting with "an eye on international usage".[65] Moreover, as stated by Paulsson, national laws themselves contain corrective norms which are formidable. They can be derived from principles contained, for instance, in the national Constitutions, or from ratified treaties—for example, regarding Human Rights—and national courts have both the duty and the authority to apply them.[66]

In addition, domestic laws are recurrently the subject of a comparative construction. It should be borne in mind that the different legal systems have open formulas granting broad powers to adjudicators, such as *good faith*, *force majeure* and *hardship*. Here, comparative law has proven very effective as an interpretative tool.[67]

This comparative construction holds even more firmly in international contracting, where there are additional reasons. As stated by Derains, it is impossible to dissociate law and the language of its expression. For instance, regarding the terms

[62] Berger (2014), pp. 89–90.

[63] Berger (2014), pp. 80–90.

[64] Brunner (2008), pp. 30–32.

[65] Goode (1992), p. 1.

[66] Paulsson (2013), p. 232.

[67] Brunner (2008), pp. 30–32. In this regard, Ralf Michaels, inter alia, notes that, "like *ius commune* and common law", the UNIDROIT Principles "serve as a global background law" for which "we find, more and more, that judges and legislators justify their decisions against a global consensus (whether imagined or real) that they find, amongst others, in the UNIDROIT Principles." They "are becoming, more and more, a sort of general benchmark against which legal arguments take place." Michaels (2014), pp. 643–668, after note 63.

consideration, implied terms, misrepresentation or frustration,[68] an ample (or broader brush) interpretation is evidently called for when one of the parties does not hail from a common law tradition.

The *broader brush* that enables usages, principles, and equity to be taken into account coincides with the visionary perspective of Martin Wolff, who, more than half a century ago, declared that a Private International Law system lacking a supranational vision would be contrary to justice.[69]

9 The Corrective Formula in Arbitration

The "broader brush" powers are expressly acknowledged in the arbitral world. Article 28(4) of the UNCITRAL Model Law states that in all cases, the terms and conditions of the contract and the commercial usage and practices applicable to the transaction are to be taken into account.[70] This formula, originally included in the European Convention on Arbitration of 1961 (Article VII), has been qualified by a leading arbitrator as one of the most significant accomplishments of the twentieth century, liberating arbitration of local perceptions.[71]

As is widely accepted, the application of a rule such as this one leads to a cosmopolitan approach and does not depend on the will of the parties, prevailing over what is determined by conflict rules. This was recognized, for instance, by an arbitral tribunal sitting in Costa Rica[72] and by an Argentinian arbitral tribunal. In the latter case, notwithstanding the fact that both parties had designated Argentinean law as applicable, the arbitral tribunal resorted to the UNIDROIT Principles as both international commercial usages and practices reflecting the solutions of different legal systems as well as international contract practice, stating that, as such, according to Article 28(4) of the UNCITRAL Model Law on International Commercial Arbitration, they should prevail over any domestic law.[73]

[68] Derains (1995), p. 6.

[69] Wolff (1958), p. 15.

[70] In the Americas, the corrective formula has been accepted for many years through Article 9 of the 1979 OAS Inter-American Convention on General Rules of Private International Law, ratified by several countries in the region. This Convention admits equitable solutions to achieve justice in particular cases, notwithstanding the provisions of national laws potentially applicable to the transaction. The spirit of this formula is replicated in Article 10 of the Mexico Convention. The solution is received in Private International Law Rules of Mexico, Venezuela and Paraguay, see Moreno Rodríguez (2016), pp. 1171–1173.

[71] Blessing (1997), p. 54. Hascher speaks of a progressive interpretation of the convention, favoring the *lex mercatoria* and international principles, see Hascher (1995), pp. 1030–1031.

[72] Ad Hoc Arbitration in Costa Rica, 30.4.2001, accessible at www.unilex.info. In turn, the arbitral Tribunal references other ICC Awards in this regard—Awards 8908/1996 and 8873/1997; Bulletin of the International Arbitration Court, vol. 10/2-Fall-1999, p. 78 ff.

[73] Ad Hoc Arbitral Award of 10.12.1997, accessible at www.unilex.info. Mayer even talks about the application of the UNIDROIT Principles in all situations, not as *lex contractus*, but specifically,

Blessing echoes the criticisms that the dual reference of provisions such as said Article 28(4) "would only complicate matters, would provide uncertainty and thus should rather be avoided, giving preference to one clear national legal system to prevail". To it, he answers that the critics "have either never had a single arbitration to adjudicate where these issues were at the heart of the dispute, or else they have not learned to realize that local or national perceptions and laws are often short-sighted, engineered under a purely local focus and do not deserve to be of an authoritative nature in a large international context".[74]

In turn, Born coincidentally sustains that the mandate given to the arbitrators "to consider trade usages underscores arbitration's historic roots in, and objective of, providing resolutions of international business disputes in a manner that accords with commercial expectations and practices. The parties' agreement that trade usages may (or must) be taken into account expresses a desire on the part of the parties that both their contract and the applicable law be interpreted in light of commercial context".[75]

Other renowned writers and practitioners point out—in a leading book commenting the ICC rules—that there are cases in which the powers of the judge or arbitrator should be used to interpret the contractual provisions and apply the usages when there is a pattern that repeats itself. When the circumstances in which this occurs in international transactions involves different laws, foreign languages or different currencies, to cite examples, "a type of jurisprudence is generated, by repeated decisions dealing with similar transnational fact patterns, which by definition cannot be derived from a purely national context" That is where the decisions such as the ICC cases, based in economic realities and the necessities of international commerce to which the specific rules of arbitration must respond, acquire force of precedents".[76]

In a recent survey among experienced arbitrators in the United States, more than a quarter of respondents "feel free to follow [their] own sense of equity and fairness in rendering an award even if the result would be contrary to the applicable law," at least some of the time.[77] Well, undoubtedly, the dual formula of the arbitration law is wise in that it permits the introduction of international standards for a transnational transaction in order to arrive at a more equitable solution.[78]

---

when the content of a determined norm of the *lex contractus* is not clearly established, or is manifestly inadequate. Mayer (2002), pp. 75–76.

[74]Blessing (1997), p. 42.

[75]Born (2014), p. 2666.

[76]Craig et al. (2000), pp. 638–639. They cite the ICC Case 4131/1982, in which an unanimous tribunal, presided by Professor Sanders, stated: "The decisions of (ICC) tribunals progressively create caselaw which should be taken into account, because it draws conclusions from economic reality and conforms to the needs of international commerce, to which rules specific to international arbitration, themselves successively elaborated, should respond" (p. 639).

[77]Stipanowich (2015).

[78]In the case *CMI International, Inc. v. Iran* of 1983 the arbitrators did not respect the selection of the law of Idaho after considering that the task of the arbitrators, as therein argued, was the search of

Are arbitrators operating *contra legem* in cases as the ones mentioned in the previous paragraphs? The answer is clearly no. When you select an applicable substantive law and a model law jurisdiction, you are also selecting Article 28 (4) with its corrective powers. The extent of this is, of course, a matter of another discussion, but evidently at least some discretion is granted to the adjudicator regarding the applicability or not of suppletive national rules.[79]

Moreover, as stated by Fernández Arroyo, Article 2A of the 2006 reform to the Model Law stresses the international origin of the model law and the necessity to promote uniformity in its application.[80] To put it bluntly, a provision like this imposes a legal mandate to the arbitrators in favour of cosmopolitism.

Last but not least, we should consider that numerous times it is a prisoner's dilemma! The parties tend to assume that the choice of non-State law will not be accepted by the courts. Even in an arbitration setting, as stated by Bortolotti, the parties often react to this uncertainty by selecting domestic laws to minimize the risks of attack based on what has been decided by domestic tribunals at the seat or at eventual places of enforcement.[81] Arbitrators can temper this using their broad powers.

Therefore, an arbitration must be clearly conducted with a cosmopolitan view, even in those cases where a national law has been selected by the parties.[82] However, the arbitrator must also be extremely careful when the parties have supported their arguments exclusively on the chosen law, to not compromise due process. The good arbitrator should make sure that the parties are able to discuss the possible scope and

justice and equity, which led them to ignore said selection. See Silberman and Ferrari (2010), p. 34, footnote.

[79]Ferrari states that the international arbitration cannot be *more* international than the national rules applicable to a given issue in a specific case allow the arbitration to be. Ferrari (2016), p. 848. Many responses can be given to defend a different view, but one of them is that when the parties select an arbitral jurisdiction that in its laws contemplates a corrective formula, this authorizes the arbitrators to reach solutions of justice.

[80]Fernández Arroyo (2013), pp. 233–234.

[81]Bortolotti (2014), p. 7.

[82]When the law was not selected, it appears that Article 28(2) of the UNCITRAL Model Law of 1985 only admits the application of non-State law when the parties chose it, not in the absence of choice. This was considered in 1987 by Lord Michael Mustill as a major blow to *lex mercatorists*. Mustill (1987), p. 181. However, subsequent case law indicates the contrary, and leading arbitral authorities, such as, *inter alia*, Emmanuel Gaillard, propose an extensive interpretation of Article 28 (2). Gaillard (2010), p. 124. An express solution in this sense (regarding arbitration specifically) can be found, for instance, in Article 187(1) of the Swiss Private International Law and in the new Article 1511 of the Procedural Code of France. Contrary to a widespread orthodox conception, it is more predictable to apply transnational rules than classic "conflictualism". Parties that have not taken the precaution of choosing the law that would govern their contract should not be surprised by the application of a rule generally accepted in comparative law. Gaillard (2010), p. 126. Based on a Von Mehren report, the 1989 Resolution of Santiago de Compostela of the Institute of International Law left aside a 1957 position, and now states, in its Article 6, that in the absence of choice, arbitrators can, if they deem it appropriate, apply general principles, that is, principles of non-State origin.

relevance of the international usages and principles that could be applicable to the case, above all, ascertaining that it is a result of what was expressly or implicitly provided for in the contract.[83]

10 In Conclusion

An arbitration is worth what an arbitrator is worth. The good arbitrator will always be mindful of supporting his conclusion in the agreement of the parties and in the facts of the case, applying, when relevant, the national law, but making sure at the same time that the legitimate expectations of the international case are considered, based on the cosmopolitan view that the adjudicator should have in this type of disputes.

This is what the "grand-old men" (the Petrocceli's of the seventies) upheld, in a spirit which will hopefully prevail again in times to come, to not jeopardize the effectiveness of this widespread means of solving international commercial controversies.

References

Arangio-Ruiz V (1994) Historia del Derecho Romano, Traducción de la Segunda Edición Italiana. Editorial Reus, Madrid

Audit B (1988) The Vienna Sales Convention and the Lex Mercatoria. In: Carbonneau TE (ed) Lex Mercatoria and arbitration, a discussion of the new law merchant, Rev edn. Juris Publishing, Kluwer International Law

Basedow J (2010) El derecho privado estatal y la economía: el derecho comercial como una amalgama de legislación pública y privada, In: ¿Cómo se Codifica hoy el Derecho Comercial Internacional?, CEDEP y La Ley Paraguaya

Benedettelli M (2016) Applying the UNIDROIT Principles in international arbitration: an exercise in conflicts. J Int Arbitr 33:653–686

Berger KP (2014) To what extent should arbitrators respect domestic case law? The German experience regarding the law on standard terms. In: Bortolotti F, Mayer F (ed) The application of substantive law by international arbitrators. Dossier XI of the ICC Institute of World Business Law, Paris

Berman HJ, Dasser FJ (1998) The "new" law merchant and the "old": sources, content, and legitimacy". In: Carbonneau TE (ed) Lex Mercatoria and arbitration, a discussion of the new law merchant, Rev edn. Juris Publishing, Kluwer International Law

[83]For instance, if the UNIDROIT Principles are going to be applied as an implied will of the parties, as far as possible, arbitral tribunals should seek confirmation from the parties at the start of the arbitration (e.g. when the terms of reference or equivalent instruments are drafted) that this was their real intention and, if it results that the issue is disputed, arbitral tribunals should give the parties a full opportunity to plead, possibly in view of a preliminary decision on the law applicable to the merits. Benedettelli (2016), p. 680.

Blackaby N, Partasides C, Redfern A, Hunter M (2009) Redfern and Hunter on international arbitration. Oxford University Press
Blessing M (1997) Choice of substantive law in international arbitration. J Int Arbitr 14:39–66
Boele-Woeli K (2016) ¿Traen consigo algún cambio los Principios de La Haya sobre la elección de la ley aplicable a los contratos comerciales internacionales? In: Fernández Arroyo DP, Moreno Rodríguez JA (eds) Contratos Internacionales, ASADIP-Organización de los Estados Americanos. Departamento de Derecho Internacional de la Secretaría de Asuntos Jurídicos, Washington
Born G (2014) International commercial arbitration, 2nd edn. Kluwer Law International
Bortolotti F (2014) The application of substantive law by international arbitrators, international chamber of commerce (ICC). DOSSIERS ICC Institute of World Business Law, Paris
Brunner C (2008) Force Majeure and Hardship under general contract principles: exemption for non-performance in international arbitration. Kluwer Law International
Craig L, Park W, Paulson J (2000) International chamber of commerce arbitration, 3rd edn. Oceana Publications
Cuniberti G (2014) The international market for contracts: the most attractive contract laws. University of Luxembourg Law Working Paper Series Paper Number 2014-02
David R (1969) The international unification of private law. Int Encycl Comp Law, Ch. 5
David R (1985) Arbitration in International Trade. Kluwer Law and Taxation Publishers, Deventer/Netherlands
Derains (1995) The ICC arbitral process. Part. VIII. Choice of the law applicable to the contract and international arbitration. ICC Int Court Arbitr Bull 6(1)
Dezalay Y, Garth BG (1996) Dealing in virtue, international commercial arbitration and the construction of a trasnational legal order. The University of Chicago Press
Drahozal CR (2003) Of Rabbits and Rhinoceri: a survey of empirical research on international commercial arbitration. J Int Arbitr 20:23–34
Fernández Arroyo DP (2013) Los precedentes y la formación de una jurisprudencia arbitral, In: Gaillard E, Fernández Arroyo DP (eds) Cuestiones Claves del Arbitraje Internacional, CEDEP y Universidad del Rosario, Asunción y Bogotá
Fernández Arroyo DP (2016) The growing significance of sets of principles to govern trans-boundary private relationships. In: International Institute for the Unification of Private Law (UNIDROIT) (ed) Eppur si muove: The age of uniform law, essays in honour of Michael Joachim Bonell to celebrate his 70th birthday, vol 1. pp 251–272
Ferrari F (2016) How international should international arbitration be? A pea in favour of a realistic answer. In: International Institute for the Unification of Private Law (UNIDROIT) (ed) Eppur si muove: The age of uniform law, essays in honour of Michael Joachim Bonell to celebrate his 70th birthday, vol 1. pp 847–855
Gaillard E (2010) Teoría Jurídica del Arbitraje Internacional, Ed. La Ley Paraguaya/CEDEP/Thomson Reuters, Asunción
Gama Jr. L, Saumier G (2011) Non-State Law in the (Proposed) Hague Principles on Choice of Law in International Contracts, El Derecho internacional Privado en los procesos de integración regional, Jornadas de la ASADIP 2011, ASADIP y Editorial Jurídica Continental, San José
Glenn HP (2001) An international private law of contract. In: Borchers P, Zekoll J (eds) International conflict of laws for the third millenium, essays in honor of Friedrich K. Juenger. Transnational Publishers Inc, New York
Goldmann B (1964) Frontières du droit et lex mercatoria. Archives de philosophie du droit 9:177
Goode R (1992) The adaptation of english law to international commercial arbitration. Arbitr Int 8:1–16
Goode R (1997) Usage and its reception in transnational commercial law. ICLQ 46:1
Hascher T (1995) European Convention on international commercial arbitration (European Convention, 1961) – commentary. In: van den Berg AJ (ed) Yearbook of commercial arbitration. Kluwer Law International, pp 1030–1031

Horvath GJ (2011) Part I: international commercial arbitration, Chapter 13: the judicialization of international arbitration: does the increasing introduction of litigation-style practices, regulations, norms and structures into international arbitration risk a denial of justice in international business disputes? In: Kröll SM, Mistelis LA et al (eds) International arbitration and international commercial law: synergy, convergence and evolution. Kluwer Law International, pp 251–271

Juenger FK (1997) Contract choice of law in the Americas. Am J Comp Law 45:195

Juenger FK (2000) The Lex Mercatoria and private international law. Louisiana Law Rev 60:1133

Lalive P (1984) On the neutrality of the arbitrator and of the place of arbitration. In: Reymond C, Bucher E (eds) Swiss essays on international arbitration. Schulthess Polygraphischer Verlag, Zurich

Lando O (2003) Principles of European contract law and UNIDROIT Principles: moving from harmonisation to unification. Unif Law Rev, 123–133

Lowenfeld AF (2002) Lex Mercatoria: an arbitrator's view. ICC International Court of Arbitration Bulletin, Special Supplement

Mayer P (2002) The role of the UNIDROIT Principles in ICC arbitration practice – Special Supplement 2002. ICC Int Court Arbitr Bull, 75–76

Menkel-Meadow CJ, Porter Love L, Kupfer Schneider A, Sternlight JR (2005) Dispute resolution, beyond de Adversarial model. Aspen Publishers, Nueva York

Michaels R (2014) The UNIDROIT Principles as global background law. Unif Law Rev 19:643–668

Micklitz HW (2016) The threefold Phenomena of constitutionalisation in private law. In: International Institute for the Unification of Private Law (UNIDROIT) (ed) Eppur si muove: The age of Uniform Law, Essays in honour of Michael Joachim Bonell to celebrate his 70th birthday, vol 1. pp 168–186

Moreno Rodríguez JA (2016) The new Paraguayan Law on international contracts: back to the past? In: International Institute for the Unification of Private Law (UNIDROIT) (ed) Eppur si muove: The age of Uniform Law, Essays in honour of Michael Joachim Bonell to celebrate his 70th birthday, vol 2. pp 1146–1178

Mosk RM (2005) Comments on enforceability of awards. In: van den Berg AJ (ed) New horizons in international commercial arbitration and beyond. ICCA Congress series N° 12

Mustill MJ (1987) The New Lex Mercatoria: the first twenty-five years. In: Bos M, Brownlie I (eds) Liber Amicorum for Lord Wilberforce. Clarendon Press, pp 149–183

Mustill MJ (1989) Arbitration: history and background. J Int Arbitr 6:43

Oppetit B (2006) Teoría del Arbitraje, translated by: Eduardo Silva Romero, Fabricio Mantilla Espinoza y José Joaquín Caicedo Demoulin, Bogotá, Legis Editores

Park W (2006) Arbitration of international business disputes: studies in law and practice. Oxford University Press, Oxford

Park WW (2016) Fidelity to contract commitments in commercial arbitration: contract language and change circumstances. In: International Institute for the Unification of Private Law (UNIDROIT) (ed) Eppur si muove: The age of Uniform Law, Essays in honour of Michael Joachim Bonell to celebrate his 70th birthday, vol 1. pp 880–895

Paulsson J (2013) The idea of arbitration. Oxford University Press

Pertegás M, Marshall BA (2014) Harmonization through the draft hague principles on choice of law in international contracts. Brooklyn J Int Law 39:975–1003

Reimann M (2006) Comparative law and private international law. In: The Oxford handbook of comparative law. Oxford University Press

Sánchez Cordero J (2016) Les processus d´acculturation juridique. Réflexions mexicaines, Eppur si muove: The age of Uniform Law, Essays in honour of Michael Joachim Bonell to celebrate his 70th birthday. International Institute for the Unification of Private Law (UNIDROIT)

Schulz F (1960) Derecho Romano Clásico, Traducción de la Edición Inglesa de 1951. Editorial Bosch, Barcelona

Silberman L, Ferrari F (2010) Getting to the law applicable to the merits in international arbitration and the consequences of getting it wrong, Law and Economics Research Paper Series. New York University School of Law

Smit H (1998) Proper choice of law and the Lex Mercatoria Arbitralis. In: Carbonneau TE (ed) Lex Mercatoria and arbitration, a discussion of the new law merchant, Rev edn. Juris Publishing, Kluwer International Law

Smits JM (2004) The Europeanisation of National Legal Systems. In: van Hoecke M (ed) Epistemology and methodology of comparative law. Hart, Oxford/Portland

Stipanowich TJ (2015) A Recent Survey of Experienced U.S. Arbitrators Highlights Areas for Further International Study and Discussion, Kluwer Arbitration Blog. http://arbitrationblog.kluwerarbitration.com/2015/02/06/a-recent-survey-of-experienced-u-s-arbitrators-highlights-areas-for-further-international-study-and-discussion/

Symeonides SC (2001) Material justice and conflicts justice in choice of law. In: Borchers P, Zekoll J (eds) International conflict of laws for the third millenium, essays in honor of Friedrich K. Juenger. Transnational Publishers Inc, New York

Teubner G (1997) Breaking frames: the global interplay of legal and social systems. Am J Comp Law 45:149–169

Várady T, Barceló JJ, von Mehren AT (2009) International commercial arbitration, a transnational perspective, 4th edn. Thomson Reuters

Vicente DM (2016) La autonomía privada y sus distintos significados a la luz del derecho comparado. In: Diego Fernández Arroyo-José Antonio Moreno Rodríguez, Contratos Internacionales, ASADIP-Organización de los Estados Americanos. Departamento de Derecho Internacional de la Secretaría de Asuntos Jurídicos, Washington

Vogenauer S (ed) (2015) Commentary on the UNIDROIT Principles of International Commercial Contracts (PICC), 2nd edn. Oxford University Press

Von Mehren AT (1992) International commercial arbitration and conflict of laws. Am Rev Arbitr 3:57

Wolff M (1958) Derecho Internacional Privado, Traducción española de la segunda edición inglesa por Antonio Marín López, Barcelona, Editorial Bosch

José Antonio Moreno Rodríguez LL.M Harvard, 1993. Member of the International Chamber of Commerce Court of Arbitration. Member of Annulment Committees of the International Centre for Settlement of Investment Disputes (ICSID). Member of the Governing Council of UNIDROIT and Chair of the Working Group on Agricultural Land and Investment Contracts. Member of the Inter-American Juridical Committee of the Organization of American States. Member of the Working Group of The Hague Conference on Private International Law regarding The Hague Principles on International Contracts. Former President of the American Association of Private International Law. Professor and Visiting Professor of several universities, among them, Heidelberg and Paris II. www.jmoreno.info.

Part III / Partie III
Workshops / Ateliers

Challenges for the Enforcement and Effectiveness of Criminal Law: The Prohibition on Illegal Drugs

Lorena Bachmaier Winter and Nora V. Demleitner

Abstract An assessment of the effectiveness of criminal law requires an initial discussion of what this concept means and what challenges the enforcement of criminal laws presents. In general, cost and effectiveness of criminal laws are difficult to ascertain. This holds particularly true for laws criminalizing activities relating to illicit drugs, such as their production, trafficking, possession, and consumption. With expectations of enforcement success often only ambiguously defined, costs insufficiently compiled, and the collateral effects of enforcement more damaging than the public health impact, drug law enforcement appears highly ineffective. This holds true for European countries as well as the United States. The enforcement of drug laws therefore remains of questionable value and may even negatively impact the standing of criminal law in its entirety.

1 Introduction

This chapter focuses on the enforcement of criminal law, which requires an initial discussion of what the concept means in this area and what challenges it presents. Cost and effectiveness of criminal laws are often difficult to ascertain. This holds particularly true for laws criminalizing activities relating to illicit drugs, such as their production, trafficking, possession, and consumption.

Drug-related offenses constitute a major challenge to the international community as a whole and virtually all countries, independent of their economic development or legal regime or tradition. Three major international conventions, which are widely ratified, require the criminalization of illicit drugs and outline an enforcement

L. Bachmaier Winter (✉)
Complutense University Madrid, Madrid, Spain
e-mail: l.bachmaier@der.ucm.es

N. V. Demleitner
Washington and Lee University, Lexington, VA, USA
e-mail: demleitnern@wlu.edu

N. Etcheverry Estrázulas, D. P. Fernández Arroyo (eds.), *Enforcement and Effectiveness of the Law - La mise en oeuvre et l'effectivité du droit*, Ius Comparatum – Global Studies in Comparative Law 30, https://doi.org/10.1007/978-3-319-93758-8_7

regime, with additional regional conventions also governing applicable measures of criminal procedure. The United Nations conventions have led to the almost universal criminalization of drugs, though enforcement differences exist. To address those, the European Union, for example, in the Framework Decision 2004/757/JHA of 25 October 2004 outlines minimum provisions required for constituent elements of criminal acts and penalties in the field of illicit drug trafficking. This chapter will detail drug law enforcement in the United States where the criminal justice regime may have led to the most draconian response to illicit drugs.

The prohibition of illicit narcotics has created major international trafficking networks that have developed into threats to state governments, the rule of law, and human rights. Some states have been labeled narco-states as traffickers appear to operate there with impunity, with government officials, including law enforcement officials and judges, either being corrupted or in fear of their lives. They also present substantial law enforcement hurdles, and have substantially impeded the effectiveness of enforcement. In addition to laws directly addressing the drug-related offenses of manufacturing, trafficking, and possession, other areas of law have been developed to remove the profits from drug trafficking. The need to target drug-related assets have led to the expansion of confiscation and forfeiture laws and to the creation of money-laundering statutes, which have, of course, also been applied to other criminal offenses.

The international character of the offense creates additional enforcement problems as it necessitates cross-border cooperation. Such cooperation is required not only at the prosecutorial and judicial stages but at the investigatory and even the preventive stages of a potential criminal case.

This chapter cannot fully discuss some of the most challenging questions in the enforcement of criminal law, especially when the effectiveness of criminal law remains in doubt, but is designed to raise them. It also shows some of the paradoxes and tells cautionary tales about criminalization. In the end, some of the developments toward alternative dispute resolution mechanisms that are prevalent in the private law area may also inform the discussion in the criminal law arena. In the United States, private and administrative laws are being used to enforce drug laws, usually as a supplement. Could such laws replace criminal law? That question is usually asked in the reverse when criminal laws supplement private and administrative law. Alternatively, could the enforcement of criminal law be privatized? Likely that approach would not be suitable to drug offenses but may be to other substantive crimes. A relevant question in light of increasing moves toward the legalization of small amounts of marijuana for personal possession is to what extent the enforcement of criminal law may benefit from decriminalization, or perhaps even legalization? On the other side, how can law assist with more effective enforcement internationally? Harmonization of laws is a crucial first step. Beyond that support for more effective collaboration, especially at the intelligence gathering stage will be crucial.

The first part of this chapter presents a theoretical discussion of enforcement, effectiveness, and efficiency of criminal law. Section 3 uses domestic drug laws in the United States to exemplify the historic development from a regulated to a criminalized area. Currently, a movement to decriminalize marijuana may foreshadow a (limited) reversal of this approach. In addition, this example also demonstrates the impact criminal law enforcement can have on a country. Changes in criminal procedure, mass imprisonment of drug offenders, and the deputization of actors and laws outside the regime of criminal laws are all part of U.S. drug law enforcement. Section 4 turns to a detailed discussion of criminal procedure as an instrument for enforcing criminal law. The emphasis here is on the transnational and organized character of drug trafficking, and the need to adjust preventive measures accordingly, without losing sight of individual rights. The examples draw heavily on the European Union and its regional conventions, but also include references to international enforcement networks.

2 Enforcement, Effectiveness and Efficiency of Criminal Law

The concept of **enforcement of law** differs when applied to private law and to criminal law.[1] Private law is usually enforced by private parties. Only when one side does not fulfill their legal obligations—derived either from torts or contracts, will the parties seek a conflict resolution scheme by resorting to arbitration, mediation or another form of alternative dispute resolution (ADR) or by filing a lawsuit. However, in the field of criminal law, the state has the monopoly of applying the law, thus the citizens never enforce the criminal law themselves. This changes the meaning of the concept of "enforcement" completely. The implementation of the criminal law falls within the exclusive competence of the state, as investigation, prosecution of criminal offenses and punishment are the function of state authorities. The *ius puniendi* is a monopoly of the state, which determines, as a rule, that the application of criminal sanctions are only legitimate after the accused "has been heard and convicted in a fair and public trial" before a court. Although lately this definition of *ius puniendi* as an exclusive power of the state is being questioned, as some call for enforcement of criminal law through private conflict solving schemes, such as victim-offender mediation, punishment after judicial proceedings is still the prevailing norm. In sum, notwithstanding the growing relevance of the restorative justice approach, and the increasing role of the victim in criminal procedure, the enforcement of criminal law lies within the authority of the state.

In criminal law, enforcement can be identified with the apprehension and punishment of lawbreakers. To that end criminal law enforcement encompasses all activities related to the detection or reporting of crime, the identification of the perpetrators, the investigative measures, the collecting of evidence, and finally the judicial sanctioning of the criminal behavior. Enforcement of criminal law refers, therefore, to all stages of criminal procedure, from the initial investigation of a

[1]On the new trends in enforcement private law, see Basedow in this volume.

possible crime, through the trial stage to the enforcement of the sanction imposed, be it custodial or not. The success of the role the different actors within the criminal justice system—police, public prosecution, judiciary, and administrative institutions—play, will determine the degree of enforcement. In short, together all elements of the criminal justice system and the rules of criminal procedure will determine the level of enforcement of the criminal law. On the other hand, the quality, proportionality and popularity of the criminal law, will also impact its enforcement. Unpopular penal statutes, as for example, the dry era prohibition laws in the United States during the 1920s led to a general acceptance of their infringement, with criminal law enforcement kept at a comparatively very low level.[2]

According to the Cambridge dictionary, the term *effectiveness* defines "the ability to be successful and produce the intended results", or in the words of the Oxford dictionary, "the degree to which something is successful in producing a desired result." Effectiveness measures the achievement of the intended results and thus it is strictly linked to determining and defining those "desired or intended" results.

This is not the place to revisit all the legal theories about the aims and objectives of criminal law, or of the goals of certain criminal norms. Broadly stated, and at the risk of simplifying too much the theoretical framework of the substantive criminal law, within this context it may suffice to state that there are two main approaches to identifying the "intended results" of criminal law.

The first aim of the criminal law is to achieve the elimination or reduction of the prohibited conduct in a society. Deterrence or the general prevention effect can be considered the main intended result.[3] To assess the effectiveness of a specific criminal norm, not only criminological studies and accurate statistics are needed but it is equally necessary to identify the exact goal desired. As the effectiveness of the criminal law will depend on the achievement of the goals, the success of the criminal law will vary depending on how those goals are defined. If success is considered the total absence of the criminalised conduct, than most criminal laws would have to be described as ineffective. But if the success is measured in terms of an acceptable rate of crimes for a society, in such case not exceeding a certain desired percentage of criminality would comply with the objectives set out, and thus allow qualifying the criminal law as effective.[4]

Suffice here to state that regarding drug offenses, the objective could be defined as the protection of society and individuals from the harm caused by the consumption of drugs, which may be defined as a public health objective.[5] When would such

---

[2]See Smith (1941), p. 16.

[3]Besides deterrence, the criminal justice system pursues other marginal goals. Among them are the rehabilitation of offenders, the disablement of offenders, the sharpening of the community's sense of right and wrong, the satisfaction of the community's sense of just retribution, and even socialized vengeance. See Hart (1958), pp. 401–402.

[4]As Beccaria (1769), p. 74-76, already stated that "the certainlty of conviction is the ideal deterrent". Therefore, adequate enforcement of the law, will increase the effectiveness of the criminal law, from the perspective of its deterrence objective.

[5]On the cost-eficeincy analyisis related to drug-abusing criminal offenders, see Manning et al (2016), pp. 24-26.

protection be considered effective? That has to be defined based on the criminal policy objectives. Again, effectiveness of criminal law enforcement in the field of drugs is always relative, because through a re-definition of the objectives the effectiveness rate can be modified. With an unrealistic or not clearly defined yardstick, however, criminal enforcement will appear ineffective. In this context, it will be interesting to see how the criminal rules on drug consumption and the new trends in marihuana decriminalization impact the dual goals of protecting public health and providing security.

Usually the effectiveness of criminal law is connected to the desired results in terms of reducing criminality, according to the objectives set out in the state's criminal policy. Consequently, the degree of effectiveness cannot be viewed as a fixed parameter to assess the adequacy of the law: by re-defining the criminal policy, the effectiveness of the criminal law will increase or decrease. Cross-national comparisons of drug law effectiveness may, therefore, be questionable unless national goals are aligned.

Even if this appears to be the standard approach to the concept of effectiveness, the desired result can also be defined differently. Efficiency in criminal law is, and should not be a singular concept. If the effectiveness of the criminal law is identified with achieving justice in a certain society and success in the fight against impunity, crime statistics indicating sanctioning of the typified conduct would determine effectiveness of such law only partially. Other criteria should be taken into account, such as enforceability, efficiency, and the capability of detecting and punishing criminal offences. From this point of view, criminal law would be considered applied effectively if it would not leave more space than desired for impunity. Effectiveness in this sense would be closely linked to the concept of enforcement, but not be identical with it. Equality as a goal would add a measure of justice to an effective criminal justice system.

Finally, the concept of effectiveness can refer solely to the enforcement of criminal law: the effectiveness of the enforcement would be the ability to investigate, prosecute and sanction criminal offences and thus to fight impunity. Effectiveness here would depend on what level of enforcement is defined as the "desired result" or objective. This effectiveness goal is closely connected to the level of financial investment a state is willing to make in enforcement. It is crucial to distinguish between the effectiveness of criminal law and the effectiveness of the enforcement of criminal law.

In sum, the two perspectives described very briefly above—the first one linked to the rates of criminality and the second one to the fight against impunity, only represent two of the possible objectives of criminal law. While they are the primary goals, they are not the only ones.

Both perspectives show that the concept of effectiveness depends on the definition of the objectives. As these can be variegated, it is necessary to express which concept of effectiveness will be followed here. In this paper, the effectiveness of criminal law will be used in the first sense, which means related to the results achieved with respect to the criminality rates. The ability to prosecute crimes committed will be considered under the concept of enforcement of criminal law.

Criminal law needs to be adequately enforced to ensure its effectiveness. To the question if criminal law has a deterrence effect, social scientists have said that "the short answer is no."[6] The criminal law by itself may not have much of a deterrence effect, but "having a criminal justice system that imposes liability and punishment for violation deters." Yet, the substantive rules on criminal liability and punishment do not materially affect deterrence.[7] The effectiveness of criminal law depends on the use of effective enforcement methods and the capture of the criminal offenders. To that end, the allocation of resources to law enforcement agencies and the use of adequate investigative techniques and gathering of evidence, will be crucial to ensure such effectiveness.

Finally, the effectiveness of criminal law is inversely proportional to its application, if by application is understood the punishment of the crime: the lesser the penalties that are imposed, the more effective a system of criminal law. Therefore, enforcement of criminal law acts in a dual way: on the one hand, it ensures effectiveness by guaranteeing the general prevention effect; on the other hand, if enforcement were not needed, the criminal law would have achieved its maximum degree of effectiveness, no crimes are committed and the legally protected good is respected.

The concept of *efficiency* relates to the way something is done, without much waste of time or effort. Effort can be measured in different ways, not only economically although in modern societies the functioning of criminal justice systems is to be measured necessarily from the economic point of view, due to existing budgetary limitations. Finding the optimal relationship between the costs and efforts of enforcing the criminal law and achieving an acceptable degree of effectiveness, i.e., reducing criminality, is the task of the criminal policy authorities.

Even though we are not directly addressing this issue here, costs play a major role in addressing efficiency and the effectiveness of criminal law in fighting drug related offenses. We refer here only to economic costs –not social costs– and only to what within the economic analysis is identified as "direct costs" and not other "indirect costs", such as a reduction in safety perceptions or health consequences. See Manning et al (2016), pp. 78–80. One data point might be illustrative: the USA government annually spends about US$30 billion in the "war against drugs" but these enormous expenditures do not appear to have led to a decrease in drug consumption or a better protection of public health.

Efficiency is always to be measured against the objectives defined, and therefore efficiency is linked to effectiveness. Efficiency is difficult to measure, as measuring the effort is always relative, not only with regard to the results achieved, but also in economic budgetary terms. It would be necessary to assess if the money spent on fighting illicit drugs, would have been better used for other purposes that would better respond to public interests and social needs.

---

[6]See Robinson and Darley (2004), p. 173.

[7]Robinson and Darley (2004), p. 174: "The behavioural sciences increasingly call into question the assumption of criminal law's *ex ante* influence on conduct".

The next section will outline the domestic enforcement of U.S. drug laws. After a brief description of the historic evolution and growth of drug enforcement forces, the section turns to questions of efficiency, effectiveness, and fairness. U.S. drug enforcement has expanded from the criminal law into other areas of the law. Recent state decisions to legalize possession of small amounts of marijuana challenge the prohibitionst approach, domestically and internationally.

3 A Case Study: Effectiveness of U.S. Drug Law Enforcement

The United States remains the largest market internationally for illegal drugs. Politically and legally, it moved the international anti-drug regime toward an enforcement focus, and has generally resisted efforts to adopt a more regulatory model. Over the last 120 years, it has steadily increased the breadth of anti-drugs laws and concomitantly increased enforcement. Procedural rules have been modified to accommodate new challenges, and sentences enhanced. Most importantly, anti-drug rules are no longer restricted to the criminal justice realm but permeate the regulatory system and other areas of law. Annual budget expenditures on combatting drugs, domestically and internationally, amount to approximately $31 billion dollars, with almost $10 billion allocated to domestic law enforcement.[8] In light of the investment, questions about effectiveness abound, and critical voices regularly declare the so-called "War on Drugs" lost.

3.1 Substantive Drug Laws: From Regulatory to Criminal Law

The manufacture, distribution, and possession of certain intoxicating substances used solely for recreational purposes is prohibited in the entire United States.[9] The federal government regulates the medical use and research of these drugs, with the U.S. Attorney General overseeing both the enforcement and regulatory approaches. In addition to federal laws and law enforcement, individual states enforce their own state drug laws within their borders.

U.S. anti-drug policy is governed by the supply reduction model, which includes "international drug control; foreign and domestic drug intelligence; interdiction; and

[8]Office of the President of the United States, National Drug Control Budget: FY 2017 Funding Highlights, February 2016.

[9]Prohibited drugs are "narcotic, psychotropic, and related substances whose production, sale, or use are restricted by [US] domestic law and international drug control agreements." Rosen (2015).

domestic law enforcement."[10] Foreign aid and military and law-enforcement assistance abroad are, therefore, part of the fight against international drug networks and the production of drugs abroad. Domestic law enforcement aims at drug users, distributors and manufacturers and includes the broad extraterritorial application of U.S. criminal laws.[11]

The federal government has controlled certain drugs since the early twentieth century. Initially some of these laws, such as the Harrison Act, set up a regulatory and tax structure for drugs such as opium and heroin. Despite its innocuous start, the Act led to prosecutions and convictions of patients and physicians when the drugs were prescribed to support an addiction. Ultimately criminal enforcement drove the practice underground.

While the public associated opium with Chinese immigration, the 1930s actions against marijuana grew out of anti-Mexican sentiments. After initial federal regulatory action, all states outlawed the possession of marijuana. Marijuana smokers were portrayed as especially dangerous, posing a threat to public safety and health.

By the 1950s penalties for drug offenses increased, with the sale of heroin to minors making a dealer death-eligible.[12] Yet, in the 1960s the legal basis for drug law-enforcement changed from the federal government's taxing power to its power to regulate interstate commerce. During these decades the government also pursued a public health approach, enhancing funding for narcotic research and resources for drug treatment.

The Controlled Substances Act of 1970 classifies substances by the danger they pose and their potential for abuse and for legitimate medical use. While marijuana and heroin have been classified as Schedule I drugs—the most dangerous, cocaine and methamphetamine are in Schedule II.

The Drug Enforcement Agency (DEA), created in 1973, works closely with other federal law-enforcement agencies, such as the Federal Bureau of Investigation (FBI), and law-enforcement agencies in the 50 states and abroad. Even though it is best known as a law-enforcement agency, it also fulfills a regulatory role by supervising compliance with registration, record keeping and required security measures of those manufacturers, physicians, pharmacies, and others permitted to work with or research these controlled substances.[13]

---

[10]Executive Office of the President, Office of National Drug Control Policy, FY2012 Budget and Performance Summary, April 2011, p. 282.

[11]Doyle (2016), p. 2. The United States frequently requests extradition of drug traffickers, and in select cases has resorted to irregular rendition in the form of abduction and even to military operations (p. 7).

[12]The death penalty for drug trafficking alone would be unconstitutional today, in the wake of the Supreme Court's decisions in *Coker v. Georgia*, 433 U.S. 584 (1977) and *Kennedy v. Louisiana*, 554 U.S. 407 (2008). On the other hand, certain types of drug trafficking carry life-without-parole sentences.

[13]Additional regulatory measures govern these bodies, and missteps in manufacturing or administering such drugs would fall within the enforcement structures of other regulatory bodies. In addition, private suits, instigated by those harmed, would arise under tort laws.

The Comprehensive Crime Control Act of 1984 permitted the Attorney General, through the DEA, to temporarily schedule new substances and authorize criminal penalties to avoid an imminent threat to public health. Such temporary scheduling can be effective up to 3 years. Even though Congress or the Attorney General may permanently schedule, remove or transfer a substance, that formal process takes substantially longer. The Department of Justice exercised that control when synthetic drugs came on the market in the late 1980s and before passage of the Anti-Drug Abuse Act of 1986 that allowed for synthetic drugs to be analogized to naturally existing drugs and classified accordingly. Separate legislation regulated the chemicals used to make synthetic drugs.[14]

With the 1970s focused on heroin and the 1980s concerned about cocaine, especially in the form of "crack," since the end of that decade synthetic drugs have been of primary concern to lawmakers and law enforcement. Methamphetamine—usually colloquially referred to as "Meth"—remains a major law-enforcement concern, with importation from Mexico and home production in rural America.[15]

Within the last few years heroin has returned as a major drug of concern, in part as a result of large-scale law-enforcement actions against prescription drug abuse.[16] In contrast to crack cocaine whose users were portrayed as urban and poor African-Americans, heroin abuse has been concentrated among rural and suburban whites. This difference may account for a change in rhetoric away from enforcement to treatment. Still heavy enforcement against drug users and sellers continues.

Drug preferences have frequently driven changes in substantive law, with more drugs over time becoming outlawed. With a national focus on the drug crisis since the early 1970s, enforcement has also expanded.

3.2 *State and Federal Enforcement*

The bulk of law enforcement actions rest with the individual states. States prosecute possession crimes and smaller dealers and small networks that operate solely within the state[17]; the federal government generally focused on large networks and on interstate or international trafficking operations. Many drug operations involve not only a host of federal agencies, such as the Federal Bureau of Investigations (FBI),

[14]Chemical Diversion and Trafficking Act makes up Title VI of the Anti-Drug Abuse Act of 1988, P.L. 100–690.

[15]The rise in the popularity of meth explains why purchasers of over-the-counter cough syrup that contains pseudoephedrine, will be registered.

[16]Muhuri et al. (2003).

[17]In contrast to the European Union member states where small possession crimes will not be prosecuted, in the United States, depending on the jurisdiction, such offenses may be brought before a court.

the Bureau of Alcohol, Tobacco, Firearms, and Explosives (ATF), or the Department of Homeland Security (DHS), but also state, local, and tribal agencies.[18] In addition to these drug task forces, numerous agencies participate in the Organized Crime Drug Enforcement Task Forces, which target major drug trafficking operations by seizing their assets and destroying their financial structure.[19] In those operations, which the federal government supports financially, a federal arrest may lead to a state prosecution, and vice versa. Theoretically, under the dual sovereignty doctrine, U.S. law permits multiple prosecutions by different sovereigns—federal and state—for the same conduct, though the more likely outcome is the government "shopping" for a jurisdiction with procedural rules and sentence structures most likely to culminate in a conviction and lengthy sentence.

In addition to congressional funding, law enforcement agencies benefit from confiscation of drug assets. The Comprehensive Crime Control Act of 1984 authorized criminal forfeiture—upon a criminal conviction—for certain federal drug offenses. This allows the federal government to retain or transfer property seized in drug cases to federal, state or local agencies. This structure has created an incentive for state agencies to participate in federal drug investigations.

Unique to the United States are so-called civil forfeitures. In these federal and state governments can proceed against property without a criminal conviction of the owner.[20] Under the laws of many states and the federal government, some or all of these forfeitures go to the seizing law-enforcement agency, which is also true in the case of criminal forfeitures. The incentive structure created has been subject to extensive criticism.[21]

In addition to enforcement within the United States, federal law enforcement also operates abroad. With the DEA as the lead agency, the Departments of State and Defense and the U.S. Agency for International Development (USAID), among others, work with foreign governments to reduce the international drug supply. This work builds on the tri-partite international treaty framework governing illicit substances,[22] and encompasses eradication and capacity building for domestic law enforcement and the judiciary.

The international anti-drug activity of the United States is designed to combat the drug supply to the United States but also address the threat organized networks pose to governments and the rule of law. Yet, critics of domestic drug enforcement have argued that U.S. government actions have destabilized communities and contributed to the largest prison population in the world.

[18]In 1988 the Office of National Drug Control Policy and its director, the so-called "drug czar," were created to coordinate the efforts of multiple federal agencies engaged in drug enforcement.

[19]Money-laundering legislation and federal regulatory structures designed to uncover and dismantle the financial infrastructure of organized drug networks are beyond the scope of this paper.

[20]For a discussion of such forfeiture in European countries, see Petter Rui and Sieber (2015).

[21]See, e.g., Demleitner (2017). For discussion of the sharing between state and federal agencies, see U.S. Department of Justice, Criminal Division, Guide to Equitable Sharing for State and Local law Enforcement Agencies, April 2009, www.justice.gov/criminal-afmls/file/794696/download.

[22]Sacco (2014).

Drug prosecutions, virtually all for trafficking, currently constitute the second largest number of criminal cases in federal courts. In state courts, however, the majority of drug cases are for possession of drugs.

Federal mandatory minimum drug sentences, up to life-without-parole, began to proliferate in the late 1980s. They were based on the type and quantity of the drug involved, which often resulted in relatively low-level offenders, so-called drug "mules", receiving especially lengthy sentences. With judges required to impose a mandatory minimum sentence if the offense of conviction demands it, federal prosecutors have become the ultimate decision-makers as only they have the authority to petition the judge to go below the mandated sanction based on the extraordinary cooperation of the offender. With high sentences looming, guilty pleas proliferated, and cooperation became a regular aspect of federal cases.[23] Those willing and able to assist the government in other prosecutions could benefit substantially from their cooperation,[24] often leading to inequities in sentences.

As the federal system prosecuted ever more drug offenders during the 1990s and the early years of the new century and the sentences imposed were lengthy, the federal prison population began to swell. Only in the last few years have federal drug prosecutions begun to ebb though the federal prison population remains large. President Obama issued a large number of sentence commutations, most of them to drug offenders who had already served many years for offenses that would qualify them now for lower sentences.

A conviction for a drug offense, even at the lowest level, however, may carry other far-reaching consequences well beyond the sanction imposed at sentencing. These so-called collateral sanctions[25] flow directly from a criminal conviction. Many of them are tied to a drug conviction. They include the denial of public housing and the optional denial of certain welfare benefits.[26] In addition, the federal government must deny educational loans to certain convicted drug offenders. Voting rights are generally restricted while someone is under a criminal justice sanction, and in some states may be denied well beyond that. A few states specifically deny driver's license privileges to those who have a drug conviction, even if the conviction is unrelated to driving. The list of such mandatory sanctions is lengthy.

Administrative agencies have the authority to bar drug offenders from benefits, such as licenses and grants. Private employers, schools, and landlords have also become agents in drug enforcement. Some employers are required, or have chosen,

---

[23]Similarly, even under the federal guideline regime, where judges retained some discretion, discounts for guilty pleas and cooperation increased the importance of prosecutors in the adjudicatory process.

[24]Studies indicated that rewards for cooperation, and the required type and level of cooperation, varied widely between different federal prosecutors' offices.

[25]For an early compilation of such collateral sanctions, see Demleitner (2002). For a current compilation of collateral sanctions generally, see Klingele et al. (2012–2013).

[26]In the case of public housing, a conviction is not even required. The government can evict tenants if they had a guest or a caretaker who had drugs on him, or if a co-tenant, often a child or grandchild, dealt drugs, even if far away from the apartment.

to conduct drug tests, at hiring and beyond. Schools have increasingly permitted police presence, and have resorted to drug searches. All of them now have the ability to check an applicant's criminal history, frequently leading to them being denied offers of employment or a rental agreement. Despite the proliferation of enforcement agents and the harshness of sanctions, drug use in the United States remains high.

3.3 From Drug Courts to Legalization

Because of the large number of drug users, however, states have developed means to divert offenders from the traditional court system. In all states specialized drug courts have been created that allow nonviolent (drug) offenders with a substance-abuse problem to be diverted from the formal criminal justice system. Such diversion may occur either before or after formal adjudication of the case. These courts, ranging from adult to juvenile drug courts, from DWI/DUI (driving while intoxicated/driving under the influence) to reentry drug courts, vary in structure, the offenders they target, and their scope. Generally, the disposition of offenders includes extensive judicial supervision of their progress in a drug treatment program and of compliance with other obligations imposed. The offender must enter the program, which some deem more onerous than a short jail sentence, voluntarily. In addition to treatment, the program includes other rehabilitative and re-entry measures, such as educational programming or job training. The judge can sanction program violations immediately, with a broad array of graduated sanctions, and reward an offender. The goals of drug courts are to end the offender's drug dependence, with no criminal record or a mitigated or waived sentence, support a law-abiding life-style, and establish a foundation for successful re-entry. Research indicates that drug courts are generally effective in ending drug abuse and in reducing recidivism.[27] Even though drug courts constitute a different model than traditional courts, to some extent the overall approach is comparable to the suspension of custodial penalties in EU countries when the convicted person accepts detoxification treatment.

Broader efforts to divert drug offenders from the criminal justice system are also underway. Since the 1970s marijuana has been classified as a Schedule I drug, which prohibits its manufacturing or possession. This prohibition has restricted medical research into the substance or its effects as the drug is labeled as having "no currently accepted medical use in treatment in the United States."[28] Changes began to occur in the 1990s when California authorized medical marijuana use, despite the federal

[27]West Huddleston and Boone (2005), p. 2. Others have argued that drug courts are not more effective than other case dispositions. Hoffman (2001–2002). Finally, the Government Accountability Office has taken the position that insufficient data collection impedes analysis. U.S. GAO, Drug Courts: Better DOJ Data Collection and Evaluation Efforts Needed to Measure the Impact of Drug Court Program, GAO-02-434, April 2002, pp. 18–20.

[28]21 U.S.C. 812(b)(1).

mandate. By 2017 close to 60% of U.S. states permit the medical use of marijuana. Different models of toleration exist. In some states the medical use is specifically authorized, in others such users are exempt from prosecution under state law.

Some states, such as Massachusetts, and some localities, have gone further and effectively decriminalized small amounts of marijuana, possessed for any personal use, by replacing criminal with civil penalties.[29] Decriminalization allows states, however, to continue with the criminal prosecution of certain marijuana offenders even for small amounts. Many states, for example, prosecute when the marijuana is "open to public view." In other cases the decision whether to pursue a violation criminally or civilly appears to be subject to official discretion.[30] Some states have moved from prosecuting the user to prosecuting those who make their facilities knowingly available for consumption, though such prosecutions are more likely for synthetic drugs.

Starting in 2012 some states, now covering 20% of the U.S. population, have legalized the possession of small amounts of marijuana for recreational use by those over 21. Those states have generally developed a regulatory and taxation scheme for the sale of marijuana.[31] While some states permit individuals to grow marijuana plants, others do not. Public consumption of marijuana and driving under the influence remain offenses.[32] Many other regulatory issues have not been fully worked out, especially in light of the conflict between state and federal laws.

The international drug conventions do not permit a country to legalize marijuana, or any other drug they have prohibited.[33] Since the United States under federal law continues to outlaw marijuana, it views itself in compliance, with the individual U.S. states potentially engaged in a pilot study. After California, with its large population, moved to legalize in November 2016, that posture may be more difficult to maintain. The major challenge to the enforcement focus under the Conventions may, however, come from Canada whose federal government is developing legalization legislation.

During the Obama administration the Department of Justice has largely respected state choices to legalize marijuana and focused its enforcement efforts on preventing criminal networks from moving into the marijuana market, distribution to minors, spillage of marijuana into neighboring states, distribution of other drugs in connection with marijuana, and violence in the marijuana market. The new administration under Attorney General Sessions appears to pursue a different approach.

[29]The federal government explicitly authorizes civil penalties in addition or in lieu of criminal sanctions. The Illicit Drug Anti-Proliferation Act of 2003 (CSA), for example, created civil penalties for "maintaining drug-involved facilities."

[30]Sacco and Finklea (2014), pp. 5–6.

[31]Colorado appears to have benefitted fiscally substantially from legalization.

[32]Sacco and Finklea (2014), p. 7.

[33]Uruguay is technically in violation of the conventions. Bolivia left the convention framework and then re-entered with a reservation regarding the chewing of coca leaves, a traditional practice in the country.

Even though even during the last decade the enforcement approach has been modified to encompass and emphasize treatment and prevention—both elements of demand reduction—to a greater extent, law enforcement expenses remain higher than those allocated for treatment.[34] Yet, the fiscal outlay on formal drug enforcement, insufficiently measures the societal investment in such enforcement.

Much of the U.S. focus on drug law enforcement is internal. At the same time, however, it plays a major role in the international arena, through the interdiction of drugs, extradition of offenders, and other related measures designed to interrupt the international flow of drugs into the United States.

4 Major Challenges for the Enforcement of Criminal Law Through the Criminal Procedure in the Field of Drug Related Crimes

The aims of criminal procedure are manifold. Its main function is to enforce criminal law, and by doing so, prevent crimes and sanction the perpetrators, and therefore enhance the sense of security in a society.[35] Additionally criminal procedure is meant to avoid the conviction of innocent persons and in general terms, protect every citizen against possible abuses of the state. In whatever way the aims are described, those aims are linked to the goals of the criminal law. Criminal procedure is ultimately a series of acts and a set of safeguards that serve to enforce the criminal law. It is therefore an instrument of an instrument.

In the next section, we will point out the main challenges for the enforcement of criminal law in the area of drug-trafficking offenses by drawing on the examples of the United States and the European Union.

4.1 Enforcement of Criminal Law, Drug-Trafficking and Organized Crime

When addressing the issue of enforcement of criminal law in the area of drug related offenses, a clear dividing line has to be drawn between possession for consumption, possession for minor distribution, consumption, and the more complex crime of drug trafficking.[36] Consumption and possession for consumption are the last link of the complex chain of the illicit drug business, the weakest part of the whole structure, as

[34]Office of National Drug Control Policy, National Drug Control Budget: FY2015 Funding Highlights, March 2014, p. 15.

[35]See Hart (1958), p. 401.

[36]It is beyond the purview of this paper to address offenses that result from addiction, such as violent and non-violent offenses aimed at gaining access to money to finance drug purchases.

the addicts could be viewed as both victims, in light of the damage to their health, and as offenders for breaking the criminal law. On the other hand, drug trafficking offenses, even if there is no direct individual victim immediately ascertainable—unless all drug consumers, or all addicts, are deemed victims—cannot be classified as victimless crime. The entire society is the victim of the public health problems, and related societal problems, drug trafficking and the resulting drug consumption cause.

For several decades already major international efforts have been focused on reducing the production, transformation, and trafficking of drugs, because they contribute significantly to undermining the rule of law and compromising in many respects the integrity of democratic institutions. In light of the sophisticated tools employed and the violence used by criminal organizations to achieve their goals, drug trafficking poses a serious threat to individuals as well as to the rule of law, and consequently to human rights.

The negative impact on national economies—and the world economic system—should not be underestimated either. Significant amounts of money are lost through tax evasion, money laundering and illicit markets, not to mention the indirect economic harm caused by organized crime as it can undermine the credibility and competitiveness of a state's financial and commercial sectors.[37] For these reasons when addressing the challenges of enforcing criminal law in the area of drug offenses, we will focus on the challenges organized crime and organized criminal drug networks pose.

Drug trafficking is one of the most profitable and grave forms of transnational organized crime. Under the United Nations Convention against Illicit Traffic in Narcotic Drugs and Psychotropic Substances of 1988,[38] States parties committed themselves to combat one of the most lucrative manifestations of transnational organized crime, international drug trafficking, by, inter alia, criminalizing laundering of the proceeds of drug trafficking and strengthening international cooperation, in particular in the field of extradition and mutual legal assistance.

Countless efforts have been made to define the terms "organized crime" and "organized criminal group."[39] The term organized crime usually refers to large-scale and complex criminal activities carried out by tightly or loosely organized associations and aimed at the establishment, supply and exploitation of illegal markets at the expense of society. Such operations are generally carried out with a ruthless disregard of the law, and often involve offenses against the person, including threats,

[37]See, for example, the Council of Europe White Paper on Transnational Organized Crime of December 2014, prepared by Bachmaier, which can be read under http://www.coe.int/t/dghl/standardsetting/cdpc/White-paper-Web.pdf.

[38]United Nations, Treaty Series, vol. 1582, No. 27627.

[39]See the long list of more than 190 definitions collected by von Lampe, under www.organized-crime.de/organizedcrimedefinitions.htm.

intimidation and physical violence.[40] As for the concept of criminal group, we follow here the definition included under Article 2(a) of the Palermo Convention on Transnational Organized Crime.[41]

As is true also for other forms of transnational organized crime, combating drug trafficking and other drug related offences requires a different and more sophisticated approach than the one adopted in combating traditional and more simple forms of criminality. Some of the core elements for detecting and prosecuting drug trafficking crimes are: extending the activities of prevention and adopting a pro-active approach; strengthening intelligence gathering and international cooperation, and using special investigative techniques, together with a legislative framework that encourages the cooperation and collaboration of those inside organized criminal groups. If international cooperation instruments do not work effectively, the fight at a transnational level is inefficient. For the recovery of assets and the detention of suspects, effective transnational investigation is needed, through the use of special investigative techniques, not only at a national level, but also via international cooperation. Only with swift international cooperation, cross-border investigation, and the targeting and seizing of assets, which make up the core element of these criminal business organizations, can the criminal laws against drug trafficking be enforced effectively. Apart from the detection and investigation of these crimes, for the sanctioning and punishing of the perpetrators and the dismantling of criminal organizations, insider cooperation and witness protection programs are highly important.

4.2 The Need for a Pro-Active Approach

With regard to *prevention,* the idea that traditional 'repressive' law enforcement bodies (police, prosecutors, courts) should have a monopoly on responding to organized crime has been revised once it has become clear that alone they are unlikely to have sufficient impact on this type of criminality. Prevention has come to the forefront in combating these types of offences.

One aspect of the prevention of organized crime focuses on the reduction of existing or future opportunities for organized criminal groups to participate in lawful markets through the investment of crime proceeds. That requires appropriate

[40]See Eighth United Nations Congress on the Prevention of Crime and the Treatment of Offenders, Havana, 27 August–7 September 1990: report prepared by the Secretariat (United Nations publication, 1990, Sales No. E.91.IV.2), chap. I, sect. C, resolution 24, annex, p. 5.

[41]United Nations Convention against Transnational Organized Crime signed in Palermo 15 December 2000, according to the UN Resolution 54/129. Article 2 (a): "Organized criminal group shall mean a structured group of three or more persons, existing for a period of time and acting in concert with the aim of committing one or more serious crimes or offences established in accordance with this Convention, in order to obtain, directly or indirectly, a financial or other material benefit".

legislative, administrative or other measures.[42] Measures should be adopted at the domestic and international level. Council of Europe Recommendation R (2001) 11 on guiding principles on the fight against organized crime[43] contains a chapter on the prevention of organized crime, outlining both sets of measures:

> Member states should identify in their legislation those provisions, which are or can be abused by organised crime groups for their own purpose, in areas such as export/import, licensing, fiscal and customs regulations, and take steps to strengthen legislation and to prevent abuse. In particular, member states should ensure mutual consistency of provisions and should have these provisions regularly tested by independent auditors to assess their "resistance" to abuse, such as fraud.
>
> Member states should establish common standards of good governance and financial discipline that enhance transparency and accountability in public administration, and should encourage the adoption of codes of conduct to prevent illegal practices, such as corruption, in the commercial and financial sectors, including public procurement.

Article 31 of the 2000 United Nations Convention against Transnational Organized Crime also contains specific provisions in this regard:

> 2. States Parties shall endeavour, in accordance with fundamental principles of their domestic law, to reduce existing or future opportunities for organized criminal groups to participate in lawful markets with proceeds of crime, through appropriate legislative, administrative or other measures. These measures should focus on: [...] (b) The promotion of the development of standards and procedures designed to safeguard the integrity of public and relevant private entities, as well as codes of conduct for relevant professions, in particular lawyers, notaries public, tax consultants and accountants; (c) The prevention of the misuse by organized criminal groups of tender procedures conducted by public authorities and of subsidies and licences granted by public authorities for commercial activity; (d) The prevention of the misuse of legal persons by organized criminal groups.

The importance of linking the prevention process to internal integrity demonstrates the complexity of the issue, the breadth of the legal areas involved, and the difficult balancing between organized crime prevention and privacy. The use of agency "intelligence" has proved to be highly useful in practice though legal scholars are hotly debating its use in criminal investigations and prosecutions.[44] After all, such information may not be tested in any adversarial proceeding, and the suspected offenders who are therefore excluded from exercising "normal" rights may not be given any opportunity to refute the allegations. Moreover the collection of intelligence information includes a broad use of information technology devices and software that are highly intrusive into the privacy of citizens, without a prior

---

[42]See the Organized Crime Best Practice Survey n° 9 of the Council of Europe, Preventive Legal Measures against Organized Crime, Strasbourg June 2003, p. 3.

[43]Adopted by the Council of Europe Committee of Ministers on 19 September 2001. The whole text of the recommendation can be found under https://rm.coe.int/CoERMPublicCommonSearchServices/DisplayDCTMContent?documentId=09000016804e603c.

[44]Intelligence gathering on drug traffickers may not be restricted to law enforcement agencies but also include other government agencies that are focused on gathering information for political or military purposes.

tested suspicion of the individuals under surveillance.[45] These methods also undermine the privacy of individuals who are not involved in drug trafficking but whose information may be collected incidentally, as a result of the focus on the target. All of these measures, which could be considered necessary to fight effectively these very complex forms of crimes, can be abused by repressive governments or even become the tools of extortion by public authorities.

Despite the controversial use of this preventive approach, criminal intelligence has been described as the lifeblood of the fight against transnational organized crime.[46] It is the foundation for all proactive investigations. It also cuts across other serious and international forms of crime since the same expertise and methodology is used for investigations of all serious crimes, including corruption and terrorism.

A fundamental component of building modern law enforcement capacity involves enhancing understanding of how criminal intelligence works and how practically to develop, share and use it. In order to operate internationally, individual Member States must have the capacity within their own law enforcement structures to collect, collate, analyze and disseminate information on criminals and the organizations within which they operate. UNODC supports criminal intelligence capabilities of law enforcement agencies through policy advice, assessment and gap analysis, and training of criminal analysts, including in using specialist analytical software. They also train front-line law enforcement agents and policy makers, including through a set of recently published criminal intelligence training manuals.

4.3 Enhancing International Cooperation

The second core element in the enforcement of criminal law in the field of drugs is international cooperation. Drug trafficking is a type of organized crime that has a clear transnational dimension. Consumers are largely, though not always, located in different geographic areas than producers, and the laundering of illicit profits tends to occur in different countries around the globe. Enforcement effectiveness, both in targeting the proceeds of the crime and the drugs themselves, requires swift and highly professionalized international cooperation. As indicated, such cooperation has to start already at the level of prevention, in the form of intelligence sharing, and then has to continue at the operative law enforcement level, mainly through Interpol, Europol, but also through bilateral agreements and joint investigation teams. International cooperation must also continue at the prosecutorial and judicial level, when it comes to evidence gathering and the detention of suspects.

At the law enforcement level, Interpol plays an essential role in this field and its global system of national central bureaux is an example of outstanding networking

[45]Bachmaier (2012), pp. 48 ff.

[46]Hirsch (2012), pp. 21 ff.; Ashworth and Zedner (2014), pp. 14 ff.

co-operation.[47] INTERPOL's system of notices and diffusions is a well-known mechanism to assist national law enforcement agencies with specific aspects of individual investigations.[48] The well-recognized activity of the United Nations Office on Drugs and Crime (UNODC) also covers setting up globally cooperative networks. Recently the International Money Laundering Information Network (IMoLIN), an Internet-based network assisting governments, organizations and individuals in the fight against money laundering has been established.[49] Another example of a network created by UNODC is the Central Asian Regional Information and Coordination Centre for Combating the Illicit Trafficking of Narcotic Drugs, Psychotropic Substances and Their Precursors (CARICC). CARICC serves to facilitate co-operation between all law enforcement agencies involved in countering illicit trafficking including the police, drug control agencies, customs, border guards and special services. It also introduces secure information exchange channels, and helps develop agreements on multilateral international operations, including controlled deliveries.

Transfer of progressive experience and best practices from one international jurisdiction to another have been established. In particular, the establishment of relations between Europol and the third countries (non-EU states), including states within Europe (Bosnia and Herzegovina, Russia, Turkey, for example) and those outside Europe, including Canada, Colombia, and the United States, could be highlighted. Eurojust carries out a similar practice. The strained EU-Russia relationship, however, exemplifies a hurdle to collaboration.

At the level of international judicial cooperation, the European Convention of 20 April 1959,[50] complemented by the Protocols signed in 1978[51] and 2001, has long governed mutual assistance in the obtaining of evidence within Europe.[52] Additionally the Schengen Agreement details rules on mutual assistance in criminal matters. Under its provisions[53] the grounds for refusing the execution of a mutual assistance request were reduced and the requirement of double incrimination was also restricted (Article 51). Moreover it provided for a simplified procedure for the transmission of extradition requests, allowing as a general rule the direct contact

[47]UNODC, Digest of Organised Crime Cases. A compilation of cases with commentaries and lessons learned, Vienna 2012, pp. 70–71, 103–104.

[48]The General Secretariat published approximately 26,500 notices and diffusions in 2011. There were 40,836 notices and 48,310 diffusions in circulation at the end of 2011, and 7958 people were arrested on the basis of a notice or diffusion during 2011 (International Notice System—Interpol). The databases and networking in the field of firearms present another good example of networking in a special area. They are channelled through ICPO, IFRT (Illicit Arms Records and Tracing Management System), iARMS, and the Ballistic Information Network (IBIN).

[49]The world's leading anti-money laundering organizations cooperated in the development of IMoLIN.

[50]Council of Europe, Treaty Series, Nr. 30.

[51]Council of Europe, Treaty Series, Nr. 99.

[52]Council of Europe, Treaty Series, Nr. 182.

[53]See specifically Articles 48 to 53.

between judicial authorities of the requesting and executing states (Article 53). These were the essential rules regarding the gathering of evidence in criminal matters in another Member State until the European Convention on Mutual Assistance in Criminal Matters of 29 May 2000 was adopted.[54] It took more than 5 years until a sufficient number of states had signed the Convention for it to enter into force on the 23 August 2005. This Convention is based upon the same principles as the 1959 Convention but represents a significant step forward in the development of judicial cooperation in criminal matters.

While international conventions reinforced and updated mutual legal assistance, the European institutions decided to improve the international judicial cooperation in criminal matters by replacing the existing international rules on mutual legal assistance with new European instruments based on the principle of mutual recognition (see the Council Conclusions of Tampere 1999[55]). Since then several action plans and programs that focused on the implementation of the principle of mutual recognition have been approved. These programs determined that the obtaining of evidence and its admissibility in criminal matters would be a priority for EU institutions.[56] The so-called "free movement of evidence" has been for years one of the goals within a European Union single area of justice and been desired as an essential element to fight cross-border and organized crime more effectively.

Finally, after lengthy discussions and debates, on 3 April 2014 the Directive 2014/41/EU regarding the European Investigation Order in criminal matters (EIO)[57] was approved. Its aim is to facilitate and speed up the gathering and transfer of evidence between the different EU member states and to harmonize the regulation of these proceedings. This Directive (to be transposed in the EU members states by 22 May 2017) will substitute the rules on transnational evidence gathering in the

[54]Council Act of 29 May 2000 establishing in accordance with Article 34 of the Treaty on European Union the Convention on Mutual Assistance in Criminal Matters between the Member States of the European Union (2000/C 197/01).

[55]Conclusions of the Presidency of the Tampere European Council of 15 and 16 October 1999, http://www.europa.eu.int/european_council/conclusions/index_es.htm, with regard to evidence, see precisely point 36.

[56]See the programme of measures to implement the principle of mutual recognition of decisions in criminal matters of 2001, OJ C12 of 15.1.2001. The point 2.1.1, concerning the obtaining of evidence states the aim: "to ensure the evidence is admissible, to prevent its disappearance and to facilitate the enforcement of search and seizure orders, so that evidence can be quickly secured in a criminal case".

[57]Directive 2014/41/EU of the European Parliament and of the Council of 3 April 2014 regarding the European Investigation Order in criminal matters, OJ L130 of 1.5.2014. On the European Investigation Order, see generally, Bachmaier (2015), pp. 47–59; Bachmaier (2017a), pp. 46–66 and also Bachmaier (2017b), pp. 313–336.

European Evidence Warrant[58] and in the European Convention on mutual assistance in criminal matters of 29 May 2000, among others.[59]

The EIO is a "judicial" resolution requesting—or perhaps more accurately ordering—the gathering of evidence that already exists or is to be obtained through investigative measures (Article 1 Directive on EIO). It can also include the request to secure or freeze evidence.[60] As stated in the Explanatory Memorandum to the Directive, this instrument is based on the principle of mutual recognition, and takes into account the flexibility of traditional mutual legal assistance mechanisms.[61] It will be applied to any "criminal" investigative measure with a European cross-border dimension, save the establishment and functioning of the joint investigation teams. The Directive aims at overcoming the undesirable fragmentation of the legal instruments regarding the collecting and transferring of evidence between the EU member states.[62]

This legal instrument shows how sovereign States continually seek to enhance the effectiveness of international judicial cooperation in the fight against transnational organized crime. However, an instrument like the European Investigation Order is only applicable within the EU while drug trafficking, a global crime, requires strengthened judicial cooperation worldwide. Practice shows that currently problems remain with the transfer and execution of requests. Practitioners indicate that among the most frequent problems are delays, mistrust, overloaded criminal justice systems, and lack of adequate knowledge of the procedure and/or language abroad.[63] Another issue law-enforcement officials frequently raise is the refusal to extradite nationals. This problem is not due to the lack of legal provisions or operative conventions but rather the unwillingness of certain states to extradite their own nationals. However, in a context of enhanced cooperation, each state should facilitate the extradition of alleged criminals to be brought to justice in the forum state. Extradition also faces other hurdles. In drug cases some countries are reluctant to extradite to the United States, for example, in light of what they often consider disproportionate sentences.

The complexity of the enforcement of criminal law in the area of drug trafficking requires different authorities, in different countries, to work together from an early investigatory stage on and continue such coordinated work throughout the

[58]Council Framework Decision 2008/9787/JHA of 18 December 2008 on the European evidence warrant for the purpose of obtaining objects, documents and data for use in proceedings in criminal matters, OJ L350 of 30.12.2008.

[59]The international conventions, framework decisions and directives that are substituted and/or amended by the Directive are listed in Article 34 DEIO.

[60]Until now regulated in the Council Framework Decision 2003/577/JHA of 22 July 2003, on the execution in the European Union of orders freezing property or evidence.

[61]Para. 6 of the Explanatory Memorandum.

[62]See para. 7 of the Explanatory Memorandum. See also Bachmaier (2013), pp. 96–98.

[63]See the study "Euroneeds: Evaluating the need for and the needs of a European Criminal Justice System" carried out by the Max Planck Institute for Foreign and International Criminal Law, http://www.mpicc.de/ww/en/pub/forschung/forschungsarbeit/strafrecht/forschungsprogramm/fp_kurzbeschreibung.htm.

prosecution and trial. In this context the creation of major law enforcement and judicial networks should be further studied. The creation of such networks should fit with the existing frameworks, taking into account the bodies and the agencies already set up at a regional level, avoiding duplication of efforts and sparing resources, and developing strategic and structural synergies with existing networks. In conclusion, it can be argued that combating complex organized crime requires new models of networking co-operation.

4.4 *Special Investigation Techniques and Collaborators of Justice*

Complex transnational criminality requires adequate measures to collect evidence through the so called "special investigation techniques". Although this term is the one used in practice and also in international legal instruments, the interception of communications, or the use of geo-localization devices and tracking instruments cannot be viewed anymore as something "special" in the field of investigating drug-trafficking offenses. In fact, this holds generally true within the criminal justice system because the use and impact of ICTs is present, to some extent, in every act and every stage of criminal prevention, investigation, prosecution, and trial. In fact, ICTs are not relevant exclusively with regard to organized crime or cybercrime, but play an increasingly important role in virtually any type of criminal offense. As indicated in the UNODC Comprehensive Study on Cybercrime, "the growing involvement of electronic evidence in all crime types is likely to revolutionize policing techniques."[64]

As was already highlighted in the AIDP General Report on "Information Society and Criminal Justice", in combating organized crime—but not only—there is need for an effective legal framework for ICT investigative measures, to allow for an appropriate balance between investigative powers and respect for individual rights, in particular the right to privacy.[65] Many of the ICT measures are carried out on the basis of general rules on search and seizure, which is not appropriate. ICTs are widely used for both information collection and in criminal investigations. Most countries, however, do not regulate the powers of law enforcement authorities in the preventive stage. The transfer of data from the preventive field to criminal proceedings should be very clearly regulated, and mechanisms and controls should be in place to avoid the illegal transfer of such elements. Well-defined rules and protocols on storing digital and electronic evidence and on guaranteeing their integrity need to be created. The defendant should have the opportunity to test the integrity of

[64]See http://www.unodc.org/documents/organized-crime/UNODC_CCPCJ_EG.4_2013/CYBERCRIME_STUDY_210213.pdf. On predictive policing based on big data, see, for example. Ferguson (2015), pp. 327 ff.; Rademacher (2017), pp. 366 ff.

[65]See for example, Bachmaier (2014), pp. 10 ff.

computer related evidence. The access to databases should be subject to stricter controls, not only at the investigative but also at the preventive stage. Mechanisms to trace which database was accessed, for which purpose and by whom, should be established. Finally, every citizen whose privacy has been encroached upon should be informed accordingly.[66]

The last element which is considered to be crucial in fighting organized crime and therefore also drug-trafficking criminal structures is providing adequate incentives for the co-operation of persons who are themselves, directly or indirectly, participants in criminal acts and thus subject (potentially) to prosecution (so-called "collaborators of justice").[67] Such insiders sometimes possess invaluable knowledge about the structure, method of operation and activities of the criminal organizations with which they are affiliated, as well as their links with other local or foreign groups. A number of international instruments require that states parties take measures, in accordance with their fundamental legal principles, to encourage the cooperation of this special category of witnesses with law-enforcement authorities. These instruments include the UNTOC (Article 26) and the UN Convention against Corruption (Article 37), as well as the more restrictive EU Council Resolution of 20 December 1996 on individuals who co-operate with the judicial process in the fight against international organized crime, and the EU Council Framework decision 2008/841/JHA of 24 October 2008 on the fight against organised crime (Article 4).

States parties to the above instruments are obliged not only to ensure that collaborating offenders enjoy *mutatis mutandis* the protection from retaliation and intimidation granted to other witnesses, but also to provide *concrete motives and inducements* to offenders to attain their cooperation in supplying information useful for investigatory and evidentiary purposes. With regard to *mitigated punishments*, most states have introduced in their Criminal Codes rules allowing the collaboration to be considered as a circumstance mitigating criminal liability, which can be taken into account by the court during sentencing.[68] However, generally no assurances are provided to the co-operating defendant in advance. As to granting immunity to the co-defendants who become collaborators of justice, many states appear not to have established such a possibility for organized criminal offenses, at least in Europe, despite the fact that the international instruments mentioned above, advocate that this possibility be considered. This continues to be a major challenge in the enforcement of criminal law in the area of drug offenses. On the other hand, the US experience

[66]On the right to privacy and the needs for notification of any encroachment see, See *Klass and Others v. Germany, Weber and Saravia v. Germany,* op. cit. (n. 30), and *Case of the Association for European Integration and Human Rights Ekimdhiev v. Bulgaria,* 28 June 2007, App. no. 62540/00; *Szabó and Vissy v. Hungary,* 12 January 2016, App. no. 37138/14.

[67]See also UNODC, Good practices for the protection of witnesses in criminal proceedings involving organised crime, New York, 2008, p. 19.

[68]Council of Europe Report on the Assessment of the answers to the questionnaire: Review of the Recommendation Rec(2005)9 on the protection of witnesses and collaborators", prepared by L. Bachmaier and Ivan Waltenburg, CDPC (2017) 21Rev, 8.11. 2017 available at https://rm.coe.int/assessment-of-the-answers-to-the-questionnaire-review-of-the-recommend/1680764f16.

with substantial discounts, though generally not immunity, for collaborators may provide a cautionary warning. Collaboration cannot become a tool for the highest level offenders to be rewarded while lower level offenders who have less information with which to collaborate feel the full brunt of the law.

5 Concluding Remarks

The effectiveness of criminal law, especially with respect to drug law enforcement, remains questionable. With expectations of enforcement success often only ambiguously defined, costs insufficiently compiled, and the collateral effects of enforcement more damaging than the public health impact, drug law enforcement appears highly ineffective. This seems particularly true when the entire cost of the venture is being considered. Decriminalization, or perhaps even some limited legalization, may present an alternative that allows other areas of law—regulatory and private—to ascend to govern the drug market more effectively.

Still, such a development is unlikely in the short run. After all, the enforcement mechanisms that have been built up in individual countries and across the globe will be difficult to dismantle. Financial investments drug traffickers have made in creating production and distribution networks have been matched by law enforcement, with both sides increasingly relying on modern technology. Enforcement requires ever more effective intelligence-led preventive efforts and global cooperation. Intelligence gathering, however, has been questioned as highly intrusive as it impedes the fundamental values of privacy and others traditionally cherished in the criminal process. The use of collaborators may also raise questions of fairness and equality. Successful enforcement counsels in favor of such tactics, however.

Despite long-standing efforts, including increased international collaboration and harsher sentences in the United States, enforcement has not shown a substantial decrease in either the supply or the consumption of drugs. The recognition of this reality should lead us to question the reflexive criminal law response and wonder whether more investment in enforcement will truly bring more effectiveness. It may be the disenchantment with the status quo that has led jurisdictions to experiment with decriminalizing consumption. It is much too early to evaluate whether this is an effective and desirable path. We may be best advised, however, to permit such experimentation at a time when the criminal enforcement approach may have run its course.

References

Ashworth A, Zedner L (2014) Preventive justice. Oxford University Press, Oxford

Beccaria C (1769) An essay on crimes and punishments, 2nd edn, London

Bachmaier L (2012) Información de inteligencia y proceso penal. In: Bachmaier L (ed) Terrorismo, proceso penal y derechos fundamentales, Madrid, 2012, pp 45–101
Bachmaier L (2013) The role of the proportionality principle in the cross-border investigations involving fundamental rights. In: Ruggeri S (ed) Transnational inquiries and the protection of fundamental rights in criminal proceedings. Springer, pp 85–108
Bachmaier L (2014) Information society and penal law. General report for the world congress of the International Association of Penal law. Int Rev Penal Law 85:6–58
Bachmaier L (2015) Transnational evidence: towards the transposition of the directive 2014/41 regarding the European investigation order in criminal matters, en EUCRIM, 2015/2, pp 47–59
Bachmaier L (2017a) European investigation order and cross-border investigation of tax offences: mutual recognition and grounds for refusal. Eur Crim Law Rev 7:46–66
Bachmaier L (2017b) Mutual recognition and cross-border interception of communications: the way ahead for the European investigation order. In: Weyembergh A (ed) The needed balances in EU criminal law. Hart publishing, Oxford, pp 313–336
Demleitner NV (2002) "Collateral Damage": no re-entry for drug offenders: no re-entry for drug offenders. Villanova Law Rev 47:1027
Demleitner NV (2017) Commodifying policing: a recipe for police-community tensions. Georgia Law Rev 51:1047
Doyle C (2016) An abridged sketch of extradition to and from the United States. Congressional Research Service, 4 October 2016
Ferguson AG (2015) Big data and predictive reasonable suspicion. Univ PA Law Rev 163:327–410
Hart MH (1958) The aims of criminal law. Law Contemp Probl 23:401–441
Hirsch MF (2012) Terrorism causing a shifting responsibility in criminal pre-trial investigation: from repression to prevention. In: Hirsch M et al (eds) Shifting responsibilities in criminal justice. Eleven International Publishing, The Hague, pp 9–29
Hoffman MB (2001–2002) The rehabilitative idea and the drug court reality. Fed Sentencing Rep 14(3–4):192
Klingele C, Roberts J, Colgate-Love M (ed) (2012–2013) Collateral consequences of criminal convictions: law, policy and practice. Thomson West
Manning M et al (2016) Economic analysis and efficiency in policing, criminal justice and crime reduction. Palgrave Macmillan, Basingstoke
Muhuri PK, Gfroerer JC, Davies MC (2003) Associations of nonmedical pain reliever use and initiation of heroin use in the United States. Substance Abuse and Mental Health Services Administration, Center for Behavioral Health Statistics and Quality, www.samhsa.gov/data/2k13/DataReview/DR006/nonmedical-pain-reliever-use-2013.pdf
Petter Rui J, Sieber U (eds) (2015) Non-conviction-based confiscation in Europe: possibilities and limitations on rules enabling confiscation without a criminal conviction. Duncker & Humblot
Rademacher T (2017) Predictive Policing im deutschen Polizeirecht. Archiv des öffentlichen Rechts 142:366–416
Robinson PH, Darley JM (2004) Does criminal law deter? A behavioural science investigation. Oxf J Leg Stud 24:173–205
Rosen LW (2015) International drug control policy: background and U.S. responses. Congressional Research Service, 16 March 2015
Sacco LN (2014) Drug enforcement in the United States: history, policy, and trends. Congressional Research Service, 2 October 2014
Sacco LN, Finklea K (2014) State Marijuana legalization initiatives: implications for federal law enforcement. Congressional Research Service, 4 December 2014
Smith B (1941) Enforcement of criminal law, The Annals of the American Academy of Political and Social Science. Crime U S 217:12–18
West Huddleston C, Boone DL (2005) Painting the current picture: A national report card on drug courts and other problem solving court programs in the United States, vol 1(2). U.S. DOJ, OJP, BJA, National Drug Court Institute

Lorena Bachmaier Winter is Full Professor at Complutense University Madrid (Spain) where she teaches on court systems, criminal procedure and civil litigation. She also teaches at Saint Louis University summer courses on Introduction to Civil Law Systems (2002–2014). She is member of the most relevant academic associations and serves on editorial boards of numerous law journals and is regular invited speaker in international conferences. She has been Alexander von Humboldt Foundation fellow at the Max Planck Institute Freiburg (2002), and FRIAS fellow at the Freiburg University, Germany.. In 2015 she was awarded an honorary doctorate by San Pedro University of Perú. She is also honorary professor of the Universidad de la Rioja, Argentina. She has written widely in the field of litigation, criminal justice systems and the rule of law, EU area of justice, international judicial cooperation and human rights. Her works have a marked focus on comparative law. She also works as international legal expert for the Council of Europe in the implementation of human rights standards and legislative reform proceedings in transitional democracies, mainly in Eastern European countries.

Nora V. Demleitner is the Roy L. Steinheimer Jr Professor of Law at Washington and Lee University (Virginia, USA), and a former dean of two U.S. law schools. During the 2017–2018 academic year, she was also a Senior Fellow at the Baldy Center for Law and Social Policy at the State University of New York, Buffalo. She teaches and has written widely in the areas of sentencing, comparative and immigration law, and on issues of legal education. Professor Demleitner is an editor of the Federal Sentencing Reporter. She held three research fellowships to the Max Planck Institute for International and Foreign Criminal Law (Freiburg, Germany) and received fellowships from the German Academic Exchange Service. She is the lead author of Sentencing Law and Policy, published by Wolters Kluwer/Aspen and her articles have appeared in leading U.S. law reviews. She is an elected member of the American Law Institute and the European Law Institute and an associate member of the International Academy of Comparative Law.

Enforcement of Contractual Obligations: Comparative Perspectives

Giuditta Cordero-Moss and Alejandro M. Garro

Abstract Much has been written, from a comparative perspective, on the different types of contractual obligations and the remedies to which the party aggrieved by a breach is entitled to pursue. But few comparative scholars have ventured to discuss the different approaches legal systems take to the actual enforcement of contractual promises. Gathering jurists from different legal systems, the IACL Congress in Montevideo gave us the opportunity to discuss, as reflected in this contribution, how courts in different parts of the world provide actual relief to the obligee in cases of nonperformance, defective performance, or delayed performance of contractual obligations.

1 Introduction

Much has been written, from a comparative perspective, on the different types of contractual obligations and the remedies to which the party aggrieved by a breach is entitled to pursue. But few comparative scholars have ventured to discuss the different approaches legal systems take to the actual enforcement of contractual promises. The topic assigned to us, gathering jurists from different legal systems, encourages us to sound out how courts in different parts of the world provide actual

This article is based on the workshop prepared by the co-authors for the 2016 Thematic Congress of the International Academy of Comparative Law ("IACL"), held in Montevideo on 18 November 2016. Special thanks are due to the IACL's Assistant to the Secretary General and PhD Candidate at Sciences Po Law School, Mr. Alexandre Senegacnik.

G. Cordero-Moss (✉)
University of Oslo, Oslo, Norway
e-mail: g.c.moss@jus.uio.no

A. M. Garro
Columbia University School of Law, New York, NY, USA
e-mail: garro@law.columbia.edu

N. Etcheverry Estrázulas, D. P. Fernández Arroyo (eds.), *Enforcement and Effectiveness of the Law - La mise en oeuvre et l'effectivité du droit*, Ius Comparatum – Global Studies in Comparative Law 30, https://doi.org/10.1007/978-3-319-93758-8_8

relief to the obligee in cases of nonperformance, defective performance, or delayed performance.

The breadth of the assignment compels us to pick and choose a few instances of nonperformance, singling out issues on which the common-law and civil-law legal traditions (or some jurisdictions within each tradition) seem to part ways, namely: the breach of a pre-contractual obligation, the possibility of obtaining performance in kind (*in natura*) as opposed to monetary damages; the enforceability of an obligation to pay money in case of nonperformance or delay in performance; and the variety of judicial mechanisms, after a final judgment has been rendered, aimed at compelling the speedy enforcement of contractual obligations.

In comparing the approaches of the legal system, some tentative conclusions can be reached. The word "tentative" is emphasized, because the divide among jurisdictions rests more on the different conceptual or doctrinal approach to an issue than genuine differences of outcome based on similar facts. For example, although the principle that the parties are bound to negotiate contracts in good faith is attributed, expressly or impliedly, to many civil law systems, one rarely finds cases in which a party is awarded damages due to the other party's breach of a pre-contractual obligation.

Another distinction generally drawn between both legal traditions points to the preference by civil law systems for specific performance, as opposed to the typical common law approach providing monetary compensation for breach of contract. Although the differences in practice are unlikely to be of major importance, different doctrinal approaches to contractual remedies remain in force. In most civil law jurisdictions it is up to the party aggrieved by the breach to decide whether the obligor should be forced to perform, as opposed to legal systems pertaining to the common law family, in which the court always retains the power to decide whether to compel performance.

Whereas the enforceability of penalty clauses is generally upheld, the traditional approach of the common law has been to invalidate all contractual penalties which do not qualify as "liquidated damages". There is widespread skepticism in the common law as to the soundness of invalidating contractual clauses stipulating the payment of an agreed sum in case of nonperformance or delay in performance.[1] Yet,

[1]Noticeably, in a relatively recent decision on the enforeceability of clauses providing for liquidated damages, the Supreme Court of the United Kingdom issued a new, more progressive test for determining whether a contractual clause should be considered penal and therefore unenforceable. See Cavendish Square Holding BV v Talal El Makdessi (El Makdessi) and ParkingEye Ltd v Beavis [2015] UKSC 67 (ParkingEye) (according to Lord Hodge, as held in *El Makdessi*, the "correct test for a penalty is whether the sum or remedy stipulated as a consequence of a breach of contract is exorbitant or unconscionable when regard is had to the innocent party's interest in the performance of the contract". See also http://www.fieldfisher.com/publications/2016/02/important-changes-to-the-english-law-rule-on-penalty-clauses-what-does-it-mean-for-franchising#sthash.4V17BN3t.dpuf. See more at http://www.fieldfisher.com/publications/2016/02/important-changes-to-the-english-law-rule-on-penalty-clauses-what-does-it-mean-for-franchising#sthash.4V17BN3t.dpuf.

differences of approach remain and it is likely to have some bearing on the promisor's decision whether to breach or not to breach a contract.

Our comparative survey of the consequences of nonperformance for breach of contract confirms that the obligee who has obtained a judicial decree of specific performance has a difficult time in actually receiving such performance unless the courts can rely on clear-cut procedural rules providing for sanctions against the obligor to encourage compliance with judicial penalties.

2 Duty to Negotiate a Contract in Good Faith and Monetary Relief

In various situations, a commercial party may be deemed to have rights against another party as a consequence of this latter party's breach of an assumed duty to negotiate in good faith.

Pre-contractual good faith obligations may arise before the parties have entered into the contract—for example, the parties may conclude a letter of intent specifying some terms of the prospective deal, leaving to further negotiations the remaining terms; or they may have signed the contract with a clause subjecting the contract to approval by the parties' boards.

A duty to negotiate in good faith may also arise during the life of the contract. For example, in case of hardship one of the parties may wish to adjust some contractual terms to supervening events, so as to reinstate the balance of the contractual performances; or some of the terms of the contract may have been left open for the parties to determine at later stages.

Legal traditions have different approaches to the duty of the parties to negotiate in good faith, both in respect to the scope of such duty, the possibility to enforce it, and, if so, the remedies available to redress such a breach. Thus, during pre-contractual negotiations the parties at common law are said to bear the risk for their own assumptions and assessments. In contrast, in many civil law jurisdictions the parties to a contract are held, to varying degrees, under an obligation to take each other's interests into consideration. Whereas in some common law jurisdictions a contract may be held to include "implied obligations", enforceable only to the extent necessary to allow for the contract to be performed, the broad principle of good faith common to all civil law jurisdictions imposes ancillary obligations going further than merely allowing the contract to be performed.

These different approaches may lead to different consequences. This is particularly so in case a party is deemed not to have carried out negotiations according to good faith—for example, because it never intended to reach an agreement. If no duty to negotiate in good faith is assumed, each party will bear its own costs and will not have a claim towards the other. If there is a duty to negotiate, its enforcement may consist of granting the aggrieved party damages corresponding to the costs it incurred in connection with the failed negotiations (reliance interest or negative contract interest). Under certain circumstances, the aggrieved party may even be granted the full range of remedies available for breach of contract, i.e. specific performance (where available) or damages putting the innocent party into the economic situation it would have been in, had the negotiations been successful (expectation interest or positive contract interest).

Contract practice aims at regulating the relationship between the parties exhaustively—thus excluding interferences by the interpreter, such as those relating to a duty to negotiate in good faith. Letters of intent often contain a clause excluding liability for a party's failure to reach an agreement. Other contracts typically include clauses specifying that the contract shall not enter into force until approved by one of the parties' board of directors. Some contracts regulate in detail the consequences of hardship, the procedures to be followed to determine open terms, etc., including a so-called "merger clause" specifying that the contract is meant to contain all obligations between the parties. Clauses of this type intend to exclude the availability of claims based on a party's breach of a duty to negotiate in good faith.

At the workshop, the jurisdictions represented in the group were: Argentina, Austria, Brazil, the Czech Republic, Finland, France, Mexico, the Netherlands, Norway, Poland, and Uruguay. Various factual scenarios had been prepared, as described below. On this basis, participants were asked to report (providing if possible full citation to legal authorities), whether courts in the participant's jurisdiction have recognized that there is a duty to negotiate in good faith, as well as the type of remedies courts in that jurisdiction granted for the breach of such duty (i.e., whether courts awarded damages for reliance (negative) or expectation (positive) interest, or ever granted an order of specific performance). If no such duty was ever recognized, participants were encouraged to discuss, with supporting reasons, what would be the most likely outcome of a case presenting the described facts. Due to time constraints, only Case 1 was discussed at the workshop.

Case 1

During pre-contractual negotiations for the establishment of a joint venture, the parties sign a letter of intent describing the main lines of the envisaged deal. The letter of intent contains a clause excluding liability for a party's failure to reach an agreement. The negotiations are carried out for a considerable period of time and are quite detailed, but they are not successful. It turns out that one of the parties never intended to reach an agreement; the only reason it engaged in negotiations was to get to know the other party's organization and its way of carrying out business. No confidential information was exchanged during the negotiations, but the parties incurred considerable expenses connected with travelling and meetings. Has there been a breach of duty to negotiate in good faith? May the aggrieved party bring a claim against the other, and, if so, how would such claim be framed (e.g., contractual, precontractual, delictual liability) and what would be the scope of recovery for damages (e.g., positive vs. negative interest). Would the result be different if the parties had not entered into a letter of intent, or if the letter of intent had not contained the clause excluding a party's liability for the failure to reach an agreement?

Case 2
A contract for the license of a certain technology is signed between the parties. The contract contains a clause conditioning the contract's entry into force to the approval of the licensor's board. The licensee is aware that the licensor has entered into similar contracts in prior occasions and assumes that the board's approval is a simple formality that will not create difficulties. Relying on this assumption, the licensee starts investing into new equipment needed for the performance of the contract. The licensor is aware of the licensee's investments, but does not deem it necessary to remind the licensee that the contract's validity remains subject to the board's formal approval. The clause in the contract is clear. At the board meeting devoted to the examination of the terms of the contract, the licensor's board resolves that good business reasons counsel a change in s strategy at this point in time, formally deciding not to grant licenses of its technology to third parties. The contract concluded with the licensee is therefore not approved by the board. Does such a decision by the (prospective) licensor amount to a breach of the duty to negotiate in good faith? May the (prospective) licensee bring a claim against the (prospective) licensor? If so, how would such claim be framed (e.g., whether in terms of contractual, precontractual, delictual liability), and what type of relief would the (prospective) licensee be entitled to (specific performance, damages, scope of recovery in terms of reliance/expectation damages, etc.)? Would the result have been different if the license contract would not have included a clause subjecting the contract's entry into force to the approval of the board?

Case 3
In a long-term contract for the periodical supply of certain material, the price is determined for only the first year of the contract. According to the contract, the price for the remaining contract period is to be negotiated by the parties in good faith. After the first year, the parties fail to agree on the price: one party proposes a price based on various objective parameters, whereas the other, for whom the contract would not be profitable at that price, proposes a price that is unreasonable under the given market circumstances. Has there been a breach of duty to negotiate in good faith? Does the aggrieved party have a claim against the other party? If so, how would such a claim be framed in your jurisdiction and what type of remedy will a court in your jurisdiction grant (e.g., reliance damages, expectation damages or specific performance)?

As all represented jurisdictions belonged to the Civil Law tradition, there were no substantial discrepancies in approach. All jurisdictions recognized a pre-contractual duty of good faith. This duty is mandatory, therefore the clause in the Letter of Intent would not be a sufficient basis to exclude liability.

This approach is quite different from the Common Law tradition, where each party is deemed to bear the risk for its own assumptions, and a party is not expected to take the interest of the other party into consideration in the negotiation phase. Moreover, in the Common Law tradition the parties are deemed to be able to allocate the risk between each other as they deem fit. Therefore, a sufficiently clear language in a Letter of Intent is deemed to achieve the described risk allocation.

As mentioned, the mandatory duty of good faith leads to different results in the Civil Law tradition. New legislative reform in Argentina, however, has introduced a provision close to the Common Law tradition. According to the new legislation, a provision included in a Letter of Intent and excluding any liability for break off of negotiations, would be enforceable literally and thus exclude liability even in a situation as the one described in the case at hand. This provision is deemed to have an exceptional character, and may therefore not be applied analogically in other situations. Thus, the primacy of the principle of good faith is maintained in all cases that do not fall directly under the new provision.

In all represented jurisdictions, the aggrieved party would be able to bring a claim for reliance interest. The aggrieved party would thus be entitled to recover the losses it incurred as a consequence of the failed negotiations. These would consist of costs and expenses, but also of loss of opportunity (for example, if the aggrieved party did not pursue negotiations with a third party because it was engaged in the failed negotiations).

3 Relief for Breach of Contract: Specific Performance vs. Damages

In comparing civil-law and common-law approaches to the legal devices by which a breach of contract may be redressed, one is inclined to restate the civilian principle that obligations, especially contractual obligations, as a rule, can be specifically enforced in accordance with the terms of the contract unless, of course, non-performance is excused or performance is actually impossible. Even if damages or other remedies remain available, in most civil law jurisdictions it is for the obligee and not for the court to choose between specific performance and substitutionary relief in the form of damages or any other non-specific remedy. This preference for enforcement in kind stands in marked contrast to the common-law approach in which monetary damages is the most common form of relief, unless its proven inadequacy makes available the extraordinary equitable remedy of specific performance.

It seems questionable, however, whether such principled difference is reflected in commercial litigation practice, domestic as well as international, monetary relief being the most common form of judgment or arbitral award to be encountered. Is it actually appropriate to assume that decrees or orders of specific performance are more readily available, while seeking the enforcement of the same type of contractual promises, in civil-law jurisdictions than in common-law jurisdictions? Would it be correct to affirm that the principle of freedom of contract in the enforcement of contracts is carried further in civil-law jurisdictions than in common-law jurisdictions? Is it true that judges in civil-law countries let the parties decide whether the promisor should be forced to perform the contract in accordance with tis terms, while their common-law brethren always retain the power to make an ultimate, discretionary decision on this point?

Participants were asked to discuss, in light of the case-scenario illustrated in the cases that follow, whether under the facts given in those cases, courts in their countries would issue a decree ordering specific performance of the contractual obligation in question, or whether an award of monetary damages is the most readily available relief for breach of contract in those cases in which such remedy is sought by the plaintiff; whether specific performance will be ordered even if the plaintiff fails to request it; and whether the courts will decide whether to grant specific performance or monetary damages irrespective of how the plaintiff frames his request for relief.

Case 1
Due to a heavy storm, an oil tanker sunk with a highly priced cargo to which the shipper also attaches a strong sentimental value. The shipper brings suit against the carrier for breach of contract, submitting convincing expert testimony to the effect that it is physically possible to recover the cargo and thus perform the contract in kind. Expert evidence also shows that such an operation would be extremely costly, lifting the ship from the bottom of the sea entailing at least twice the monetary value of the cargo. Is the shipper entitled to specific performance of the contract of carriage in such a case?

With respect to case 1 the Uruguayan participants in the group were of the view that Uruguayan law permitted recovery by the shipper involving the lifting of the ship from the bottom of the sea, even though that cost was at least twice the monetary value of the cargo, subject to the possibility that a force majeure clause existed in the contract and that the conditions described in the problem that the oil tanker sank due to a heavy storm amounted to force majeure. The Brazilian member of the group also expressed the view that, under Brazilian law, there was no discretion in the judge not to award specific performance apart from the circumstance where performance was impossible.

In the Netherlands, under the Civil Code as revised in 1992, the shipper would have the choice between specific performance and damages. If the shipper chose specific performance, then the contract must be fulfilled unless to do so was unreasonable or unfair.

In France, from 1 October 2016, pursuant to the amended Article 1221 of the Civil Code, the shipper would be entitled to specific performance unless the execution of the obligation was impossible or there existed a manifest disproportion between the costs for the debtor and the interests of the creditor.

In Canada, it was said to depend on the terms of the contract and the judge would have a discretion whether or not to decree specific performance depending upon the nature of the goods. The case scenario refers to the fact that shipper attaches "sentimental value" to the cargo, yet a cargo of oil, does not seem particularly unusual and it is unlikely to attract a decree of specific performance. Also, aside from the "sentimental value" that the obligee attaches to the cargo, the normal common law approach in Australia, would not be to grant specific performance in a case of this nature, due to the unremarkable nature of oil as a cargo and the disproportionate costs of raising the oil from the sea bed. One would have to expect, however, that environmental authorities would want the cargo of oil removed from the sea bed if possible to avoid it causing environmental harm.

Case 2
A buyer located in "Costa Dorada", a developing country where foreign exchange is very scarce, decides to purchase valuable machinery from a seller located in "Goldcoast", a highly industrialized country where such sophisticated machinery is manufactured and exported all over the world. The seller receives payment in full of the contract price before delivery. A few weeks later, when the time comes for the seller to perform, he refuses delivery of the machine, offering instead a full refund of the price he received, plus interest. The seller submits persuasive expert testimony to the effect that buyer may obtain a similar machine from "Ruritania", another industrialized country close to "Goldcoast", also ready to export the same type of machinery available from "Goldcoast". Should the buyer be obliged to import the machine from "Ruritania", receiving full monetary compensation from the seller, despite the scarcity of foreign exchange in "Costa Dorada", or is the buyer entitled to demand specific performance from the seller, forcing him to deliver the machinery he promised to sell? The view expressed by the civilian jurisdictions represented, Argentina. Brazil, Uruguay, the Netherlands and France, was that in this case, dealing with the purchase of valuable and sophisticated machinery, specific performance may be asked for and would be granted and that the absence of ready access to foreign exchange would be a further justification for the issuance of a decree of specific performance.

The Canadian and Australian members of the group also thought it more likely that a judge would order specific performance in a common law jurisdiction having regard to the unusual nature of the machinery, the absence of any proper discretionary reason to refuse specific performance, and the potential difficulty for the purchaser of accessing foreign exchange to purchase a substitute machine.

4 Enforcement of the Parties' Agreement to Pay a Specific Sum of Money in Case of Non-Performance or Delay in Performance

A promisee of a contractual promise interested in obtaining actual and timely specific performance, foreseeing the possibility that the contract under negotiation may not be specifically enforceable, or contemplating the difficulties and cost of proving the amount of its losses in case of breach, may consider whether he may be protected by inserting a clause in the contract itself whereby the party in breach is bound to pay a sum of money if such a breach were to occur.

The validity of such an agreement to pay a sum of money in case of nonperformance is most likely to be upheld in most civil law countries, whose judges are bound to award the agreed-upon sum. In many civil-law countries courts retain discretion to reduce to a reasonable amount a sum of money that is manifestly excessive, even if the parties refuse to confer such powers on the court.

In the absence of such extraordinary circumstances, once the parties agreed on a specific sum to be paid as a penalty for nonperformance or delay in performance, courts in most civil law jurisdictions are not allowed to award a smaller or larger sum than the one fixed in the contract. By way of exception, in a few number of civil law jurisdictions, the obligee is entitled to recover damages in excess of the agreed-upon sum, provided such damages are proven and the obligor is found liable for his failure to perform. Even in a smaller number of jurisdictions inspired by French law, the court is even empowered to increase the agreed-upon sum to a reasonable amount in case it is "ridiculously small" in proportion to the loss suffered by the aggrieved party.

This civilian approach stands markedly in contrast with the one traditionally adopted in most common-law jurisdictions, which consider such clauses unenforceable on grounds of public policy as long as the stipulated sum is high and clearly intended as a penalty, i.e., for the purpose of pressure the obligor into rendering actual and timely performance, rather than as a liquidated damages clause intended to estimate the monetary compensation a court of law could award as damages resulting from a contemplated breach.

The soundness of the classical approach invalidating all penalty clauses which do not qualify as liquidated damages has been put into question, especially in common law jurisdictions where the parties otherwise enjoy ample freedom to shape their contracts. There are many situations in which specific performance is unavailable for all practical purposes, or in which neither damages or specific performance provide reliable protection for environmental or other non-pecuniary interests. Under these circumstances, it seems questionable for any legal system to invalidate such clauses, whether intended as a penalty or as a reasonable pre-estimate of damages, as long as the parties have freely assented to its incorporation into the contract and the court retains the power to review it is not used in an oppressive manner. As reported previously, a decision handed down in 2015 by the UK Supreme Court, "El Makdessi", departed from the traditional common law approach, acknowledging that, as long as the stipulated sum is not exorbitant or unconscionable, a party may hold a legitimate interest protected by a contractual penalty which does not have to be a genuine pre-estimate of loss.[2]

Participants were are asked to report whether courts in their jurisdictions would upheld the validity of a contractual clause providing for the payment of a fixed sum of money in cases of breach described in the cases that follow. They were also asked to indicate whether courts in their countries retain the power to reduce or increase the

---

[2]See Cavendish Square Holding BV v Talal El Makdessi (El Makdessi) and ParkingEye Ltd v Beavis [2015] UKSC 67 (ParkingEye).

fixed sum to be paid by the breaching party on the ground that insistence on paying such sum would be oppressive, abusive, or otherwise in violation of the principle of good faith.

Under the given facts in the hypothetical cases presented for discussion, participants were asked whether under the law in force in their jurisdictions, the obligee would be entitled to recover a sum larger than the agreed-upon sum, indicating the reasons why the court would be entitled to grant such an award. Assuming that courts would invalidate clauses for the payment of a fixed sum in the factual context presented by these cases, participants were also requested to indicate whether the enforceability of this type of clause is subject to the obligee's proof that the fixed sum is a reasonable bona fide pre-estimate of the loss that he could have incurred in case of breach.

Case 1

"A" undertakes to deliver to "B" within 1 year 100 tons of sugar at $1000 per ton, the parties agreeing on a penalty of $200 per ton. "A" fails to deliver 50 tons, but by the end of that year the sugar's market price has fallen to $500 per ton, so that "B" has in fact saved $500 per ton on the 50 tons which "A" has failed to deliver. Please discuss whether courts in your jurisdiction:

(a) Will simply authorize "B" to recover the penalty in full (50 × $200 = $10,000)? Or would such determination depend on whether the fixed sum qualifies as a "reasonable pre-estimate of the loss which "A" would have incurred a year ahead upon the "B"'s failure to deliver the sugar?;
(b) Will be allowed to reduce the penalty on the ground that it is excessive in relation to the actual loss suffered (specifying whether the court can only reduce the penalty or, in the exercise of this discretion, wipe it out completely, reducing the penalty to zero, on the ground that no loss has been incurred);
(c) Will have the power to reduce the penalty, but depending in any way on the characterization of the obligor as a "merchant".

Case 2

"Bobby" is a loving puddle whose market value is only $75, but whose owner Peter ("P") is extremely devoted to him. Being required to leave town due to a family emergency, P entrusts Bobby's custody to "David's Kennel" ("D") for five days at the rate of $90 per day. "P" and "D" agree that Bobby is to have a daily portion of one-half of filet mignon, and "D" promises to pay $1000 for every day on which Bobby should fail to receive the stipulated food. Thinking that "P" would never find out, "D" gives Bobby nothing but scraps. One of "D"'s disgruntled employees informs "P" upon his return of the type of food received by Bobby, so that "P" seeks to recover from "D" $5000.Please discuss whether in your jurisdiction:

(a) "P"'s claim would be enforceable, or whether such stipulation would not be enforceable;
(b) Assuming the stipulated fixed sum for nonperformance is not enforceable, what type of damages would "P" be able to recover from "D"?;

(c) Assuming the stipulated fixed sum is recoverable, would the court be entitled to reduce the amount? Would the court's power to reduce the amount depend on whether "D" is a "merchant"?;
(d) Assuming that Bobby's mistreatment result in material (pecuniary) damages whose amount "P" is able to establish in excess of $5000 (which was the amount stipulated by the parties), could "P"'s recovery in such a case exceed the fix sum of $5000?

The time available for discussion was unfortunately not enough to address the questions raised in light of the specific facts of the cases presented. Yet, some conclusions of a general nature were helpful to determine contrasting approaches.

The majority of the jurisdictions represented in this group pertained to the civil law tradition (Argentina, Brazil, Germany, Italy, Uruguay). Courts in their countries, accordingly, were inclined to enforce "penalty clauses" as written. Potential abuses were expressly addressed by giving courts discretion to decrease the amount of the penalty in case of the fixed sum agreed by the parties were to be found "manifestly" or obviously disproportionate to the actual damages likely to be suffered by the obligee.

French law and German law, in turn, provided for two exceptional features, generally not followed in other jurisdictions. Whereas the German Commercial Code expressly provides that the agreed sum may not be decreased if the obligor were to qualify as a "merchant", the French Civil Code expressly grants discretion to the courts to raise the amount of the agreed sum in case such sum were to prove "ridiculously" or "absurdly" (*dérisoire*) small.

5 Post-Judgment Mechanisms Aimed at Ensuring the Full and Speedy Enforcement of Contractual Promises

It seems clear that the obligee who has obtained a judgment or an award in her favor would have won a hollow victory unless she can actually and speedily obtain what is owed under the contract. Accordingly, the ideal implementation of the golden principle that contracts ought to be promptly performed in accordance with their terms very much depends on the mechanisms of enforcement available in the various jurisdictions once a judgment or arbitral award has been rendered.

The effectiveness of the enforcement remedies and mechanisms may not vary much as long as the obligation is to pay a liquid sum of money. However, if the enforcement of a contractual obligation implicates an order or decree of specific performance, ordering the judgment debtor to deliver, to do, or not to do something, then the effectiveness of the enforcement of contracts very much depends on the legal tools available to judges or other officers of the court (bailiffs, marshals, sheriffs, *huisiers*, etc.) to enforce such court order of performance.

The enforcement of contractual promises may not only depend on the nature of the obligation (i.e., payment of a sum of money vis-à-vis rendering services, delivering property, or abstaining to do something). Rules and practices governing post-judgment enforcement are also likely to vary according to the specific object of the performance—that is, whether it consists of an obligation to transfer title to land or deliver possession of real property; deliver possession or title to chattels (whether fungible or not) or register title to intangibles. Whether the obligor's acts may be undertaken by a third person or can be carried out only by the obligor (*intuitu personae*) is likely to play a relevant role on whether performance of the obligation may be rendered in kind.

Differences across jurisdictions on this point are also subject to the common-law/civil-law divide. It is well known that common-law courts retain their inherent equitable power of "*contempt of court*", whereas enforcement mechanisms in civil law jurisdictions tend to be weaker. Some civil-law jurisdictions, however, have granted statutory powers to the court, after appropriate warnings, to impose monetary fines and even imprisonment in case such fines cannot be collected due to the debtor's unreasonable refusal to perform. Other civil-law systems have no statutory provisions aimed at coercing the judgment-debtor to comply, yet in some of those jurisdictions judges have assumed, *sua sponte* or via case-law, the power to impose judicial penalties in the form of a sum of money (*astreintes*, *sanciones conminatorias*) which in many countries may be collected by the plaintiff even if such sum exceeds the plaintiff's actual damages. Many have questioned the constitutional legitimacy of post-judgment procedures entailing judicially-imposed fines, or decreeing the imprisonment of a recalcitrant debtor for unreasonably refusing to pay a sum of money—especially in those cases in which the effectiveness of the enforcement very much depends on the power of the court to exert pressure "*in personam*".

The purpose of the inquiry pursued among members of this group was to inquire, on the bases of the case-scenarios that follow, on the post-judgment mechanisms available in different jurisdictions aimed at allowing the obligee to recover whatshe is owed after a judgment or award has been rendered and all opportunities to appeal had been exhausted. Time permitting, participants were asked to address issues such as:

(a) which court or courts would have jurisdiction to follow-up with the enforcement of the judgment;
(b) how long it may take for such judgment to become final and not subject to further appeals or recourses of any kind;
(c) when will the obligee actually pocket the money owed to her, receive possession of the property owed to her, have the services due actually performed, counting such time-period from the time the judgment or order becomes final and the time the obligee actually receives the performance owed to her;
(d) how much, as per each participant's own estimate, would cost to the obligee (in terms of court and attorneys fees as well as other court costs) to carry out such enforcement mechanisms (if possiblecalculating such value in US dollars at the rate of exchange in force closest to our discussion in Montevideo.

In order to address those issues in light of a specific factual context, participants were asked to consider the following hypothesis:

In exchange for fixed sum of money, payable in advance, "A" agrees to build a standard house for "B". The contract provides that the house should be finished by February 1, so that "B" can hold an important family event during the first week of February. Work in the house is quite advanced by January 15, but it appears obvious that the house will be far from complete by February 1 unless "A" speeds up his work, probably hiring many more workers capable of putting additional hours of work so that the house may be ready for the agreed date.

1. Assuming that "A" inexcusably fails to complete the house by February 1, and in the absence of a contract term addressing this issue, is "B" required to put "A" "in default" (i.e., providing some kind of warning or admonition to perform) in order to bring a claim against "A" for breach of contract?
2. Also assuming that "A" inexcusably fails to take any measure to speed up the completion of the house in order to comply with the February 1 deadline, and that, anticipating "A"'s failure to comply with such deadline, "B" obtains in mid-January a judgment in his favor ordering "A" to speedily complete the house. Can "B" also obtain a court order in your jurisdiction aimed at exerting pressure on her to perform by, for example:
   (a) Directing "A" to pay a monetary fine for each day that he fails to complete the contract (and, if so, whether such penalty should be paid to "B" or to the public treasury and if payment of the penalty to "A" would exclude "B"'s liability for damages), or
   (b) Ordering the imprisonment of "A" if he were to stubbornly and in bad faith continue to refuse to perform the contract.

Again, the time available for discussion was not enough to address the questions presented in light of the specific facts of the case presented, but most participants had the opportunity to exchange enough information so as to permit reaching some general conclusions. None of the representatives from civil law jurisdictions (Brazil, Colombia, Paraguay,Uruguay) reported anything remotely comparable to the strong powers of "contempt of court" inherent to the function of judges belonging to the common law tradition. Yet, in some of those civil law jurisdictions (Argentina, Brazil, Uruguay) courts receive express statutory authority, modeled after the "judicial penalty" (*astreinte*) originally devised by the French judiciary, to apply a fine against a recalcitrant obligor refusing to comply with a judicial decree ordering the performance of an obligation. Noticeably, whereas in Argentina and Brazil the amount of the fine goes to the pocket of the plaintiff, Uruguayan law provides that half of the penalty goes to the plaintiff and the other half to the public treasure.

Giuditta Cordero-Moss is a Professor at the University of Oslo (Director of the Department for Private Law in the period 2012–2015). A former corporate lawyer, she has acted as arbitrator in international disputes since 2002; judge of the Administrative Tribunal of European Bank for Reconstruction and Development; delegate for Norway to the UNCITRAL Working Group on Arbitration; Vice Chairman of the Board of the Financial Supervisory Authority of Norway. She is a member of the Norwegian Tariff Board and a member of the Norwegian Academy of Science and Letters. Author of numerous books and articles in Norway and internationally, she lectures at universities and organisations, including the Hague Academy of International Law (Party Autonomy in International Commercial Arbitration (2014)).

Alejandro M. Garro is Adjunct Professor of Law and Senior Research Scholar of the Parker School of Foreign and Comparative Law of Columbia University. He is also Honorary Professor at the National University of Buenos Aires School of Law (UBA). His areas of teaching focus on comparative law and international commercial law (international sales, secured transactions, international arbitration, and litigation). Professor Garro is the author or editor of books on international commercial arbitration, international sales, and secured transactions, as well as books, scores of scholarly articles and contributions to edited volumes. He is admitted to practice in Buenos Aires, Madrid, and New York. He is a titular member of the International Academy of Comparative Law.

Intra-Family Torts: From Immunity to Special Rules in Criminal and Civil Law

Salvatore Patti

Abstract This article examines the development of the rules concerning Criminal and Civil Law against family violence. It analyses the social changes and legal evolution from a mutual immunity of spouses to a widespread legal protection of victims of domestic violence. It aims to depict the tendencies towards the application of general Tort Law in Civil Law cases and towards special rules providing more and specific protection within Criminal Law. In this context the article also critically considers the latest international, European and Italian legislation.

Crime statistics coming from many States show that domestic abuse concerns every year millions of women and men.

Legislators have reacted: in addition to the present rules in the criminal codes regarding homicide, assault, battery, rape etc., specific rules have been added, which in the last years provided measures such as non-harassment orders, restraining orders, non-molestation orders and occupation orders, etc.

In particular, the occupation order has been introduced *inter alia* in the legal systems of Italy and England and Wales (along with the instrument of the non-molestation order) in order to govern the occupation of a family home. In fact, it can be used to exclude the abuser to enter the home and give the victim of the abuse the right to enter and remain in the family home.

Thus, the first feature that is worth highlighting is the interdisciplinarity of the regulatory material that has to be analyzed by the scholar of Comparative Law and that is linked to the complexity of the remedies which necessarily had to be developed in order to respond to a complicated issue that for centuries did not receive an adequate regulation. In the course of time, the rules concerning Criminal and Civil Law against family violence developed from a mutual immunity of the spouses—in fact of the husband—to a widespread legal protection of victims of domestic violence.

S. Patti (✉)
University of Rome "La Sapienza", Rome, Italy
e-mail: segreteria@pattilex.com

N. Etcheverry Estrázulas, D. P. Fernández Arroyo (eds.), *Enforcement and Effectiveness of the Law - La mise en oeuvre et l'effectivité du droit*, Ius Comparatum – Global Studies in Comparative Law 30, https://doi.org/10.1007/978-3-319-93758-8_9

The legislation covering the topic of domestic violence includes the Council of Europe Convention on preventing and fighting violence against women and domestic violence, the Directive 2012/29/EU of the European Parliament and of the Council of October 25, 2012, establishing minimum standards on the rights, support and protection of victims of crime (replacing Council Framework Decision 2001/220/JHA. In Italy, Law no. 119/2013), implements the aforementioned European directive.

Hence, along with the rules of Criminal Law, a path of protection against family abuse has been set in Civil Law and, as one can see, the legal systems around the world have been studying ways to adapt Civil Law rules to the problem, starting from the relationship between husband and wife (to be read as including, in the different legal systems, the various forms of domestic partnerships as far as *ad hoc* regulations have been issued by the legislators) as the center of a family.

In fact, the problem of tort liability between husband and wife has been subject to studies in Anglo-American Law more than in other legal systems and culminated in a doctrine of interspousal immunity. In order to understand such a doctrine, one needs to know its historical context and grounds, such as the economic dependence of the wife on her husband, the limitation of the wife's legal capacity, including her right to sue and to be sued, etc. In fact, it has to be taken into consideration that, in the past, marriage meant that, even though the married woman formally still had the capacity to own property, the right to use and to enjoy her assets was assigned to her husband, with the consequence that the wife became its mere title holder. Besides, the act of marriage deprived the woman of her legal capacity to act as well as to be a party to a judicial process, and any actions for the compensation of the damage caused to the married woman could only be initiated by her husband. This resulted, amongst others, in the unavailability of an independent cause of action between the spouses. It therefore appears that the provision granting immunity from tort liability to the party committing a tort within the spouses' relationship constituted the logical corollary of the limitations imposed upon the wife's legal capacity. The justification for such immunity following the marriage was originally deducted from the principle of 'unity of spouses', which stated that husband and wife legally were considered a unity.

The 'unity of spouses' doctrine, which has had a huge impact on the former Anglo-American legal thinking throughout the years, led to the principle of 'interspousal immunity' as the basis for the handling of controversies involving injuries between husband and wife as well as to the non-applicability of tort liability rules. Given the fact that the law considered the spouses to be 'one person', the spouses—as one subjective identity—could not be liable when causing damages to one another, whether undertaken willfully or negligently. This meant that the woman, who was not able to sue except in the name of her husband, for many years, did not have any protection against the latter.

Over the years, the fiction of the 'unity of spouses' was abolished, granting the married women *inter alia* more property rights.

The courts, however, established another basis for the immunity between the spouses, which was then followed for several decades in the jurisprudence. In particular, driven by the aim to support the protection of the family harmony and the domestic peace, judges considered that those principles should prevail over the ones that justified the application of the tort liability rules. The idea was that involving tribunals in matrimonial conflicts would cause damage to the family harmony and to the domestic peace and should, therefore, be avoided at the expense of any sanctions due to tortious conduct.

In this context, special attention needs to be paid to the marital rape exemption, which provided criminal immunity to the husband regarding the rape of his wife. This exemption, granted to the husband, has been developed by the Common Law as a consequence of the principle of the 'unity of spouses' and was adopted by nearly all American jurisdictions. According to the older case law, the spouses were to be considered as one entity, leading to the result that—since the husband "*may not rape himself*"—rape between the spouses during marriage was simply unimaginable. Consequently, the principle regarding the 'unity of spouses' not only spared the husband from the application of the Civil Law rules, but also from criminal prosecution. Another argument used to justify the husband's criminal immunity was based on the property rights he had in relation to his wife. While the husband was entitled to take actions in order to protect his property rights in case of a rape of his wife by a third party, the use of violence by himself against his wife was the equivalent of the exercise of those property rights and thus not to be considered illegal.

However, the decline of the abovementioned concepts after some decades did not lead to a complete renouncement of the immunity principle. Instead, the American jurisdiction searched for new grounds on which to base this principle and to guarantee immunity from criminal liability in case of a rape of the married woman by her own husband: the 'consent' given by the former. It was argued that by celebrating marriage the wife also agreed to engage in sexual intercourse with her husband as well as to accept all of his demands. Thus, a refusal from her side would legitimate her husband to use violence towards his spouse.

Compared to the United States of America, the legal situation in Europe differed with regard to this subject. In fact, aside from England which also had a similar 'unity of spouses' and immunity doctrine, continental legal systems such as those of Germany or Italy did not follow such principles. However, there was no different *modus operandi* of the rules on tort liability in continental legal systems: the rules regarding tortious conduct were not applied as legal actions generally were not initiated, e.g. the damaged family member refrained from suing judicial relief.

For example, in Italy, more than in other continental legal systems, tortious conduct of the spouses has long been without sanctions. As it can be read in some old cases, the general rule was to hold the husband as not liable for actions taken while exercising the *jus corrigendi*, him being the "head of the family". In fact, he was granted the right to discipline his wife by "*violent but moderate means*", as stated by the Italian Supreme Court (*Corte di Cassazione*) at the beginning of the last century. The 'violent but moderate means' implied that the husband, contrary to the American system, nevertheless would be held liable whenever his damaging actions exceeded the normal limits of the *jus corrigendi*. As a result, even though the husband actually had the power to correct his wife physically and the immunity principle has never been fully accepted in Italy, only few legal proceedings can be found.

Reflecting on the fundamental changes in social customs and traditions, e.g. the conception of equality between husband and wife and the respective Family Law reforms, the doctrine of interspousal immunity declined in the course of the last century.

Nevertheless the abolition of the 'fiction' of the 'unity of spouses' in the Anglo-American Law did not at first lead to a different approach in the legal praxis as courts then based the spouses' immunity upon the idea of protecting family harmony and domestic peace (like, as seen, the approach in the continental legal systems). These principles were deemed to be prevailing and precluded the application of general tort liability rules.

Only following legislative interventions (especially as late as in the second half of the twentieth century) by means of statutes providing gradually more and more comprehensive rights for one spouse to sue the other one due to the tortious conduct of the latter, the courts gradually dismissed the idea of immunity. Corresponding court rulings (e.g. new case law) then established the grounds for further legal actions based on general tort rules. In England, such legislative intervention took form in the 'Law Reform Husband and Wife Act' of 1962 which expressly granted spouses the right to seek damages against each other "as if they were not married".

In the continental legal systems, without the obstacle of constant case law affirming inter-spousal immunity, general Tort Law could be and was indeed applied, as for instance with regards to the Italian provision of Article 2043 of the Civil Code. However, the problem arose as to what extent this general application was possible among family members; it was discussed in Italy whether or not general norms of civil liability were applicable besides the special norms regulated in the Family Law book, such as the remedy of divorce. Many authors opposed such a wide scope of application, placing emphasis on the 'closed' character of the Family Law book contained in the Civil Code and arguing that, under a wide scope of application, no appropriate treatment of the special relationship between spouses could be granted. Over time this opinion was overruled in the Italian legal doctrine, with the consequence that general norms of civil liability also governed cases of compensation for damages caused and suffered by family members.

Legal immunity between spouses was not only a issue belonging to the field of Civil Law; actually in the field of Criminal Law the overall picture that has to be drawn differs from the evolution that emerged on the horizon of Civil Law. Indeed, in Italy, for example, judicial decisions condemning the tortious conduct of a rape between spouses can be dated back to the year 1976. From thereon, it was perceived that the physical integrity of an individual involved a matter of public interest and as a consequence any 'consent' by a married woman to injuries concerning her human body was inadmissible and the respective principle was deemed to be obsolete. Furthermore, the problem of prior and little convincing argumentation according to which a woman would have had sufficient alternative remedies outside Criminal Law and to which limitations would have been necessary in order to avoid the risk of abusive false charges, was overcome. Nevertheless, the evolution of Criminal Law provisions against violence in families seems, maybe more than in the area of Civil Law, a continuous 'work in progress' until recent times. In fact, it can be observed that the long-fought application of general rules is *de facto* not sufficient to protect wives in intra-family violence cases.

Under this perspective the development of special norms on the international level, as well as their implementation and consideration on the national level over the last decade, is of particular interest. So, the Council of Europe Convention on preventing and fighting violence against women and domestic violence (Istanbul Convention), which was opened for signature on May 11, 2011 in Istanbul (Turkey) and which came into force on August 1, 2014 is one of the most interesting legal instruments in the present context. As of June 2015, the Istanbul Convention has been signed by 39 countries, including Italy, and is the first legally binding instrument creating a broad and comprehensive legal framework. In fact, it focuses on preventing domestic violence and all forms of violence against women, protecting victims, prosecuting any offenders as well as foreseeing a possibility of treatment for the abusive person. Moreover, the Convention shall contribute to the elimination of all forms of discrimination against women and promote substantive equality between women and men.

Several definitions established in the Istanbul Convention are worth mentioning, as they reveal a new attitude of the legislator concerning the rights of women. For instance, by examining Article 3a) of the Istanbul Convention, according to which 'violence against women' is defined as a violation of human rights and a form of discrimination against women, the relationship between the protection of women, human rights and rules regarding discrimination is illustrated. Moreover, the definition is quite broad and comprises all forms of gender-based violence that result in, or are likely to result in, physical, sexual, psychological or economic harm or suffering to women including rape, stalking or sexual harassment as well as any threat of such acts. Another noteworthy definition is seen in Article 3b) of the Istanbul Convention concerning 'domestic violence', which means any of the above-mentioned acts that occur within the family or domestic unit, irrespective of biological or legal family ties, whether or not the perpetrator shares or has shared the same residence with the victim. Due to the fact that no joint residence is required, violence committed after the end of a relationship is thus also covered by the definition. Domestic violence mainly comprises the violence between current or former spouses or partners (intimate-partner violence) or the inter-generational violence between parents and children, regardless the gender, putting the focus on the role played, whether victim or offender. The final definitions worth highlighting are those regarding 'gender' and 'gender-based violence against women' set forth in Articles 3(c) and (d) of the Istanbul Convention. The former means the socially constructed roles, behaviors, activities and attributes that a given society considers appropriate for women and men. In order to overcome these gender roles, Article 12(1) of the Istanbul Convention actually foresees that the obligation to eradicate prejudices, customs, traditions and any other practices that are based on the idea of the inferiority of women or on stereotyped roles for women and men is one of the general obligations of the Istanbul Convention. The second kind of conduct (gender-based violence against women) is defined as violence directed against a woman because of the fact that she is a woman or because the violence affects women disproportionately to men.

The countries having signed the Istanbul Convention are obliged to criminalize various offences, *inter alia* psychological violence, stalking, physical violence, sexual violence including rape, forced marriage, female genital mutilation, forced abortion and forced sterilization as well as sexual harassment (see Articles 33 to 40 of the Istanbul Convention). The protection becomes effective in the light of Article 52 of the Istanbul Convention, according to which the judge is entitled to order the party committing domestic violence to leave the victim's household and to prohibit any further contact.

Moreover, the governments that ratify the Istanbul Convention also agree to train professionals who will work in close contact with the victims and perform such activities as run awareness-raising campaigns, also through the involvement of the media and the private sector; the latter means have to be used also to eradicate gender stereotypes and to promote mutual respect. The Istanbul Convention also focuses on the perpetrator and, therefore, the ratifying States are bound to set up treatment for the abusers.

On the European level, the Directive 2012/29/Eu of the European Parliament and of the Council of October 25, 2012 ("Directive") is another noteworthy regulation. As mentioned in Recital 13 of the Directive, the latter applies in relation to "criminal offences committed in the Union and to criminal proceedings that take place in the Union". Unlike the Istanbul Convention, that can be considered a very special treaty of rules, as it aims to prevent and fight violence against women in particular and domestic violence, the Directive is a more general treaty and provides protection for any "victims of crimes", regardless of the victim's sex. According to the Directive's subtitle, it establishes minimum standards on the rights, support and protection of victims of crimes. In particular, Article 1(1) of the Directive entitled "Objectives", states that the purpose of this Directive is to ensure that victims of crime receive appropriate support, protection and information and are put in the position to participate in criminal proceedings. Article 2(1)a) of the Directive provides the definition of 'victim' as a "*natural person who has suffered harm, including physical, mental or emotional harm or economic loss which was directly caused by a criminal offence*" or "*family members or a person whose death was directly caused by a criminal offence and who have suffered harm as a result of that person's death*". With this regard, 'family members' means "the spouse, the person who is living with the victim in a committed intimate relationship, in a joint household and on a stable and continuous basis, the relatives in direct line, the siblings and the dependents of the victim" (see, for example Article 2(1)b) of the Directive).

Violence in relationships and families as well as violence against women in particular are mentioned in the Recitals of the Directive; for instance, Recital 18 of the Directive refers to violence committed in a close relationship and establishes that such an offence is committed by a person who is a current or former spouse or partner or family member of the victim, whether or not the offender shares or has shared the same household with the victim. In accordance with what has been foreseen in the Istanbul Convention, the Directive does not necessarily require that the person committing the violence and the person being victim to such violence do live or used to live together in order for the Directive to apply; however, there must be or must have been a special relationship. In these cases, the Directive acknowledges that victims of violence special protection measures, as the offending person is a person whom the victim of violence should be able to trust and the violence has been committed while being in a close relationship. The Directive goes even one step further and recognizes that this type of violence mainly affects women and that the situation can be even worse if the woman is economically and socially dependent on the offender or depends on him with regard to her right to reside in the family home.

The Directive, just like the Istanbul Convention, pays special attention to the protection against gender-based violence. For example, Recital 17 of the Directive deals with such kind of violence defining it as violence that is directed against a person because of that person's gender, gender identity or gender expression or that affects persons of a particular gender disproportionally. This is, of course, inclusive of but not limited to women, and also takes into account physical, sexual and psychological as well as economic violence.

Furthermore, under Chapter 2 the Directive contains several provisions for information and support for the victims, including, *inter alia*, the victim's right to receive information from a first contact with a competent authority (Article 4), the victim's right to receive information about his/her case (Article 5), or the victim's right to access victim support services (Article 8). In order to provide an adequate protection also in case that the intra-family violence involves persons of different nationalities, Article 7 of the Directive foresees the victim's right to interpretation and translation of the information essential to exercise his/her rights in criminal proceedings. This aspect is linked to the right of the victim when participating in criminal proceeding. Moreover, the Directive, in its Chapter 4, deals with the victim's right on protection. By November 16, 2015, the Member States shall bring into force the laws, the regulations and the administrative provisions in order to comply with the Directive.

Next to the protection and the rights granted to the victim, one interesting aspect is surely the status of the perpetrator. In fact, by strengthening the victims' rights, the Directive consequently weakens the legal status of the person accused of having committed violence. By way of example, Article 6 of the Directive foresees that victims shall be notified when the person who is remanded in custody, prosecuted or sentenced for criminal offences concerning them is released from or has escaped detention. The understandable and legitimate need to protect victims from further violent attacks, however, must not hide the fact that the offender remanded in custody has to be presumed innocent. Indeed, it is not yet determined at that time whether he has committed the crime and whether he is a (further) threat to the victim. The same applies to Article 22 of the Directive, which provides for a timely and individual assessment, in accordance with national procedures, to identify specific protection needs of the victims and to determine whether and to what extent they would benefit from special measures in the course of criminal proceedings. Such timely performance of the assessment of the victim could be in conflict with the presumption of innocence of the person accused. Given the fact that the lack of an actual victimization cannot be ruled out during the preliminary proceedings, at that point of time one could only speak of a presumed victim. Therefore, an early determination of the accusing person as a victim with specific protection needs could be close to a prejudgment of the offender contrary to the rule of law. When examining the situation in Italy, its newspapers regularly report on cases of marital and domestic violence, often leading to the death of the woman and, thus, the prevention of such crimes is even more necessary.

Moving shortly to the situation, past and present, in Italy, the regulation and the overall concept of marital and domestic violence did not and does not differ from that in other European countries. However, it needs to be stressed that Italian judges, already from the last century onwards, granted compensation for victims of intra-family torts. Such compensation included not only the economic loss suffered but, more importantly, non-material losses like moral damage, mental suffering etc., thus recognizing the existence of an injury and, more important, of a victim.

In the light of the pressure to adjust the Italian Law to the international conventions, the European directives and the jurisdiction of the European Court of Human Rights as well as the continuous news regarding domestic violence, the Italian legislator, by means of the Italian Law no. 119 of 2013, implemented the aforementioned Directive and also took into consideration what has been established in the provisions of the Istanbul Convention. A significant novelty has been the new provision regarding the immediate removal of the perpetrator from the family home and the order for them to stay away from the victim, namely Article 384 of the Code of Criminal Procedure. In case of such a removal and restraining order, the victim has the right to receive information from the first contact with a competent authority. This is, in fact, of great importance, as very often the victims—mostly women—do not dispose of any knowledge concerning these new rules.

A sentence worth mentioning, that describes the development of the rules concerning Criminal and Civil Law against family violence over the last century, illustrating the core behind them and their nature surely is: "*Principles belonging to other historical periods may not be the instrument of injustice in a profoundly different community*." Both, the Anglo-American and the continental Europe legislations changed their perspective in this legal field, which was accompanied and influenced by profound social evolutions, mainly in the area of gender equality.

The methods and ways in which those changes were implemented, for example, case law, new legislative acts etc., of course differed from country to country due to the varying legal systems. Nonetheless, the common aim that has been pursued by taking these different paths regarding family torts is an application of the general Tort Law in Civil Law cases and, as it can be noted in more recent developments, a tendency towards special rules providing more and specific protection within Criminal Law. It is with regard to the latter that the latest international, European and Italian legislative developments represent the modern understanding of necessary requirements for granting an adequate protection of family violence victims. Even though the level of protection in this field has never been on a higher legislative level, reality and practice will evaluate and show the actual impact of these new rules. Looking at an alarmingly high number of domestic violence cases also in recent times, it seems that the legislation still needs to prove its capacity of being a valuable instrument for achieving and securing the ideas and standards of modern society.

Salvatore Patti was admitted to the National Italian Bar in 1974, while he was certified to plead before the Italian Supreme Court in 1987. After his professorship at the Universities of Sassari and Trieste, since 1995 he is Professor of Private Law (Ordinario di Diritto Privato) at the University of Rome I "La Sapienza". He has been a member of the Commission on European Family Law and of various associations, among others, the Scientific Committee of the Consiglio Superiore della Magistratura. Professor Patti is currently member of the International Academy of Comparative Law and of the Gesellschaft für Rechtsvergleichung. He is author of more than 300 scientific publications in many languages as well as scientific director of the review "Familia" and editor or co-editor of various law reviews. He is an associate member of the International Academy of Comparative Law.

The manufacturer's authorised representative in the EU is Springer Nature Customer Service Centre GmbH, Europaplatz 3, 69115 Heidelberg, Germany. If you have any concerns regarding our products, please contact ProductSafety@springernature.com

Printed and bound by CPI Group (UK) Ltd, Croydon, CR0 4YY
30/09/2026
02225664-0019